T0385428

The
Graphic
Design
Bible

The
Graphic
Design
Bible

Theo
Inglis

ilex

Theo Inglis is a freelance graphic designer, writer and university lecturer. His debut book, *Mid-Century Modern Graphic Design*, was published by Batsford in May 2019. He was a freelance reporter for *Grafik* magazine and Monotype from 2016–17. He has written for AIGA's Eye on Design, *Communication Arts*, *Creative Review*, *The Financial Times*, *Computer Arts*, and *Apollo* magazine. Freelance clients have included Pentagram, Penguin Random House, The Poetry School, Arts Emergency, openDemocracy, The International Society of Typographic Designers and a variety of independent literary publishers. From 2021–22 he was senior designer for the leading literary magazine *Granta*. Theo holds a BA in Graphic Design from Norwich University of the Arts and an MA in Critical Writing in Art & Design from the Royal College of Art.

Contents

Above: 'Give 'em both barrels' poster for United States Office for Emergency Management, Jean Carlu, 1941.

Below: 'America's answer! Production' poster for the United States Office for Emergency Management, Jean Carlu, 1941.

Introduction

'Design is the method of putting form and content together.
Design, just as art, has multiple definitions: there is no
single definition. Design can be art. Design can be aesthetics.
Design is so simple, that's why it is so complicated.' Paul Rand[1]

'Graphic design isn't so rarefied or so special. It isn't a
profession, it's a medium. It's a mode of address, a means of
communication. It's used throughout culture at varying levels of
complexity and with varying degrees of success. That's what's
important about graphic design. That's what makes it interesting.
And it is at work every place where there are words and images.'
Tibor Kalman, J. Abbott Miller and Karrie Jacobs[2]

Graphic design is a broad subject matter: it is a medium, a practice, a craft, a discipline, a profession and an entire industry, and it intersects with almost every aspect of human society – from business and politics to art and culture. To tell the full story of graphic design requires reference to such disparate world events as the development of the alphabet some 4,000 years ago, the work of ancient Roman and Greek stone carvers, the manuscripts of medieval scribes, the birth of the printing press, the advent of the Industrial Revolution and the modern consumer capitalism that followed it, all the way to the invention of the internet in the late 20th century, and beyond into the unknown future.

Some outcomes of graphic design, when done correctly, go unnoticed as we go about in our daily lives, while others have the power to make or break the commercial success of a company or product. Graphic design can be mundane or glamorous, creatively inventive or rigorously organizational, ornamentally beautiful or functionally utilitarian, socially worthwhile or ethically questionable, technologically advanced or brutally simple in its means. To borrow the words of the great American poet Walt Whitman, graphic design is large, it contains multitudes.

A piece of graphic design can become iconic, historically significant, widely reproduced, internationally collected and exhibited, but it is more likely to end up in landfill than a museum. Most graphic design, by its very nature, is ephemeral, ordinary, transitory, yet it always tells us something about the society that produced it. With every passing decade, every new area of culture, every technological development, graphic design evolves. While it may change irrevocably in many ways, it remains the same in others, maintaining core principles and concerns that weather the storm of changing fashions and aesthetic trends. As graphic designer and historian Richard Hollis put by: 'Eyes and brains have worked the same way over generations. The environment changes but the principles of visual communication survive.'[3]

The key aspect that ties together distinct creative pursuits under the umbrella of graphic design is the goal of communication: a work of graphic design has to transfer some kind of meaning to the audience; it has to have been produced with a specific functional aim, be it to promote, to inform, to identify, to attract or to direct. Defining graphic design is a slippery task, as is deciding exactly when it emerged historically or where it is heading; while disentangling it from interrelated disciplines - such as printing, advertising, typography, illustration, art or media (let alone design more generally) - is nigh-on impossible. As designer and writer David Reinfurt notes, graphic design has 'no real subject matter of its own'; it is 'always working with outside content. It's a method applied to working with other subjects.'[4] This is not to say that graphic design is a marginal pursuit - just try imagining a world without it!

About This Book
The Graphic Design Bible is a book about the history, ideas, theories and contexts of graphic design, as well as the issues that surround it as a contemporary practice. It is not intended to be a 'how-to book'. If you want to learn practical graphic design skills, there are other books and, in our modern digital age, other ways that are perhaps better suited to the rapid technological developments currently impacting how design is done. Nor is *The Graphic Design Bible* an encyclopedia: there are inevitably many areas that have not been covered and further depth that could have been added to each section if space allowed. Where possible, I have included suggested further reading and, within the text, referred to other sources that can provide additional, less concise, information. All of the sections in this book could easily have an entire book dedicated to them - most of them do already. Such is the complex world of graphic design - the deeper you dig, the more there is to discover and ponder.

This is not a book dominated by images. The subject is, of course, entirely visual, but it requires text to be explained and explored properly. Thankfully, in our internet age, books are no longer the primary

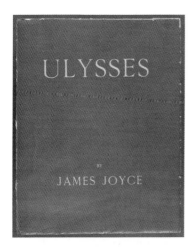

Above Left: First edition cover of James Joyce's *Ulysses*, 1922.

Above Right: *O: Kurske, O Komsomole, O Mae*, cover design by Ruvim Mazel, 1924.

Below Right: 'Handle with care' poster, Missouri W.P.A. Art Project, 1943.

Below Left: 'Gay 90's Art Ball' poster, Illinois W.P.A. Art Project, 1939.

Overleaf: 'Mass communication of complicated issues' poster design for MIT, Dietmar R. Winkler, 1970.

MASS
MASS
MASS
MASS
MASS
COMMUNICATION
COMMUNICATION
COMMUNICATION
COMMUNICATION
MASS
OF COMPLICATED
OF COMPLICATED
OF COMPLICATED
COMMUNICATION
OF COMPLICATED ISSUES
OF COMPLICATED ISSUES
ISSUES
ISSUES
ISSUES
ISSUES
MASS
MASS
MASS
COMMUNICATION
MASS
COMMUNICATION
COMMUNICATION
COMMUNICATION
MASS
OF COMPLICATED
OF COMPLICATED
OF COMPLICATED
COMMUNICATION
OF COMPLICATED ISSUES
OF COMPLICATED ISSUES
ISSUES
ISSUES
ISSUES
ISSUES

MASS
COMMUNICATION
OF COMPLICATED
ISSUES

Karl Taylor
Compton Seminar
Series

Massachusetts
Institute of Technology
Kresge Auditorium

Wednesday,
February 25, 1970
8 pm

Free Tickets available
Monday,
February 23, 1970
10 am
Lobby Building 10.

Moderator:
Dr. James R. Killian
Chairman of the
MIT Corporation

Panelists:
Fred W. Friendly
Former Vice President,
CBS News

Mike Wallace
Correspondent,
CBS News

Edwin Diamond
Former Senior Editor,
Newsweek

Thomas Winship
Editor
Boston Globe

source of visual examples for graphic designers. My entire life as a designer has been an online one, and I truly believe that looking at as much graphic design, and as wide a variety as possible, is incredibly valuable for all designers, aspiring or established; it has certainly shaped my own ideas and interests. As designers, we learn mostly by looking and by doing – trying things out – but there are all kinds of aspects to graphic design that are missed if you only look and do. What we do is, of course, what we are judged on (and mostly paid for), but without the why and how there would be no graphic design. This is particularly important at the time of writing, as AI-generated images are becoming widespread and a hot topic of debate; if the role of the graphic designer is to simply replicate what is already out there, creating images without an understanding of why or a clear rationale, we can expect to be obsolete pretty imminently.

Thankfully, graphic design remains a human pursuit for now; the best graphic design involves creativity, ideas and concepts, requiring a mixture of heart, soul, brain and taste, not just eyes. Some elements of graphic design will inevitably be taken out of our hands – it has already become far less labour-intensive, and much faster than it was a few decades ago – but, if anything, this just makes the use of the intellect, a knowledge of ideas and theory, and a critical mind more important for designers if we are to stay necessary, relevant and, above all, gainfully employed.

The Graphic Design Bible is made up of five chapters, covering History, Theory, Practice, Typography and Mediums, each of which is split into smaller sections, ranging from two to eight pages in length, and illustrated with varying amounts of images. Typography is arguably a separate discipline from graphic design, but the understanding and use of type are of such importance to graphic designers that it would be remiss not to include it. The boundaries surrounding graphic design are porous, even fuzzy at times, and this is particularly true of graphic design and typography.

Although the history of graphic design constitutes only one of the five chapters (which is more of a whistle-stop tour than a complete chronology), much of this book is concerned with historical explanations, something partly suggested by the implications of a 'bible'. To understand where contemporary design is, it is important to be aware of how we got here, what has changed, and what has stayed the same. Removed from the zeitgeist concern with trends, and with the benefit of hindsight, understanding the *why* of graphic design is easier from a historical perspective. In studying design history, we can learn skills that help us better understand the present along with ideas and approaches that we can bring to our contemporary work. The downside of history is that it is overwhelmingly homogeneous, particularly the dominant narrative of graphic design's development: its figures are mostly white, male, American or European, reflecting who dominated the 20th-century society from which the discipline emerged. This does not mean that students and young designers

Clerkenwell, London EC1
c.1700 ¶ Wells, Springs,
Waters, Trees, Gardens,
Orchards, Fields, Bowl-
ing greens. ¶ Jewellery, Hor-
ology, Bookbinding & Printing.
¶ the typography workshop 1992.

should dismiss history, but it is important to acknowledge that this dominant history is only one potential story of many, and much valuable work is being done to highlight and unearth more diverse alternatives. As the architectural historian Sigfried Giedion wrote: 'History is not static but dynamic. No generation is privileged to grasp a work of art from all sides; each actively living generation discovers new aspects of it,' adding that one must be 'permeated by the spirit of his [sic] own time' to 'detect those tracts of the past which previous generations have overlooked'.[5]

There are sections of this book – those on race, gender, sexuality, politics and appropriation – that would appear out of place to some graphic designers of previous generations, raised on ideas of neutrality and form over content (Paul Rand wrote in 1992: 'A student whose mind is cluttered with matters which have nothing directly to do with design [...] overwhelmed with social problems and political issues is a bewildered student').[6] However, they reflect not just my own views, but wider societal changes that have impacted graphic design in recent years, and will rightly continue to do so.

Above: Broadside 5, Alan Kitching / The Typography Workshop, 1992.

Opposite: 'Dgtl fmnsm – Lab #disconnect' poster, Anja Kaiser, 2019.

dgtl fmnsm Lab
ticket@hellerau.org
Tickets +49 351 264 62 46
www.hellerau.org

Chapter 1: History

Graphic Roots

Where does the history of graphic design begin? The term itself is often attributed to the American book designer W.A. Dwiggins (1880-1956), who used it in an article in 1922.[1] Dwiggins, however, surely was not the first to combine 'graphic' – whose etymological origins lie in the ancient Greek *graphikós* (pertaining to drawing, painting, writing, etc.) – with 'design' - a word derived from the Latin *designare* meaning to 'mark out, point out; devise; choose, designate, or appoint'.[2] 'Graphic design' was not widely used until the latter half of the 20th century: 'commercial art' had been dominant before, while 'graphic art' was also used.

In educational settings, commercial art started to become graphic design around mid-century. In 1948, London's Royal College of Art (RCA) switched its course title from Publicity Design to Graphic Design. It was a visit by RCA staff to Yale in the fifties that encouraged the American university to change its degree programme (the first in the country) from Graphic Arts to Graphic Design.[3] This was indicative of the evolving role of the designer in a rapidly changing world. Any connection to 'art', still widely thought of as having a primarily decorative role, was unhelpful for designers. Nor was being wedded to 'commerce' – designers were interested in how their skills could be put to use beyond publicity and advertising. More recent course name changes in higher education from Graphic Design to Graphic Communication or Visual Communication point to the ever-expanding scope of the practice today.

The semantics of whether 'graphic design' is a suitable label aside, there have been considerable debates about where to begin its origin story, particularly with the growth of graphic design history as a scholarly discipline. As Italian designer Massimo Vignelli (1931-2014) said in his keynote speech at The First Symposium on the History of Graphic Design at the Rochester Institute of Technology (RIT) in 1983, 'Graphic Design has been kept in the dark, we need a little flashlight, if not a floodlight, cast on history.'[4] For some, such as Josef Müller-Brockmann (1914-96), Philip B. Meggs (1942-2002) and Paul Rand (1914-96), this history begins with prehistoric cave paintings. Another popular starting point for the history of graphic design is in the 15th century, with the printing, in Mainz (in present-day Germany), of the Gutenberg Bible, the first full book printed in Europe using movable type and a printing press (moveable type had been used earlier in China and Korea to print both paper money and books).

A key difference between the Gutenberg Bible and an earlier illuminated manuscript is the fact that it was perfectly mechanically reproducible, with a metal-cast typeface allowing for a consistency impossible for scribes to match. The ability to mass-produce exact copies is often seen as a key factor in differentiating graphic design from craft. However, does this mean that a 19th-century printer setting a block of text for a poster is more of a graphic designer than an ancient Roman shopkeeper combining text and image when painting a sign on a terracotta tablet? The use of both text and image together was widespread in the pre-industrial age when literacy was rare, and is commonly seen as a key factor in differentiating graphic design from more purely pictorial disciplines like illustration or painting.

One aspect that seems to tie together disparate creative pursuits under the umbrella of graphic design is the goal of *communication*. A work of graphic design has to transfer some kind of *meaning* to the audience; it has to have been produced with a specific functional aim, be it to promote, to inform, to identify, to attract or to direct. Defining graphic design is a slippery task, like deciding exactly when it was invented, while disentangling its history from that of related disciplines, such as printing, advertising or media, is nigh-on impossible. As US designer and writer David Reinfurt (b. 1951) notes, graphic design has 'no real subject matter of its own'; it is 'always working with outside content. It's a method applied to working with other subjects.'[5]

Many historians of graphic design agree that it was in the printed poster that the discipline first truly emerged. Posters of the early 19th century were dominated by typography, printed mostly using big woodblock typefaces and perhaps a single-colour woodcut illustration. The invention of full-colour lithographic printing took posters from being the exclusive realm of printers, allowing artists to produce work that is closer to today's idea of graphic design. Colour lithography, perfected by French artist Jules Chéret (1836–1932) in the 1860s and enabled by advances in ink technology, required artists to separate their work into three differently coloured layers,

Above: Bill posters on the cover of *Gebrauchsgraphik*, 3, by Michael Engelmann, 1956.

Previous Spread: Detail from *A London Street Scene*, John Orlando Parry, 1835.

which were each etched onto stone and then overlaid through the printing process.

This approach, utilized on posters (often advertising night-life-related events) by artists like Chéret, Henri de Toulouse-Lautrec (1864–1901), Alphonse Mucha (1860–1939) and Aubrey Beardsley (1872–98), became emblematic of the Belle Époque era, epitomizing a highly decorative art nouveau style. The lithographic process required flat blocks of colour, giving images a highly 'graphic' look, an approach partly inspired by the popularity of Asian art.

Although they would have considered themselves artists rather than designers, the creators of these posters utilized a mixture of technical know-how, conceptual thinking and artistic prowess in works that integrated text and image and were communicative and mass-reproducible.

Colour lithographic techniques soon spread around the world, and an increase in the volume and quality of posters was reflected in the growth of publications dedicated to the subject, such as *Art in Advertising* (American, 1890-9), *Les Maîtres de l'affiche* (Masters of the Poster; French, 1895-1900), *The Poster* (British, 1898-1900) and *Das Plakat* (German; 1910-21). Further developments in printing technology, combined with rapid growth in commerce, led to posters becoming increasingly common by the early 20th century. Meanwhile similar techniques were being applied in other areas, such as on magazine and book covers, in an ever more visual world.

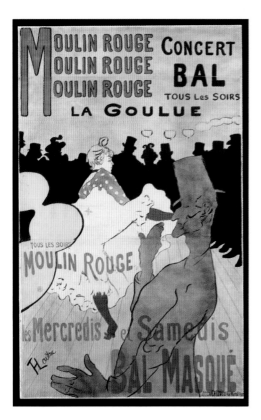

Further Reading →

Sara De Bondt & Catherine de Smet, *Graphic Design: History in the Writing* (Occasional Papers, 2014)

Richard Hollis, *Graphic Design in the Twentieth Century* (Thames & Hudson, 2021)

Philip B. Meggs & Alston W. Purvis, *Meggs' History of Graphic Design* (Wiley, 2016)

Above Left: 'Moulin Rouge: La Goulue' poster, Henri de Toulouse-Lautrec, 1891.

Below Right: Poster for *The Chap-Book*, Will H. Bradley, 1894.

Below Left: Poster for Dutch camera company Capi, Johann Georg van Caspel, c.1899.

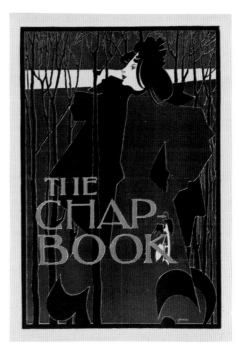

The Avant-garde

'We intend to sing the love of danger, the habit of energy and fearlessness.'
Filippo Tommaso Marinetti, *Manifesto of Futurism*, 1909

'The time of destruction is at an end. A new age is dawning: the age of construction.'
De Stijl: Manifesto V, 1923

The flowing and expressive art nouveau, dominant during the early days of commercial art, was fading by the time World War I began in 1914. However, it had helped to popularize the concept of a *Gesamtkunstwerk* (a German word meaning 'total artwork') – the synthesis of various areas of art, design and crafts under a unified aesthetic – which would inspire the majority of movements that followed. Many important art nouveau figures, such as Charles Rennie Mackintosh (1868–1928) and Henry van de Velde (1863–1957), developed styles that could be applied as easily to graphic design as to buildings or furniture.

The organic forms of art nouveau were replaced by a more angular and streamlined approach, which has been labelled retrospectively as art deco, an early modernist aesthetic that celebrated technological innovations and speed. Graphic designers working in this mode included the French Cassandre (Adolphe Jean-Marie Mouron, 1901–68) and American Edward McKnight Kauffer (1890–1954), who, in 1938, wrote that 'the artist in advertising is a new kind of being'.[6] Their influences came mainly from the movements causing shock waves in European art, notably Cubism, which rejected traditional conventions of perspective, and Surrealism, which mined the imagery of dreams and the unconscious.

Such movements, which were marked by new international networks enabled by print media and improved communication technology, were part of what would be labelled the avant-garde, from the French term for the soldiers first into battle. The avant-garde was a label applied to any form of art that broke new ground and challenged the status quo, whether in terms of aesthetics, ideas or even politics. The influence of radical political ideas such as socialism, communism and fascism were often influential on artists who saw their work at the vanguard of a force reshaping society. The avant-garde movements forged in early 20th-century Europe would form the crucible of what would become known as the Modern Movement, or modernism, as artists, designers and writers sought to experiment with new forms of expression appropriate for a time of rapid modernization and intense social change.

One of the earliest movements originated in Italy: Futurism was launched by poet Filippo Tommaso Marinetti (1876–1944) in 1909 with a manifesto celebrating industry, speed, technology, youth and even war, while calling for the destruction of museums and libraries to free Italy from the 'gangrene of professors, archaeologists, tourist guides and antiquaries'.[7] While some modernist movements' calls for extreme measures was merely

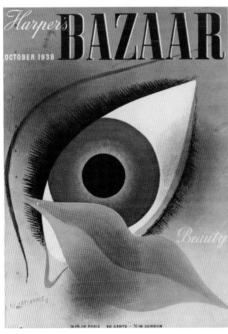

Top: Advertisement for Gilbey's Invalid Port, Edward McKnight Kauffer, 1933.

Above Right: 'Keep Clean', poster for the Federal Art Project, Erik Hans Krause, c.1936–9.

Above Left: Cover for *Harper's Bazaar* magazine, Cassandre, 1938.

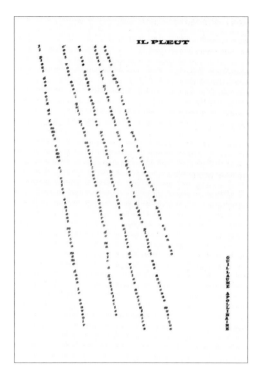

Above Left: 'Il pleut' (It Rains), poem from *Calligrammes*, Guillaume Apollinaire, 1918.
Above Right: Book cover for *Zang Tumb Tumb*, Filippo Tommaso Marinetti, 1914.

provocative rhetoric, Futurism had strong connections with Italy's ultra-nationalistic movement, fascism, and truly celebrated the destructiveness of war and Italian colonialism. Marinetti and other Futurists, like the painter and designer Fortunato Depero (1892–1960), were outright fascists who supported Italy's fascist leader, Benito Mussolini. Futurist designers' embrace of capitalistic progress meant that they were particularly suited to work in commercial design fields; Fortunato Depero designed posters for Campari and covers for *Vanity Fair*. One of the best examples of Futurist graphic design was Marinetti's book *Zang Tumb Tuuum*, inspired by his experience at the Battle of Adrianople in 1912. Published in 1914, it used varied typefaces in different sizes and dynamic, anarchic layouts to convey the overwhelming chaos of mechanized war. A short-lived British take on Futurism, Vorticism, inspired by Ezra Pound's (1885–1972) concept of 'the vortex' – defined by the American poet as 'the point of maximum energy'[8] – was launched by painter and writer Wyndham Lewis (1882–1957) in 1914 through the magazine *Blast*, whose magenta cover and heavy sans-serif typography in asymmetrical layouts shocked England.

Marinetti's use of text as a visually expressive element in its own right, as well as the embrace of machine typography, was particularly influential on other avant-garde movements' experiments with text. Similar techniques would be used by French poet Guillaume Apollinaire (1880–1918) in his poetry collection *Calligrammes* (1918), visual poems where the arrangement of words aided their meaning.

While the predominantly right-wing Futurists embraced war as 'the world's only hygiene',[9] World War I left much of Europe looking on in horror. One group formed with strong anti-war, anti-bourgeois, left-wing tendencies was Dada, a nonsensical name chosen by German poet Hugo Ball (1886–1927) and applied to a small circle of pan-European artists and poets who met at his satirical Zurich nightclub Cabaret Voltaire.

They shared an interest in anarchy, nonsense, irrationality and nihilism as a response to the senseless brutality of war. Key Dada techniques included collage, assemblage (the seemingly random combining of objects), the clash of text and image, the use of typographic symbols and eclectic typefaces in chaotic compositions that emulated the spirit of Dada's energetic cabaret nights. Dada ideas were disseminated widely through printed journals, giving impetus to artists, such as Tristan Tzara (1896–1963), Raoul Hausmann (1886–1971) and Kurt Schwitters (1887–1948), to experiment and develop a distinctive Dadaist graphic aesthetic marked by an anti-establishment disregard for convention. Schwitters's *Merz*, which featured modernist layouts, acted as a meeting point for various European movements. Schwitters later became a key component of the 'New Typography', designed an experimental typeface that aimed to replicate phonetic

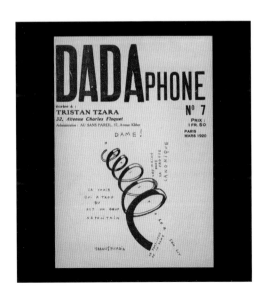

Above: *Merz matinéen* event flyer, El Lissitzky, 1923.

Left: *DADA Phone no.7* cover, Francis Picabia, 1920.

Above Left: '*Kino Glaz*' (Film Eye) poster for six films by Dziga Vertov, Alexander Rodchenko, 1924.

Above Right: Cover, *Merz* magazine, Issue 1 (January 1923): 'Holland Dada', Kurt Schwitters.

sounds, and was a founding member of the Ring Neue Werbegestalter (Circle of New Advertising Designers), a group of pioneering European designers applying avant-garde techniques to late twenties publicity.

One of Schwitters's collaborators was Theo van Doesburg (1883–1931), a founder of the leading art faction in the Netherlands, known as De Stijl (The Style) after a journal of the same name founded in 1917. Other key figures in the movement were painter Piet Mondrian (1872–1944) and furniture designer and architect Gerrit Rietveld (1888–1964), both of whom are best known for geometric work that

made use of vertical and horizontal lines in a limited colour palette of black, white, red, blue and yellow. De Stijl, also known as Neo-plasticism, was far more rational and minimalistic than either Futurism or Dada, and this was reflected in the group's approach to graphic design, as mostly developed by Van Doesburg. The limitations imposed by the prevalence of right angles led to innovative blocky typography and abstract geometric compositions, inspired by a rejection of the excesses of Dutch Expressionism.

Many influences on De Stijl came from Russia, a country where avant-garde ideas and radical politics came together during the 1917 Revolution which overthrew the monarchy, instigating a socialist republic. One early development in Russian modern art was Kazimir Malevich's (1897–1935) Suprematism, which represented perhaps the first attempt at pure-geometrical, non-representational abstract painting, beginning in 1915 with a black square on a white background. Malevich's inspiration was 'the supremacy of pure feeling or perception in the pictorial arts' and a rejection of merely replicating 'the visual phenomena of the objective world'.[10] This celebration of new possibilities went hand in hand with the revolution, and in a reorganized educational system Malevich became an influential teacher. One of his acolytes, El Lissitzky (1890–1941), developed a Suprematist approach to graphic design, using ample white space, limited colour and dynamic angles.

In the early Soviet days, artists were keen to make their work socially and politically useful, so graphic design was a logical area for exploration. This idea was summed up in the Russian journal *LEF* in 1923, where theorist Osip Brik (1888–1945) wrote: 'You must go into real work, carry your own organizational talent where it is needed – into production.'[11] Brik was writing about artist and designer Alexander Rodchenko (1891–1956), who in 1915, with architect Vladimir Tatlin (1885–1953), had founded Constructivism. Although visually similar to Suprematism, Constructivism was less concerned with 'sensations' and aimed to be utilitarian, taking inspiration from modern industrial production and embracing the camera.

Further Reading →

Jeremy Aynsley, *Pioneers of Modern Graphic Design* (Mitchell Beazley, 2004)

Johanna Drucker, *The Visible Word* (University of Chicago Press, 1997)

The Bauhaus

'Let us strive for, conceive and create the new building of the future that will unite every discipline, architecture and sculpture and painting, and which will one day rise heavenwards from the million hands of craftsmen as a clear symbol of a new belief to come.' Walter Gropius, 1919

Opened in Weimar, Germany, by architect Walter Gropius (1883-1969) in 1919, the Bauhaus (which translates as 'house of building') was the most influential art and design school of the 20th century thanks to its innovative staff and multi-disciplinary approach which cut across various traditional discipline boundaries in an attempt to unite the arts. The school's founding values were utopian, building on proto-modernist and avant-garde principles, as well influences from the Arts and Crafts movement in Britain, particularly William Morris (1834-96) and John Ruskin (1819-1900).

The Bauhaus was inherently political: Gropius's founding manifesto spoke of creating 'a new guild of craftsmen [...] free of the divisive class pretensions that endeavoured to raise a prideful barrier between craftsmen and artists'.[12] Although the school's staff did not necessarily share their politics, their theories often had clear socialist overtones, proposing that creativity, technology and radicalism would bring beauty to the masses, break down class barriers and create an equal, modern society. Unity in all things was the goal, whether that was between societal divides, art and technology, art and industry, and across art, architecture, crafts and design. Despite being progressive, the Bauhaus upheld widely held sexist views: women (whom Gropius collectively described as 'the beautiful

sex') were allowed at the Bauhaus, but were pushed towards crafts in the traditionally feminine decorative and domestic spheres, such as ceramics and textile weaving.

While it is often assumed that the Bauhaus had a distinct, consistent modernist aesthetic from the outset, this was not the case, and it took time and experimentation for the characteristics now associated with the school to develop. Many early Bauhaus tutors still experimented with Expressionism, and the school was far from being a bastion of science and reason: mysticism and spirituality were of great interest to staff such as Paul Klee (1879-1940), Wassily Kandinsky (1866-1944) and Johannes Itten (1888-1967), the last the original tutor on the school's mandatory first-year 'foundation' class where students studied across disciplines. Writing in the catalogue for a Bauhaus exhibition at the Museum of Modern Art, New York, in 1938, Alexander Dorner wrote: 'to speak of a cut and dried "Bauhaus style" would be to revert to the cultural paralysis of the 19th century [...]. Its integral part, namely the functional foundation of design, was just as full of changing possibilities as our own technical age.'[13]

Graphic design and typography were not among the subjects initially taught at the Bauhaus but soon became important, particularly once László

AU SS TE LL UN G

EUROPÄI
-SCHES
KUNST-
GEWERBE
6.MARZ
10.SEPT
1927
LEIPZIG
GRASSIMUSEUM
an der Johanniskirche

Left:
Catalogue
cover for
the European
Applied Arts
Exhibition,
Herbert Bayer,
1927.

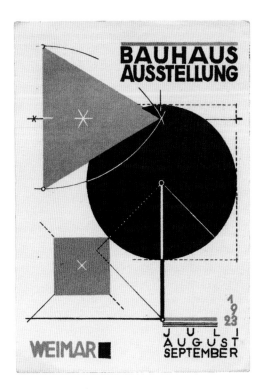

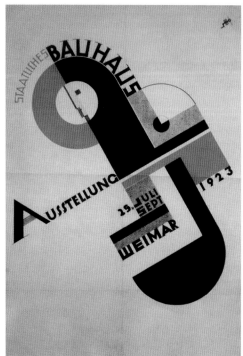

Above Left: Bauhaus Exhibition poster, Herbert Bayer, 1923.

Above Right: Bauhaus Exhibition poster, Joost Schmidt, 1923.

Below: Drawings for Universal Type alphabet, Herbert Bayer, c.1925.

Moholy-Nagy (1895-1946) joined in 1923. Other important figures in the growth of Bauhaus graphics were three students turned teachers: Herbert Bayer (1900-85), Josef Albers (1888-1976) and Joost Schmidt (1893-1948), who all helped to translate the school's principles into a graphic visual language. Albers was particularly interested in colour theory, and Bauhaus design was dominated by the use of bright flat colours, particularly the primaries - blue, yellow and red. This triad was joined by another, the three basic shapes - circle, triangle and square - which when rendered in the primary colours became emblematic of Bauhaus principles. It was Kandinsky, a trailblazer of abstract art, who cemented the use of primary colours and basic shapes as key to the visual language of the Bauhaus.

Bauhaus layout designs developed by Moholy-Nagy, Schmidt, Bayer and their students were characterized by utilitarian asymmetry, rational minimalism, absence of ornamentation, generous negative space, limited colours, and geometric shapes as organizational devices. Influences came chiefly from earlier avant-garde movements such as Constructivism and De Stijl, and a desire to find a suitable and efficient visual language for the machine age.

Bauhaus typography was dominated by bold, geometric sans-serif typefaces. Serifs were considered an unnecessary ornament, and any connection to typographic tradition was avoided. Developing appropriate new typefaces was a concern for Bauhaus designers, Albers created experimental stencil alphabets from modular elements, including 'Kombinationsschrift', made by combining squares, triangles and quarter-circles exclusively. The best-known Bauhaus typeface is Bayer's Universal Type (1925), a purely rational, geometric sans-serif that eliminated uppercase letters and was used on signage at the Gropius-designed Dessau campus. Exclusively lowercase type became a hallmark of the Bauhaus, with capitals seen as unnecessary. Bayer wrote in 1926: 'Doesn't one say the same thing with one alphabet as with two alphabets?'[14] Neither Bayer's nor Albers's fonts became commercially available, but they were influential and spawned imitations and revivals in the late 20th century.

Abstraction and geometry were promoted over illustration, which was seen as anachronistic, and machine-produced 'objective' photography was promoted as the realm in which Bauhaus graphic designers should experiment with imagery. Moholy-Nagy was particularly innovative in the use of photography: he experimented with photograms created in the darkroom, integrated typography and photography through his 'Typophotos', and created graphic design entirely through the camera, such as his prospectus and book cover for *Bauhausbücher 14*.

The Bauhaus burned bright in its 14-year lifespan, but the political situation in the Weimar Republic forced the school to leave conservative Weimar for Dessau in 1925, then for Berlin in 1930, where it lasted three years in a reduced capacity amid the uncertainty caused by the rise to power of Hitler and the Nazis. Gropius resigned as director in 1928 and was replaced by architect Hannes Meyer (1889-1954), whose political focus on social needs made him unpopular with Dessau's right-wing local government.

He was replaced in 1930 by Ludwig Mies van der Rohe (1886-1969). While it remained open, the Bauhaus's influence was spread through students' work and various exhibitions and publications. Upon closure, most staff emigrated to the United States, where they further spread the Bauhaus modernist ethos through both their work and teaching: Breuer and Gropius taught at Harvard, Albers at Yale and Mies van der Rohe at the Illinois Institute of Technology, while also designing its campus buildings. Herbert Bayer did not teach in the United States but was prolific and influential there.

The Bauhaus has boasted of many spiritual successors, notably Moholy-Nagy's New Bauhaus opened in Chicago in 1937, and the Ulm School of Design (HfG), founded in Germany in 1953 and led by Swiss designer and former Bauhaus student Max Bill (1908-94), who took inspiration from his alma mater, instigating a progressive, theory-rich cross-disciplinary approach.

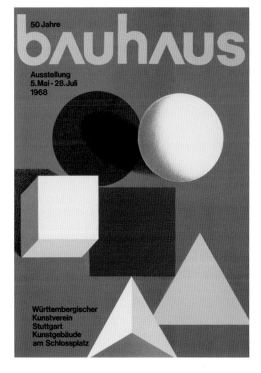

Above Left: *Bauhausbücher 14* prospectus cover, László Moholy-Nagy, 1928.

Above Right: *Bauhausbücher 14: From Material to Architecture* cover, László Moholy-Nagy, 1929.

Below: 'Bauhaus 50 Years' exhibition poster, Herbert Bayer, 1968.

Further Reading →

Bauhaus Typography at 100 (Letterform Archive, 2022)

Magdalena Droste, *Bauhaus* (Taschen, 2021)

Ellen Lupton and J. Abbott Miller, *The ABCs of the Bauhaus* (Thames & Hudson, 1993)

The New Typography

'The essence of the new typography is clarity. This puts it into deliberate opposition to the old typography whose aim was "beauty" and whose clarity did not attain the high level we require today. This utmost clarity is necessary today because of the manifold claims for our attention made by the extraordinary amount of print, which demands the greatest economy of expression.' Jan Tschichold, 1928.[15]

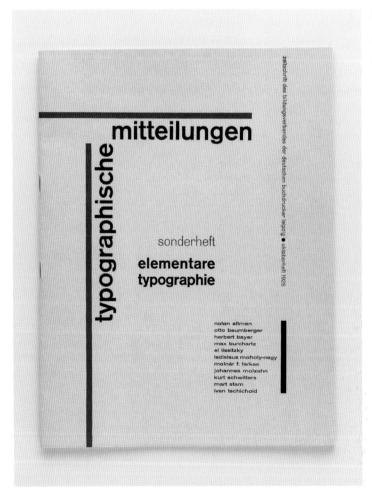

Left: Cover of a special issue of *Typographische Mitteilungen* on 'Elemental Typography', Jan Tschichold, 1925.

Further Reading →

Paul Stirton, *Jan Tschichold and the New Typography* (Yale University Press, 2019)

Jan Tschichold, *The New Typography* (University of California Press, 2006)

The European avant-garde movements of the early 20th century had key aspects in common: a desire to develop new, modern forms of expression and a rejection of outmoded traditions. However, they did not share all of the tenets now associated with modernism, such as utilitarianism, rationality, minimalism, denigration of ornament and the abandonment of historical references. In architecture, the modernist approach became particularly clear, with maxims like Louis Sullivan's (1856–1924) 'Form follows function' and Mies van der Rohe's 'Less is more' becoming explanations of what it meant to think like a modernist.

In graphic design, certain tendencies shared across movements crystallized a modernist approach, particularly in typography where it could be best described as logical, asymmetrical layouts with ranged-left sans-serif type. Jan Tschichold (1902–74) would eventually codify this modernist typographic approach with his coinage of the term 'die neue Typographie' (the New Typography) in his influential 1928 book. Tschichold had trained in traditional calligraphy and book layout design, but had his worldview challenged at the first Weimar Bauhaus exhibition in 1923. Two years later, in a special supplement titled 'Elemental Typography' published by the trade journal *Typographische Mitteilungen*, Tschichold put forward his ideas about functional modern typography alongside work by Herbert Bayer, El Lissitzky and Moholy-Nagy. Tschichold's design for 'elementare Typographie' (elementary typography) was clear and striking, especially in comparison to contemporaneous issues of the same journal.

Tschichold's impetus was not rejection of tradition for its own sake, but was rather about striving for maximum clarity in communication. As he put it in *Die neue Typographie*: 'When in earlier periods ornament was used, often in an extravagant degree, it only showed how little the essence of typography, which is communication, was understood.' He argued that asymmetry and standardization would better 'express the diversity of modern life'. However, Tschichold was not advocating for a one-size-fits-all approach: the typographer's role was to 'give pure and direct expression to the contents of whatever is printed'.[16] Forced to flee Germany during Nazi rule, Tschichold later denounced his restrictive modernism and reverted to a classical style, notably for Penguin books, and would reflect that he saw parallels between the New Typography and fascism.

Mid-Century Modern

Although not a term used at the time, 'Mid-Century Modern' found currency by the late 20th century as a label for a loose set of tendencies found in art and design in the middle of the century. Difficult to pin down exactly, Mid-Century Modern is generally categorized as a softer, more relaxed and more playful evolution of harder-edged, formalist modernism. Designers took ideas developed by the European avant-gardes and tried to make them appropriate for a public that was sceptical about the radical, austere nature of many expressions of modernism. In the United States at least, the post-war economy was booming, and there was optimism and a desire for positivity in the wake of conflict. The focus was less on creating a utopian future through radical prescriptive measures or on emulating outmoded traditions, and more on celebrating the present. As American magazine *House Beautiful* told its readers in 1955: 'to be contemporary, is to relax in the 20th century, to avoid completely the modern strain of straining to be modern.'[17]

The emigration of European modernists to work and teach in the United States was vital in the development of Mid-Century Modern, as was the dissemination of avant-garde art and design through books and magazines. Paul Rand (1914–96), who as a young American graphic designer produced archetypal Mid-Century Modern work, credited his interest in design to a chance teenage encounter with two European journals (*Commercial Art* and *Gebrauchgraphik*) in which he 'learned about contemporary commercial design

and its kinship to the arts and was introduced to the Bauhaus notion that good design was an integral part of everyday life.'[18]

The Mid-Century Modern style in graphic design can be characterized by a moving away from the anonymous, objective 'machine aesthetic' of much interwar modernism and back towards a more individualistic, expressive approach, that shared much with the creativity of modern art pioneers like Pablo Picasso (1891–1973), Paul Klee (1879–1940) and Joan Miró (1893–1983), with dashes of Dada anarchy and Surrealist whimsy.

Commercial culture was growing, with greater emphasis on the use of imagery and design to attract customers in ever more competitive marketplaces. This placed the impetus on designers to create work that was unique and eye-catching. Increased commercial opportunities meant that designers had more room to experiment with eclectic approaches, including graphic simplicity, flat colours in bright optimistic palettes, the use of handwriting or varied typography in dynamic layouts, organic shapes, torn paper illustrations, collage, abstraction, informality, childlike naivety and, most of all, visual playfulness. The mid-century era was a time when the boundary between graphic design and illustration was blurred, and most designers employed a combination of illustration, photography, typography, lettering and abstract shapes in their work.

Creative freedom was integral to mid-century designs. Rather than being enthralled to a particular manifesto or dogma, the order of the day was finding an appropriate and effective

Above: Advertisement for Coronet Brandy, Paul Rand, c.1952.

Below: Glenn Gould album cover for Columbia Records, S. Neil Fujita, 1959.

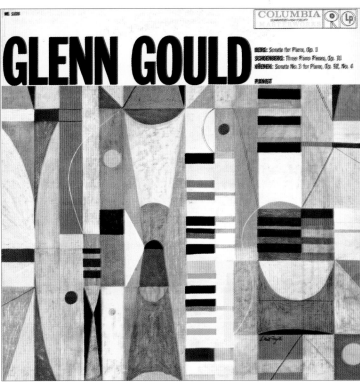

approach for the specific project. Given the horrors of World War II, it is unsurprising that many designers found their tolerance for rigid *isms* diminished. Alvin Lustig, whose book covers for New Directions are brilliant examples of Mid-Century Modern, explained his viewpoint thus: 'As we become more mature we will learn to master the interplay between past and present and not be so self-conscious of our rejection or acceptance of tradition. We will not make the mistake that both rigid modernists and conservatives make, of confusing the quality of form with the specific forms themselves.'[19] The Cold War between the Soviet Union and the United States and their allies (1947-91) was another important context for Mid-Century Modern; freedom - personal, creative or commercial - was inherently political. The dominant characteristics of Mid-Century Modern made it ideally aligned to the image the United States wanted to project to the world, in particular its space for personal, individualistic styles (many designers even signed their work), a lack of overriding rules, and its embrace of capitalist consumerism.

Although some had their specialisms, most designers did not limit themselves to one industry and worked on posters, advertisements, record sleeves, magazines and books, with many also illustrating children's books. A few of the names most associated with Mid-Century graphics include Rand and Alvin Lustig (1915-55), as well as Saul Bass (1920-96) - best known for his film posters and opening title sequences - Alex Steinweiss (1917-2011) - widely credited with inventing the album cover - Ray Eames (1912-88), Leo Lionni (1910-99), Elaine Lustig Cohen

(1927-2016), Rudolph de Harak (1924-2002), Ivan Chermayeff (1932-2017), Jerome Snyder (1916-76) and Erik Nitsche (1908-98). These figures all worked in the United States during the fifties, but the Mid-Century Modern aesthetic was not unique to any country: the same tendencies were found in Latin America, Europe and Japan. The rise of the International Typographic Style led many mid-century designers back towards rationalism, although by the 'swinging sixties' others became even more eclectic. It was the growing dominance of photography over illustration that was most responsible for causing Mid-Century Modern styles to diminish.

Above Left: *Staff* magazine cover, Alvin Lustig, 1944.

Above Right: *The Romantic Agony,* book cover for Meridian Books, Elaine Lustig Cohen, 1956.

Below: Press advertisement design for the Container Corporation of America, Jerome Snyder, 1947.

Further Reading →

Greg D'Onofrio & Steven Heller, *The Moderns: Midcentury American Graphic Design* (Abrams, 2017)

Theo Inglis, *Mid-Century Modern Graphic Design* (Batsford, 2019)

R. Roger Remington, *American Modernism: Graphic Design, 1920–1960* (Laurence King, 2013)

The Swiss Style

Building on the principles of various avant-garde European movements in art and design (particularly the International Style of architecture), modernist graphic design became particularly strong in Switzerland, especially post-World War II. This small country, famed for its industrial precision and geopolitical neutrality, developed what would become known as the Swiss Style of rationalist, modernist graphic design.

Key features of the Swiss Style, which strove for neutral objectivity and efficiency over superfluity, was the use of sans-serif typefaces (especially Akzidenz-Grotesk, Helvetica and Univers), flat strong colours, strict asymmetric grid-based layouts, and a preference for the use of typography, photography and geometry over illustration and hand-lettering. Interests in mathematics, science, semiotics, systems and Gestalt psychology were key influences, while there was also a political side to the search for non-ideological neutrality and utopian efficiency. Key figures included Emil Ruder (1914-70), Armin Hofman (1920-2020), Josef Müller-Brockmann (1914-96), Thérèse Moll (1934-61), Hans Neuburg (1904-83) and Karl Gerstner (1930-2017), as well as designers also known for hard-edged abstract paintings such as Richard Paul Lohse (1902-88) and Max Bill, who were both part of the concrete art movement. An early influence on Swiss modernist graphic design was Ernst Keller (1891-1968), who taught in Zürich from 1918 to 1956, educating many who would go on to find fame for their designs. Posters were the main outlet for these designers, as well as printed publications and packaging. Their Swiss clients included pharmaceutical and chemical company Geigy and a wide variety of state and cultural organizations.

While it was dominant, what we now describe as the Swiss Style was not the only approach taken in the country at the time. Designers such as Celestino Piatti (1922-2007) and Herbert Leupin (1916-99) continued to use playful, illustrative styles, while book designers such as Jost Hochuli (b. 1933), Rudolf Hostettler (1919-81) and Jan Tschichold were not averse to applying a more traditional methodology when suitable. Many of the designers whose work epitomized the Swiss Style would surely have objected to the 'style' label altogether, as they were guided by aesthetic, rational and even moral principles rather than by fashion. By the seventies, thanks to designers like Wolfgang Weingart (1941-2021) and Rosmarie Tissi (b. 1937), the Swiss Style evolved through the injection of postmodern principles like deconstruction and experimentation, resulting in pioneering work that continued the country's reputation for cutting-edge graphic communication.

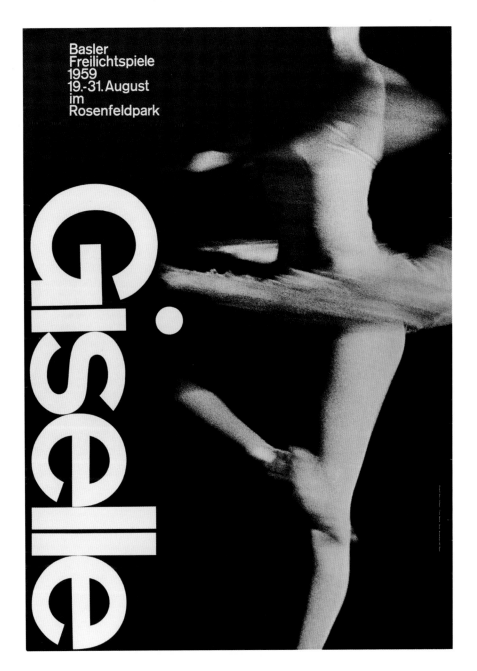

Above: 'Giselle' ballet poster, Armin Hofmann, 1959.

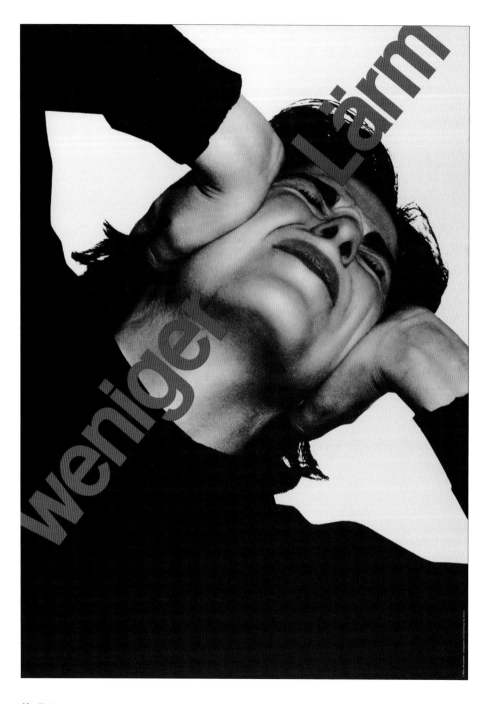

Left: 'National Sport' poster,
Karl Gerstner, 1960.

Below: Geigy Micorène prospectus
cover, Thérèse Moll, 1958.

Opposite: 'Less Noise' poster,
Josef Müller-Brockmann, 1960.

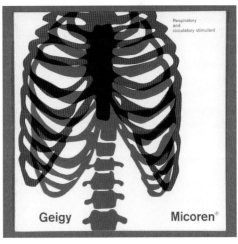

Further Reading →

100 Years of Swiss Graphic Design
(Lars Müller Publishers, 2015)

Richard Hollis, *Swiss Graphic Design*
(Laurence King, 2006)

Emil Ruder, *Typography: A Manual of
Design* (Verlag Niggli, 2009)

The Creative Revolution

Advertising changed hugely during the fifties and sixties thanks to the post-war economic boom. Prosperity, combined with the growth in mass media (particularly television) and pop culture, caused advertising agencies to rethink their approach. Out went the pushy 'hard sell' approach that had developed during the Great Depression (1929-39), which bombarded consumers with convincing information. Such adverts usually relied on 'long copy' - blocks of text filled with hyperbole, product claims and facts and figures, while the accompanying images were often only illustrative, showing the product or its users in a literal way through saccharine imagery.

Consumers had changed, and there was more competition for their attention. Advertising had to work harder to be memorable. The approach that replaced the hard sell was sometimes termed 'the new advertising' and has been retrospectively labelled as 'the creative revolution in advertising'. It came mostly from New York's Madison Avenue, but soon spread worldwide (particularly to London) and was characterized by a more intelligent, creative, conceptual and emotive approach. A key factor was stronger links between text and image, with both becoming more sophisticated through a focus on directness and simplicity as well as on 'ideas', rather than information overload. 'Soft-sell' techniques that became common included wit, humour, irreverence and emotion.

While copywriter and art director remained separate job roles, those holding these titles worked more collaboratively. Art departments no longer just churned out realistic pictorial illustrations for advertisements led by text; they had ideas and wanted to be inventive and stylish. David Ogilvy (1911-99), a British-born executive who founded an American agency in 1949, famously quipped that 'the customer is not a moron'; treating consumers as intelligent meant that advertising could be, too. One of the most influential agencies was Doyle Dane Bernbach, best known for its era-defining Volkswagen advertisements. Bill Bernbach (1911-82), credited with many innovations that changed the industry, argued that advertising should be creative, not formulaic. 'Persuasion', he wrote, 'happens to be not a science, but an art.'[20]

Will we ever kill the bug?

You don't have to be Jewish

to love Levy's
real Jewish Rye

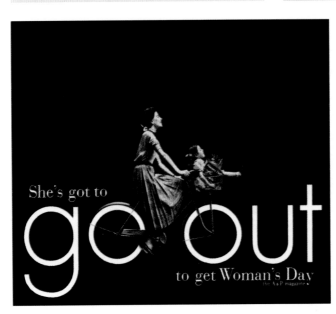

She's got to go out to get Woman's Day

Above Left: Volkswagen advertisement, art direction by Len Sirowitz, copy by Hal Silverman, photograph by Wingate Paine, Doyle Dane Bernbach, 1966.

Above Right: Levy's rye bread advertisement, art direction by William Taubin, photograph by Howard Zieff, copy by Judy Protas, Doyle Dane Bernbach, 1967.

Below: Advertisement for *Woman's Day*, Gene Federico, 1953.

Design Agencies

The agency model, where designers produce work collectively and are joined by people working in other roles (such as copywriters, managers, and administrators) first emerged in advertising. Originally advertising agencies acted merely as an intermediary between companies and publications with advertising space, but by the end of the 19th century agencies were increasingly described as 'full-service', meaning they would write and design the advertisement, too. Early freelance designers were reliant on agencies' art directors for commissions, with the most influential connected long-term to a particular agency - for example Charles Coiner (1898-1989) at N.W. Ayer, Ashley Havinden (1903-73) at W.S. Crawford, and Herbert Bayer at Dorland.

Although there were sometimes creative duos, the 'commercial artist' of the early 20th century was usually an individual who gained work based on their personal style and abilities. Some successful designers had uncredited assistants to do the more menial work but retained control of the creative process. Many early graphic designers were happy to work alone, but some were business-minded, taking inspiration from advertising agency models but with designers, not business executives, at the management level.

An early example is Studio Boggeri, founded in 1933 by Antonio Boggeri (1900-89) in Milan, which utilized modernist graphic designers for clients like Pirelli and Olivetti. Boggeri helped bring Swiss influences to Italy; shared modernist principles meant that the studio could maintain a consistent approach beyond just the personal style of an individual.

Outside simply graphic design there was the Design Research Unit (DRU), founded in London in 1943 by advertising executive Marcus Brumwell (1901-83), art critic Herbert Read (1893-1968), architect Misha Black (1910-77) and graphic designer Milner Gray (1899-1997). DRU saw design as problem-solving and was equally comfortable working on interior design, industrial design, graphic design and architecture. The modernist principles of efficiency, professionalism and consistency were factors that led to designers increasingly working in groups, offering their expertise at the top levels of industry.

The rise of 'corporate identity' design meant that the scope of a designer's work increased beyond that which one person could reasonably be expected to produce. This - combined with a decline in individualistic, hand-done techniques - meant that post-World War II the agency or studio gradually began to replace the lone designer. In some cases, designers who had found fame working solo started studios, for instance Henri Kay Henrion (1914-90), who founded Henrion Design Associates in 1951. Other key studios included Brownjohn, Chermayeff & Geismar (1957), Total Design (1963), Unimark International (1965) and Wolff Olins (1965).

Even designers whose work remained based on more eclectic styles and illustrative techniques found that there was strength in numbers. The best example is Push Pin Studios, founded by Milton Glaser (1929-2020) and Seymour Chwast (b. 1931) in New York City

in 1954, whose members benefited from
a shared office space and collaborative
promotional materials. The vibrancy of
New York's post-war advertising scene
was an influence on many designers who
would end up founding agencies. One
important figure was Bob Gill (1931–2021)
who moved to London in 1962 and joined
with two English designers, Alan Fletcher
(1931–2006) and Colin Forbes (1928–2022),
to form Fletcher/Forbes/Gill (FFG), which
was one of the earliest designer-led
agencies in sixties London. FFG became
Pentagram in 1972, which remains one of
the world's best-known independent design
studios, with offices in three countries.

Above: London bus advertisement for Pirelli slippers, Fletcher/Forbes/Gill, 1962.

The International Style

The influence of Swiss Style graphic design was disseminated widely by the sixties through international exhibitions, magazines like *Neue Grafik*, designers flocking to be educated in Switzerland, and conversely, Swiss designers travelling to teach and work in other countries, particularly the United States. Armin Hofmann, for example, had a long association with Yale: between 1970 and 1990 he ran an intensive workshop for students once a year. Another key influence in the United States was Zurich-born Fred Troller (1930-2002) who moved to New York to work for Geigy's American office before opening his own studio in 1968 and teaching variously at Cooper Union, the School of the Visual Arts, and Rhode Island School of Design (RISD). Max Bill was one of the founders of the Ulm School of Design in Germany in 1953, which became a bastion of modernist education, with Swiss and Bauhaus influences predominant. Books like *The Graphic Artist and His Design Problems* (1961) by Joseph Müller-Brockmann, *Graphic Design Manual: Principles and Practice* (1965) by Armin Hofmann and *Typography: A Manual of Design* (1967) by Emil Ruder helped bring Swiss design to the masses in multilingual German, French and English editions.

With the Swiss approach becoming popular globally – particularly in the context of an increasingly multinational corporate world – what became known as the International Typographic Style saw non-Swiss designers applying principles pioneered in Zürich and Basel. The idea of an International Style, necessary when not all proponents were Swiss, was a term borrowed from architecture, where it was used for the high modernism of architects like Philip Johnson, Mies van der Rohe, Le Corbusier and Walter Gropius. Key names associated with the International Typographic Style include Rudolph de Harak (1924-2002), Jacqueline S. Casey (1927-92) and Muriel Cooper (1925-94) at the Massachusetts Institute of Technology (MIT), Otl Aicher (1922-91), and Massimo Vignelli (1931-2014) and Bob Noorda (1927-2010), who were two of the founders of Unimark International.

The goals of clarity, simplicity, legibility and objectivity were appropriate for an age where companies were thinking globally and wanted designs that would work effectively across national, cultural and linguistic divides. The use of grids and logical layouts (see page 128-31), as well as a limited range of sans-serif typefaces and colours, was helpful for designers whose output needed to be more adaptable; to work in different languages and to be standardized across an ever-wider variety of products with the rise of brands and the need for a consistent corporate identity. Swiss principles were particularly influential on the brand guidelines or standards manuals that many companies and organizations developed in the fifties and sixties in an effort to make the corporate design process more efficient and to maintain a quality at volumes where it was impossible for one individual designer, or even one office, to oversee all visual output.

The ever-increasing availability of Swiss typefaces, particularly Helvetica and Adrian Frutiger's Univers

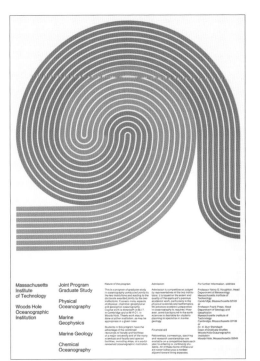

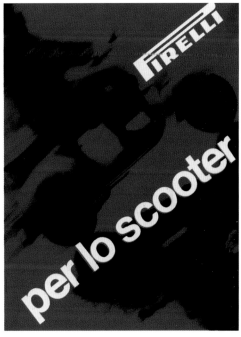

Above Left: Poster for MIT's Woods Hole Oceanographic Institution, Dietmar R. Winkler, 1960.

Above Right: Pirelli Scooter advertisement, Pino Milàs at Centro, Pirelli's in-house design agency, 1963.

Below: Page from the *United States Environmental Protection Agency Graphic Standards System*, Steff Geissbühler at Chermayeff & Geismar Associates, 1977.

(both 1957), helped spread the Swiss Style approach. This was especially true following the rapid growth of phototypesetting, which meant that designers were less hamstrung by the limitations of which typefaces local printers had, which in some countries still overwhelmingly meant old serifs.

Many designers felt that the ubiquity of the International Typographic Style, which had inevitably shed some of its more utopian principles as it gained widespread popularity, had led to the visual landscape of graphic design becoming monotonous. Designers growing up in the wake of World War II often found modernism boringly familiar, rather than excitingly modern, while in the countercultural sixties and seventies the association with big business and authority was another potential turn-off for a new generation. However, there have remained particular areas of graphic design, particularly in informational and signage contexts, where the rational efficiency of the International Style remains a strong influence. Many of its more scientific and psychological principles have found a new life in the digital age in areas such as user interface (UI) and user experience (UX) design (see pages 302–5). The push for greater accessibility and usability has also seen aspects of the International Style gain new relevance as designers once again aim to create work with universality.

Above Left: 'Coffee Hour' poster for the Massachusetts Institute of Technology, Jacqueline S. Casey, 1979.

Above Right: The National Theatre 1967/68 Booking Period Programme, Ken Briggs, 1967.

Below: Record sleeve for Vivaldi's *Gloria* on Westminster Records, Rudolph de Harak, 1963.

Further Reading →

Jens Müller and R. Roger Remington, *Logo Modernism* (Taschen, 2015)

Massimo Vignelli, *The Vignelli Canon* (Lars Müller Publishers, 2015)

Wim de Wit (ed.), *Design for the Corporate World 1950–1975* (Lund Humphries, 2017)

Counter-cultures

Creative pursuits have long attracted bohemians seeking an alternative to societies' norms. This was especially true of many movements of the early twentieth century, particularly Dada, Futurism and Surrealism, where the artists involved sought to smash the conventions imposed by the dominant cultural and political hegemony through their work, ideas and very way of life. Although influential in artistic circles, and retrospectively lauded, the radical groups of the interwar period had limited scope to bring their anti-establishment messages to the masses.

In the fifties many young people found themselves questioning societal values. In the United States this led to what became known as the Beat Generation, or 'beatniks' - a disaffected, nonconformist youth subculture whose adherents took no solace in the economic prosperity around them or the values espoused by their parents. Influences on the Beats included Existentialism, Eastern mysticism, the anarchic freedom of jazz, and the mind-expanding power of drugs, while they rallied against the racism, sexism, materialism, nationalism and conservatism of society at large.

By the sixties the generational divide was greater than ever and some of the ideas that had been incubating during the beatnik era became a worldwide counter-culture thanks to the growth in mass media and pop culture, disseminating ideas quickly to a youth audience in the 'global village'. The term 'counter-culture' was popularized by Theodore Roszak's 1969 book *The Making of a Counter Culture,* which explored the phenomenon sociologically. Roszak argued that 'most of what is presently happening that is new, provocative and engaging, in politics, education, the arts, social relations (love, courtship, family, community), is the creation either of youth who are profoundly, even fanatically, alienated from the parental generation, or of those who address themselves primarily to the young.'[21]

This was certainly true of graphic design during the second half of the sixties, when the 'hippie' movement spawned psychedelic rock music inspired by mind-altering substances, which in turn led to an experimental approach to design utilized for associated album covers and posters. Psychedelic graphics - epitomized by American designers like Victor Moscoso (b. 1936), Wes Wilson (1937-2020) and Bonnie MacLean (1939-2020) - took an anti-modernist approach, eschewing rationalism in favour of an organic, flowing, hand-drawn style in bright clashing colours that borrowed from art nouveau. A new generation of young graphic designers were encouraged to 'turn on, tune in, drop out' and their anti-consumerism tendencies left them looking to use their skills in ways that did not serve the mainstream. Beyond pop culture outputs like gig posters, this often manifested in work servicing causes they believed in, such as peace, feminism, gay rights, anti-racism and ecology.

Protest was one of the main ways counter-cultural ideas were expressed during the second half of the 20th century; posters and placards proved to be a fruitful area for graphic expression. The most influential examples came out of the May 1968 strikes in France and

USA PULL
yourself
together!!

Black
Power

RETALIATION TO CRIME: REVOLUTIONARY VIOLENCE
RÉPONSE AU CRIME: LA VIOLENCE RÉVOLUTIONNAIRE
RESPUESTA AL ASESINATO: VIOLENCIA REVOLUCIONARIA

Above Left: 'USA Pull Yourself Together' poster,
Paul Peter Piech, undated.

Above Right: 'Larry Baldwin of Fluxus International
presents FluxFest' poster, Ida Griffin, 1967.

Left: 'Black Power' poster, Alfredo Rostgaard for
the Organization of Solidarity of the People of
Asia, Africa, and Latin America, 1968.

Left: Poster,
B. Martin
Pedersen, 1970.

Above Left: '*Soutien aux usines occupées pour la victoire du peuple*' (Support the occupied factories for the victory of the people) screen-print poster, Atelier Populaire, 1968.

Above Right: 'Committee of 100' anti-nuclear poster, Robin Fior, 1961.

the output of the Atelier Populaire, a workshop run by students at the occupied École des Beaux-Arts in Paris. The group's posters, silkscreen-printed on cheap paper and using a simple style with rough lettering, were produced quickly in high volumes and reflected its Marxist, anti-bourgeois views and opposition to the government. The silkscreen technique was economical as well as portable; located in an occupied building the workshop was under constant threat. The limitations of screen printing dictated the basic style of the May '68 posters; detail was hard to achieve, but screen-

printing has remained a popular choice among activists and dissident groups due to its economy, ease and ability to print on paper and fabric.

In 1969 members of the Atelier Populaire wrote a statement on their work, showing that they were aware that any item of design could become a commodity. They declared: 'The posters produced by the Atelier Populaire are weapons in the service of the struggle and are an inseparable part of it. Their rightful place is in the centres of conflict, that is to say, in the streets and on the walls of the factories. To use them for decorative purposes, to display them in bourgeois places of culture or to consider them as objects of aesthetic interest is to impair both their function and their effect.'[22]

The example set by Atelier Populaire, and common technical constraints, helped establish an aesthetics of resistance; similar designs were produced by protesting students across Europe, and in the United States where the impetus was challenging US imperialism. The malign influence of America was a key theme in the output of the Organization in Solidarity with the People of Africa, Asia, and Latin America (OSPAAAL), a group producing posters and magazines in communist Cuba with a distinctive Pop art-inspired style, and the aim of promoting global, anti-imperialist solidarity. The widespread racism of American society was another subject OSPAAAL was keen to highlight and it borrowed images by Emory Douglas (b. 1943), the 'Minister of Culture' for the Black Panther Party, responsible for creating many of the group's striking visuals.

During the Cold War there was protest against nuclear weapons, with the British Campaign for Nuclear Disarmament (CND), founded in 1957, perhaps the best known. The CND utilized designers like Robin Fior (1935-2012), Ken Briggs (1931-2013), Ian McLaren and Ken Garland (1929-2021) who took an uncompromisingly direct modernist approach, using bold sans-serif fonts to drive the message home. The CND logo (Gerald Holtom [1914-85], 1958) became better known as the peace sign – a symbol for the entire hippie movement.

The hippies spread their 'peace and love' ideas, but it was the Vietnam War (1955-75) that proved a watershed for the anti-war movement gaining broader backing. Many designers from a commercial background created posters in opposition to the war, such as Tomi Ungerer (1931-2019), Seymour Chwast and Milton Glaser (b. 1929), who all worked in a pop-influenced, illustrative style. Chwast, like many protesting Vietnam, subverted Uncle Sam, the symbol of American patriotism. Chwast and Glaser both also designed posters for Earth Day, an early ecological movement.

Beyond posters and protest, it was publishing where the counter-culture flourished and developed a distinctive rough DIY aesthetic. Underground magazines like *OZ* and the *International Times* spread counter-cultural messages, while also giving artists and designers a chance to experiment creatively. The results were often the polar opposite to mainstream commercial design, celebrating a more spontaneous or amateurish approach, or aiming to offend and challenge. Use of sexual imagery became a contentious point as a more permissive, liberal generation clashed with their conservative elders. One of the most famous cases was *Eros*, an arty erotica magazine designed by Herb Lubalin (1918-81), which landed its publisher, Ralph Ginzburg (1929-2006), in jail for violating obscenity laws. Ginzburg would go on to work with Lubalin on two further magazines, *Fact* and *Avant Garde*, which were not as explicit as *Eros* but were overtly political and challenged the status quo of late-sixties America, while making full use of Lubalin's typographic innovations.

By the mid-seventies, as the hippie movement became increasingly diluted,

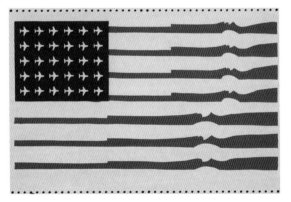

Above Left: 'Give Earth a Chance' poster, Milton Glaser for Earth Day, 1970.

Above Right: 'Come Together in Peace' poster, the Strike Poster Workshop, 1969.

Below Right: Anti-Vietnam War poster, 1970.

Below Left: 'End Bad Breath' poster, Seymour Chwast, 1967.

a new harder-edged, in-your-face
subculture, punk, emerged in response to
economic recession and a looming sense of
societal collapse. Do-it-yourself was the
spirit of the day, and self-publishing
continued, with a preference for homemade 'fanzines' over slicker magazines.
The aesthetic was rough and ready,
anarchic and often aggressive, aiming to
shock the respectable world and challenge
its values. Jamie Reid (b. 1947),
designer for the Sex Pistols, typified
the punk graphic approach with his
ransom-note style typography and use of
low-quality found imagery. Much of what
epitomized punk – the deconstruction, the
rejection of meaning, the cynicism and
the parody – places it squarely into a
wider postmodern context.

Further Reading →

James Birch & Barry Miles, *The British Underground Press of the Sixties: A Catalogue* (Rocket 88, 2017)

Geoff Kaplan (ed.), *Power to the People: The Graphic Design of the Radical Press and the Rise of the Counter-Culture, 1964–1974* (University of Chicago Press, 2013)

Suzy Prince and Ian Lowey, *The Graphic Art of the Underground: A Countercultural History* (Bloomsbury, 2014)

Postmodernism

Postmodernism is a complex term that defies easy explanation. Coming to prominence in the 1970s, it does not refer to one specific style or philosophy, but rather is an umbrella term under which a variety of visual aesthetics, cultural trends and intellectual theories sit together through a loosely shared sensibility. As the name implies, postmodernism is intimately connected to modernism, with *post* meaning 'after'. Postmodernism can be seen as a reaction to modernism. In many cases this meant a direct rejection of modernist principles; however, the relationship was not always purely oppositional, modernism becoming something to reference and borrow from. For some artists, designers and theorists, it was clear that many of the ideals espoused by modernism - such as pure reason, universality, objectivity, logic, clarity and the importance of rules - were either no longer relevant or never plausible in the first place.

The Tate website defines postmodernism thus: 'postmodernism was born of scepticism and a suspicion of reason. It challenged the notion that there are universal certainties or truths. Postmodern art drew on philosophy of the mid to late twentieth century, and advocated that individual experience and interpretation of our experience was more concrete than abstract principles […] [P]ostmodernism embraced complex and often contradictory layers of meaning.'[23] The philosophies that were influential on postmodernism include structuralism, post-structuralism (mainly a French development from writers like Michel Foucault, Jean Baudrillard and Gilles Deleuze), deconstruction (generally attributed to Jacques Derrida) and Roland Barthes' idea of 'the death of the author' which contends that interpretation transcends intent.

While such ideas were brewing in philosophical arenas, similar characteristics were developing in visual fields, such as Pop art's collapsing of the boundaries between high and low culture by celebrating everyday consumerist objects, and conceptual art's prioritizing of the process and idea behind an artwork over the finished object itself. In architecture, where postmodernism came to early prominence, boredom with the International Style led to a flowering of new ideas that aimed to inject fun, variety, uniqueness and personality back into buildings. Particularly important in the development of postmodern architecture were the ideas of Robert Venturi (1925-2018) and Denise Scott Brown (b. 1931). Writing in 1962, Venturi advocated for 'a complex and contradictory architecture based on the richness and ambiguity of modern experience', adding that he liked elements which are 'hybrid rather than "pure," compromising rather than "clean," distorted rather than "straightforward," ambiguous rather than "articulated"'.[24]

Postmodern graphic design, also known as 'New Wave', followed in the footsteps of architecture, sharing an almost identical impetus. In *No More Rules*, an exploration of postmodern graphic design, Rick Poynor defines postmodern cultural objects as displaying 'fragmentation, impurity of form, depthlessness, indeterminacy, intertextuality, pluralism, eclecticism and a return to the vernacular'. Poynor adds that 'originality, in the imperative modernist sense of "making it new", ceases to be the goal; parody, pastiche and the ironic recycling of earlier forms proliferate. The postmodern object "problematizes" meaning, offers multiple points of access and makes itself as open as possible to interpretation.'[25]

An early figure in postmodern graphic design was the German-born Wolfgang Weingart (1941–2021). Trained by Swiss Style designers, Weingart respected the approach that had long dominated his adopted country, Switzerland, where he settled in 1963, but also found the restrictions and dogma stifling, causing him to rebel and experiment. The end result was a kind of deconstructed and 'blown-up' Swiss Style, maximalist rather than minimalist, highly personal and ambiguous. Weingart pushed the legibility of bold sans-serifs and integrated his typography into complex images, using collage to blend photography and graphic textures into work that was fragmentary and intriguing, often in muted grey colour schemes. Although much imitated, Weingart's work was distinctive and relied on the mastery of technical production and new techniques such as phototypesetting and Xerox photocopying. The use of grids and halftone dot patterns shows Weingart's interest in drawing attention to the techniques and processes of graphic design itself, this

Above Left: *WET* magazine, Vol. 4 Issue 2, April Greiman and Jayme Odgers, 1979.
Above Right: Poster for Art Directors & Artists Club Sacramento, McRay Magleby, 1984.

kind of 'meta', self-reflective quality being often found in postmodern media.

Weingart was highly influential through his publishing in magazines such as *Typografische Monatsblätter* and posters for the Kunsthalle Basel, but especially through his teaching in Basel. Two graphic designers who became important New Wave figures were taught by Weingart, Dan Friedman (1945-95) and April Greiman (b. 1948), and they took his influence back across the Atlantic with them to teaching positions, Friedman at Yale and Greiman at the California Institute of the Arts (CalArts). Greiman's work shared some of the complexity, textures and layering of Weingart's and Friedman's work but was brighter, sharing much with the contemporaneous work of the Memphis Group, an Italian design collective founded by Ettore Sottsass (1917-2007)

in 1980, whose clashing colours and playful shapes and patterns defined the eighties' postmodern aesthetic. Early in her career, Greiman worked with Californian designer and photographer Jayme Odgers (1939-2022) on several projects such as a poster for the 1984 Los Angeles Olympics, covers for *WET* magazine and a poster for CalArts. One of her most famous solo works was a 1986 issue of *Design Quarterly* titled 'Does It Make Sense?', which comprised a double-sided, 180cm-long (6ft) printed piece featuring a video-computer generated image of Greiman's naked body alongside other digital imagery. Greiman was one of the earliest adopters of the Apple computer and pioneered its use in graphic design, its limitations giving her work a distinctive pixelated effect that soon became commonplace.

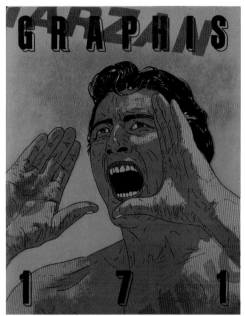

Above: From the programme for *Bring in 'da Noise, Bring in 'da Funk*, The Joseph Papp Public Theatre, designed by Paula Scher, *1996*.

Right: *Graphis* magazine 171, Tadanori Yokoo, 1974.

Opposite Left: *The Ian Dury Songbook* cover, Barney Bubbles, 1979.

Opposite Right: *The Face* magazine, Issue 49, Neville Brody, 1984.

California became a hub of postmodern graphic design. Beyond Greiman and CalArts there was *Emigre*, a hugely influential magazine as well as typeface foundry based in Berkeley, which show-cased the work of postmodern digital typographers like Zuzana Licko (b. 1961), Rudy VanderLans (b. 1955), Jeffery Keedy ('Mr Keedy', b. 1957), P. Scott Makela (1960-99) and Jonathan Barnbrook (b.1966). *Emigre* magazine, one of the first to be designed entirely digitally on an Apple Macintosh, became a venue for many important, critical discussions of graphic design in the eighties and nineties. *Emigre*'s challenging aesthetic and disregard for modernist precepts irked many old-guard designers.

The California surf and skate scene led to one of the best-known postmodern designers, David Carson (b. 1955),

getting his start as a designer at magazines like *Transworld, Beach Culture* and *Surfer*. Carson, who is famed for his work on the Gen X alternative-culture magazine *Ray Gun* from 1992 to 1995, was known for his punky, intuitive and rule-breaking approach, use of distressed grunge fonts, deconstructive techniques and, at times, lack of respect for the content he was arranging. As with much postmodern design that pushed against legibility, it could be argued that Carson's creation of visual interest, combined with the level of attention required to decipher the text, meant that readers were more likely to pay attention, particularly in an era where the written word was frequently losing out to other forms of media.

California was also home to the Women's Design Program at CalArts,

BLAH™

£2.50 DM 11.50 Issue No.01 April 1996   the rebirth of print

01

everything's gone
blur-shaped...
DAMON ALBARN *VS* IRVINE WELSH

Bis
LTJ Bukem

Igor Pop
Larry Clark
Daft Punk

Foo Fighters

Beastie Boys
Beck

Northern Uproar
Fluffy

Ash
Madonna
K Foundation

The Prodigy

Above: *Typografische Monatsblätter* magazine, Issue 3, Wolfgang Weingart and Lauralee Alben, 1979.

Opposite: *Blah Blah Blah* magazine #1, April 1996, design by Chris Ashworth, Neil Fletcher and Amanda Sissons.

initiated by the feminist designer Sheila Levrant de Bretteville (b. 1940) which ran alongside a similar fine art course spearheaded by Judy Chicago (b. 1939) and Miriam Schapiro (1923-2015). Many of these figures would leave CalArts, struggling to enact change in a male-dominated environment, to found the Woman's Building, a non-profit art centre focused on education and feminism in Los Angeles. Levrant de Bretteville's design work was not always characteristic of postmodern aesthetics but she was a fierce advocate for a theory-driven,

expanded idea of graphic design, while postmodernism's interest in subjective experiences and breaking down of old orders made it a natural fit for the women's movement. In 1990 Levrant de Bretteville became director of the Graduate Program in Graphic Design at Yale, where her teaching – which 'was pluralistic and pushed design as a proactive practice (rather than focusing solely on corporate service)'[26] – would influence and inspire generations of designers over the next three decades. Once a bastion of modernism, an ardent postmodern feminist's appointment at Yale was controversial among the old guard and caused Paul Rand to resign in protest while encouraging Armin Hoffmann to do the same – a move seemingly tinged with sexism. Rand would go on, in 1992, to author an attack on postmodernism, titled 'Confusion and Chaos: The Seduction of Contemporary Graphic Design' for the American Institute of Graphic Arts (AIGA). Here he advocates for graphic design as an apolitical pursuit based on 'immutable laws of form', adding that making 'the classroom a perpetual forum for political and social issues for instance is wrong; and to see aesthetics as sociology, is grossly misleading'.[27] While Rand made some important points in the article about the value of practical experience and historical knowledge, he comes across as uncomfortable with the world changing around him. As Mr Keedy wrote in *Emigre* in 1998: 'Designers began to realize that as mediators of culture, they could no longer hide behind the "problems" they were "solving".'[28]

Beyond California, another bastion of American postmodernism was the Cranbrook Academy of Art, where graphic design

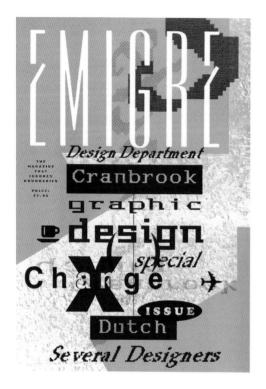

Above Left: *Emigre* #10: Cranbrook, Glenn Suokko, 1988.
Above Right: *Stop American Cultural Imperialism,* Virus Fonts poster, Jonathan Barnbrook, 2001.

course leader Katherine McCoy (b. 1945) moved away from her modernist background following the influence of deconstruction, post-structuralism and *Learning from Las Vegas*, a book that celebrated America's 'commercial vernacular' architecture. McCoy, who wrote that she was 'not so much interested in the layers of form as the layers of meaning', taught many important postmodern designers such as Keedy, Elliott Earls (b. 1966), Allen Hori (b. 1969) and Edward Fella (b. 1938).[29] Fella developed a highly personal illustrative typographic style inspired by everyday things including roadside

signage and designs created ad hoc by non-professionals. Other influential Cranbrook graduates from McCoy's tenure include Lorraine Wild (b. 1953), Andrew Blauvelt (b. 1964) and Lucille Tenazas (b. 1953).

Outside of America, another area of postmodern graphic design was Britain, where designers tended to start out working for the New Wave, post-punk music scene. Particularly influential was Barney Bubbles (1942–83), a designer who began creating album covers in a psychedelic mode but soon was making work that was a pastiche of Mid-Century

Modern or utilized historical avant-garde references for musicians like Elvis Costello and Ian Dury. Bubbles influenced a younger generation of designers in the music industry, such as Peter Saville (b. 1955), Malcolm Garrett (b. 1956) and Neville Brody (b. 1057). Brody, whose early work made heavy use of Constructivism, became famous for his work on cutting-edge cultural magazines such as *The Face* and *Arena*. The revival of historical styles, pastiche, appropriation and parody were key ingredients of postmodernism, and were not unique to these British designers, Americans such as Paula Scher (b. 1948) and Tibor Kalman (1949-99) often used historical source material in their work. In Britain, by the early nineties, there was also a trend for complex, maximalist approaches typified by Tomato, 8vo, The Designers Republic and Jonathan Barnbrook (b. 1966).

From Rand's critique to Vignelli's comments on *Emigre* and Steven Heller's (b. 1950) famous 1993 article 'The Cult of the Ugly', in which he wrote that '[w]hen the layered, vernacular look is practiced in the extreme, whether with forethought or not, it simply contributes to the perpetuation of bad design', Postmodernism in graphic design was always divisive and hotly debated.[30] Complex intellectual ideas irrevocably changed the way many designers thought about themselves, but the eclectic 'no rules' aesthetic was easily imitated and became a cliché. Regardless of one's viewpoint, postmodernism changed graphic design for ever. As Mr Keedy, writing in *Emigre* in 1998, concluded: 'Postmodernism isn't a style; it's an idea about the time we are living in, a time that is full of complexities, contradictions, and possibilities. It is an unwieldy and troublesome paradigm. However, I still think it is preferable to the reassuring limitations of Modernism.'[31]

Further Reading →
Glenn Adamson and Jane Pavitt, *Postmodernism: Style and Subversion, 1970–1990* (V&A Publishing, 2011)
Judith Gura, *Postmodern Design Complete* (Thames & Hudson, 2017)
Rick Poynor, *No More Rules: Graphic Design and Postmodernism* (Laurence King Publishing, 2013)

Digital Graphic Design

'Change is underway and is moving swiftly, with or without us. The choice is ours. The computer does not rob us of creative initiative; it sets us free.'
Sharon Poggenpohl, 'Creativity and Technology', 1983.[32]

The advent of digital technology and the widespread availability of computers by the last decade of the 20th century ushered in the greatest change to ever occur to graphic design. What had once been an entirely physical activity became dematerialized. From typesetting and layout arrangement to the manipulation of photographs and creation of new images, graphic design could all be done (albeit crudely in some cases early on) digitally on a computer. Desktop publishing made it easier for individuals to do graphic design without the need for external experts who controlled or managed the various areas of production. Although early computers were prohibitively expensive and slow and had limited capabilities, they signalled the start of a process that would break down historical barriers to entry to the profession, as well as a speeding up of the process of graphic design itself.

The rise of computers caused trepidation among the design community: some were excited by new possibilities, but others were worried that the boundaries between amateur and professional would break down, making graphic design an unviable career. A common concern was that the limitations of the computer, as a tool, would dictate design aesthetics too much, and that, as Paul Rand put it, 'whatever "special effects" a computer makes possible' would seduce designers to ignore graphic design's foundational principles of communication.[33] As a phrase often attributed to Marshall McLuhan holds, 'We shape our tools and thereafter our tools shape us.' This was true in the early days of the computer when designers such as April Greiman (b. 1948) and Zuzana Licko (b. 1961) turned the low-resolution, pixelated look into a conscious design choice (see page 239). However, technology is never static and computers soon represented an opening up of limitless possibilities, rather than being prescriptive.

The dawn of digital design overlapped with the rise of postmodernism, and the possibilities of the computer, particularly the breaking down of boundaries and the ability to quickly generate alternatives and variations, were exciting to many designers who had tired of modernism. The fact that it was difficult at first to create clean, perfect designs coincided with the emergence of grunge as a musical genre and subculture: graphic designers like David Carson and Elliott Earls used computers to create complex, rough work that was ambiguous, intriguing and often hard to decipher. They made use of layering techniques and irregular textures to tap into the messy aesthetic that was ubiquitous in alternative visual culture by the nineties. Grunge was not necessarily new: before computers many designers interested in DIY techniques had achieved similar imperfect effects, such as Vaughan Oliver (1957–2019),

Above: 'Snow White + the Seven Pixels' lecture poster, April Greiman, 1986.

Further Reading →

Helen Armstrong (ed.), *Digital Design Theory* (Princeton Architectural Press, 2016)
Muriel Cooper 'Computers and Design', *Design Quarterly*, No. 142 (1989).

French group Grapus and Dutch studio Hard Werken.

Computers were not just of interest to postmodern designers: Paul Rand designed identities for PC manufacturers like IBM and NeXT, and Bauhaus graduate Walter Allner (1909-2006) is credited as the first designer to use a computer-generated image on a magazine cover. For *Fortune* in 1965, he generated a graphic showing different upward arrows on a PDP-1 computer which were shown on an oscilloscope screen and photographed. The 'machine aesthetic' was something that many modernists strove for - an objective, rational approach freed from individualistic styles - so, unsurprisingly, many modernist principles would inspire the development of areas of digital design, such as information architecture, graphical user interfaces (GUIs) and icons. Modernists like Ladislav Sutnar (1897-1976) and Karl Gerstner (1930-2017) were pioneers in design programmes and systems for the organization of complex information. Some 60 years after Otto (1882-1945) and Marie (1898-1986) Neurath developed Isotype - a modernist visual pictogram language - Susan Kare (b. 1954) at Apple was using the same principles when developing graphic icons for the Macintosh, which debuted in 1984 and was the first operating system to run a user-friendly GUI. Kare also designed many of the Mac's in-built fonts, including Cairo, a pixelated dingbat font which foreshadowed the rise of emojis.

Another modernist pioneer of interface design and computer advocate was the American Muriel Cooper (1925-94), who spent much of her career at the Massachusetts Institute of Technology

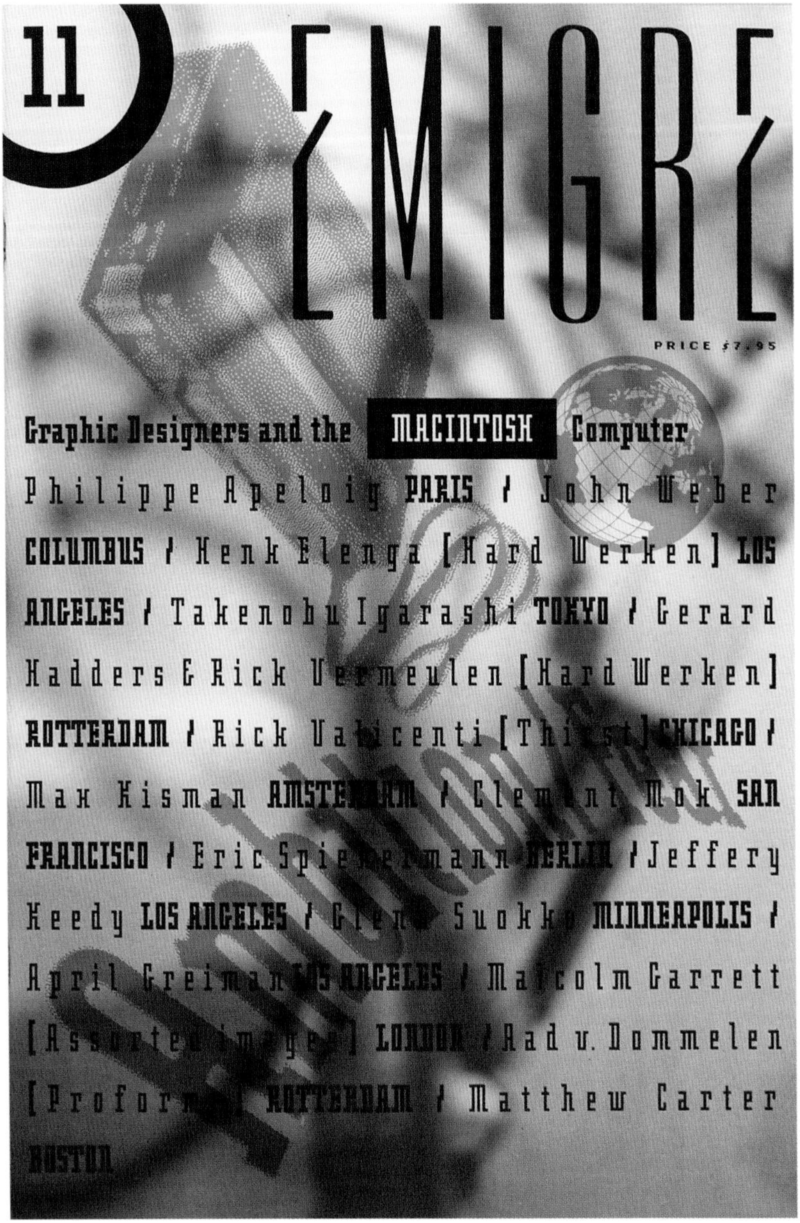

Above: *Emigre 11: Ambition/Fear*, Rudy VanderLans, 1989.

(MIT). Cooper co-founded MIT's Visible Language Workshop and was passionately interested in the computer's ability to reduce the 'gap between process and product' and to liberate graphic design from its mostly static, two-dimensional confines. Writing in 1989, Cooper commented: 'Traditional graphic design skills will continue to be important for display and presentation, but a new interdisciplinary profession, whose practitioners will be adept in the integration of static and dynamic words and images, will be required to organize and filter information growing at an exponential rate.'[34] The first tenured female staff member at MIT's Media Lab, Cooper worked with students who would go on to dominate the new field of 'interaction design', developing innovative digital graphic interfaces.

The early years of digital graphic design produced a range of different programs and tools, as software companies and hardware manufacturers competed for customers and utilized technological developments to offer new capabilities. Eventually, Apple's computers became industry standard for designers, and Adobe's suite of graphics programs developed a near monopoly, replacing now mostly forgotten software such as MacPaint, Quark XPress, PageMaker, Freehand and CorelDRAW.

Designers' fears of being replaced, either by computers themselves or non-professionals, linger on. With design tools freely available as software, apps and through web browsers, it is easier than ever for someone with no training to dabble in simple graphic design, while the continued rise of artificial intelligence (AI) and machine learning

means that it is inevitable that aspects of graphic design will be automated. In 1965 Walter Allner commented on his computer-generated *Fortune* cover: 'If the computer puts art directors out of work, I'll at least have had some on-the-job training as a design machine programmer.'[35]

Nearly 60 years later, art directors still have jobs, but as technology evolves the role of the designer will continue to morph with it. Whether it will eventually make us obsolete remains to be seen. For optimists, it may be that AI will free designers from the more tedious aspects of graphic communication, allowing for a more expansive definition of the practice. However, designers also have an ethical responsibility in the development of new technology. As Muriel Cooper noted before her death in 1994: 'Some people believe that the computer will eventually think for itself. If so, it is crucial that designers and others with humane intentions be involved in the way it develops.'[36]

The Canon

The term 'canon' - works selected as the most important historically in a field - originated in literature, but has been applied to most areas of culture, including graphic design. One of the first people to explore this idea was Martha Scotford in 'Is There a Canon of Graphic Design?', an article published in the journal of the American Institute of Graphic Arts in 1991. Scotford concludes that a canon creates the idea of 'heroes and superstars', adding that by 'singling out individual designers and work, we may lose sight of the range of communication, expression, concepts, techniques, and formats that make up the wealth of graphic design history'.[37]

Graphic design history is shaped by the fact that, during the 19th and 20th centuries, society was dominated by white males from Europe and North America, and that visual culture was reflective of those who held the power. Designers who did not fit into this narrow confine have been less likely to win recognition through awards and membership of professional bodies, have their work collected by museums and be featured in books and magazines. All these factors mean that designers from any kind of minority who historically did succeed are much less visible than their 'majority' counterparts. Often, the names that have become the most prominent in design history belong to those who were not shy about self-promotion and, more importantly, were given a platform to do so.

Graphic design historians usually attempt to create a logical, tidy narrative to explain the development of the discipline. However, as Scotford concluded, the effort to reduce history to a 'smaller and perhaps more manageable package' comes at the detriment of an expanded canon that is 'intentional, conscious, responsible and truly meaningful for all'.[38] It is now over 30 years since Scotford's article was published: change has been slow but finally, in the last decade particularly, there have been valuable and sustained attempts to diversify and 'decolonize' the canon of graphic design history, acknowledging the discriminations of the past, and considering what names may have been undervalued or ignored completely, and why. Major pushes in particular aim to shine a light on the often-uncredited or undervalued role of women in the history of the discipline, and to uncover the work, perspective and experiences of BIPOC (Black, Indigenous and People of Colour) designers.

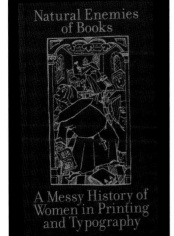

Above: 'The Black Experience in Graphic Design', article by Dorothy Jackson in *Print* magazine, Volume 22 Issue 6, 1968, featuring a poster for Pamoja Gallery by Bill Howell and symbols by Alex Walker.

Left: *Natural Enemies of Books: A Messy History of Women in Printing and Typography* by MMS [Maryam Fanni, Matilda Flodmark, Sara Kaaman], designed by Eller med a, 2020.

Further Reading →

The Black Experience in Design: Identity, Expression & Reflection (Allworth Press, 2022)

Briar Levit (ed.), *Baseline Shift: Untold Stories of Women in Graphic Design History* (Princeton Architectural Press, 2021)

If the designer is to make
a deliberate contribution to society,
he must be able to integrate
all he can learn about
behavior and resources,
ecology and human needs;

taste and style just aren't enough.

For information regarding admission,
graduate & undergraduate study, and financial aid
write:

School of Design

California Institute of the Arts
2404 West 7th Street
Los Angeles, California 90057

opening fall 1970

design: Sheila de Bretteville

Chapter 2:
Theory

Semiotics

Semiotics is an area of philosophy concerned with the study of 'signs', which in this case does not mean just the conventional definition of a sign, but refers to anything that communicates. Emerging in the 19th century through the writing of linguists and philosophers such as Charles Sanders Peirce (1839–1914) and Ferdinand de Saussure (1857–1913), semiotics seeks to understand the nature of human communication – how meaning is formed and conveyed – not just through language, but beyond into the wider sensory world. It was Saussure who proposed the most important aspect of semiotics, the concept of 'signifier' and 'signified' – the two elements that come together to create a 'sign'. The 'signifier' exists in the 'plane of expression' – for instance a verbal sound, a written word or a visual representation – while the 'signified' is the idea or concept that the 'signifier' represents, so is not just limited to an actual physical object.

An important point for Saussure was that the connection between signified and signifier, although they are inseparable, is arbitrary – the word 'apple', for instance, would be meaningless to someone who knows no English; rarely does a word have any obvious connection to the thing it refers to. Beyond the question of language barriers, there are also the specific symbolic meanings that signs hold, which are not natural or universal but culturally and historically specific. To return to the apple, one may associate it with health, temptation, or the technology company that shares its name, but each of these require prior knowledge rather than being intrinsic to the apple itself. Symbolic meaning can develop from something experienced in the natural world – for example, red means hot (fire glows red) – but it is more common that symbolic meaning is a human invention and has become a convention over time – for example, red meaning stop and green meaning go, or a cross meaning no and a tick meaning yes. However, these cannot be considered universal – in China, red is a lucky, joyful colour and is used for lines on charts showing positive growth. Nor are meanings historically fixed. Consider the gender associations of colour for children: pink for girls and blue for boys. Historically, there is evidence that in the early 20th century some people considered the opposite to be appropriate, while in the 21st century such rigid associations are being challenged, so it is plausible to imagine a future where colours hold no such gender associations.

Peirce sought to understand the different functions he observed between signs, proposing three categories – icon, index and symbol. The 'icon' resembles the thing being signified, so might be a photograph or an accurate drawing. However, as explored by the Surrealist artist René Magritte (1898–1967) in his famous painting *The Treachery of Images* (1929) a representation is not the thing itself – although it may look the same, its function is entirely different. The 'index' is something that can stand in for a different item it is related to – for instance, smoke for fire or a dark cloud for rain. The final category, 'symbol', refers to examples which are arbitrary and human-specific and acquire meaning only through convention and context – for

Above: *Design* magazine, Issue 166, Bob Gill, Fletcher/Forbes/Gill, 1962.

Previous Spread: Three-dimensional poster for the School of Design, California Institute of the Arts, Sheila Levrant de Bretteville, 1970.

instance, an abstract brand logo must be seen on a product or in an advertisement for any association to form in the mind of the consumer.

For graphic designers, semiotics explains how and why pieces of visual communication function, and suggest ways in which our work could be more successful at delivering messages. Often obscured by difficult philosophical jargon, semiotics generally seeks to explain phenomena that can seem fairly obvious once you understand the points being made. Designers, to succeed, should have an innate awareness of, and interest in, the creation of meaning and the different ways of achieving effective communication. Using all three types of sign - icon, index and symbol - is second nature in graphic design.

Unsurprisingly, semiotics began to interest graphic designers during the era of post-World War II modernism, particularly at the Ulm School of Design thanks to the Argentine designer and painter Tomás Maldonado (1922–2018). Designers were looking to science, mathematics, technology and theory as a way to rationalize design - away from the subjective vagaries of taste, and towards objective efficiency and universality. This coincided with a growing interest in psychology and consumer research in advertising and branding. By the fifties writers like Roland Barthes (1915–80) turned a semiotic eye onto everyday culture, analysing adverts for an Italian food brand or laundry detergent packaging. Barthes' book *Mythologies* (1957, first English edition 1972), was hugely influential on the growing field of cultural studies and used semiotics

to 'demystify' how various forms of media and design function, and to reveal the ideological motives that lay hidden behind ideas of 'naturalness' and '*what-goes-without-saying*'.[1]

Above Left: Roland Barthes, *Mythologies*, book cover, Philip Castle, 1973.

Above Right: 'I Love NY More Than Ever' poster, Milton Glaser, 2001.

Below: Noto Color Emoji font, Google.

Further Reading →

David Crow, *Visible Signs: An Introduction to Semiotics in the Visual Arts* (Bloomsbury, 2018)
Sean Hall, *This Means This, This Means That: A User's Guide to Semiotics* (Laurence King, 2012)

Aesthetics

A term that has come in recent decades to refer more generally to how something looks, aesthetics (coined in 1735 by German philosopher Alexander Gottlieb Baumgarten [1714-62]) technically refers to a complex branch of philosophical study concerned with beauty and taste. While many ancient philosophers, most notably Plato (428/427 or 424/423-348/347 BCE), believed that there was an 'ideal' version of any object against which the things we experience in reality are imperfect imitations, Enlightenment thinkers such as Immanuel Kant (1724-1804) moved aesthetics away from such unreachable truths, towards rationality and individual judgement.

For many philosophers, taste was intrinsically connected with morality; beauty went hand in hand with 'goodness', while at the other end of the scale the now debunked pseudoscience of phrenology proposed that a misshapen skull was indicative of an evil or criminal character. Ludwig Wittgenstein (1889-1951) memorably proposed that 'Ethics and Aesthetics are one', by which he hoped to point out that both are rooted in lived experience and combine both individual subjective judgement and wider societal standards. For Søren Kierkegaard (1813-55), the 'aesthetic life' was one devoted to individualistic pleasures; an idea taken up by the writers, artists and designers of the Aesthetic Movement in the late 19th century who 'aimed to escape the ugliness and materialism of the Industrial Age, by focusing instead on producing art that was beautiful rather than having a deeper meaning'.[2] Associated with this movement was the designer William Morris (1834-96), who famously said: 'Have nothing in your houses that you do not know to be useful or believe to be beautiful.' Modernism would later combine these two seeming opposites, promoting the idea that utility was itself beautiful (in contrast to the classical view of aesthetics that beauty was entirely separate from meaning or function). Later, postmodernism would challenge this, embracing again the subjectivity of taste, and challenging traditional notions of beauty.

As with any academic field, there are different schools of thought within aesthetics. For instance, from a Marxist perspective it would be argued that 'good taste' is imposed from above by those with social, political and economic power, and that, under capitalism, aesthetic trends are a tool to drive profit by encouraging consumers to replace products often.

In design, there have been constant attempts to identify methods that might be utilized in the pursuit of objective beauty: ideas gleaned from psychological research, around visual harmony or mathematical precision. However, explaining why a piece of graphic design is appealing usually involves the vagaries of feeling.

Further Reading →

David Pye, *The Nature and Aesthetics of Design* (Airlife Publishing, 1995)

Design and Aesthetics: A Reader, ed. Mo Dodson & Jerry Palmer (Routledge, 1996)

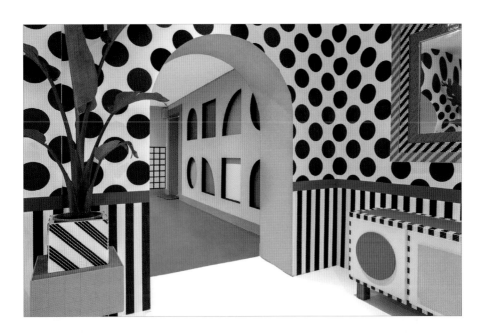

Above: *House of Dots* installation for The LEGO Group, Camille Walala, 2020.

Below: Herman Miller holiday campaign image, Wade & Leta, 2019.

Gestalt

A German word with no exact equivalent in English, *gestalt* means how something has been put together or arranged, and is associated with a movement in psychology that emerged in the early 20th century in Germany and Austria. Gestalt psychology was born out of a belief that it was essential to study things as a 'whole', rather than in their constituent parts, to mirror how human perception itself works.

Visual perception was one of the first areas where gestalt theory developed, and its relevance to design is strong. Graphic designers bring together different elements to form a whole, which is taken in by the viewer in one go. The audience will not consider each individual part of a designer's work before deciding how it makes them feel. Upon seeing a bottle of Coca-Cola, a viewer does not first think about the colour red, then consider the logo's script lettering and finally the bottle's distinctive shape, but instead takes the information in and processes it all at once. This holds for even the most basic examples – on seeing a piece of text, the reader simultaneously takes in what it says and the chosen font.

Gestalt psychology highlights the importance of understanding how, in our minds, the receiving and processing of information are not separate, but one unified whole. Gestalt theorists identified many principles that are important for graphic designers to understand, for instance the 'figure-ground' relationship, which is used to understand how viewers perceive the difference between foreground and background in a two-dimensional image. Factors impacting this relationship include contrast, scale, position and use of space. However, it is possible to create images where the figure-ground relationship is unstable and viewers can alternate between seeing one thing and another, the famous example being the 'Rubin Vase'. Figure-ground has been much used by graphic designers and image makers, such as in creating a two-in-one image with negative space, or using ample white space to make an element come to the foreground.

In 1923 Max Wertheimer (1880–1943), one of the pioneers of gestalt, introduced eight gestalt principles, or 'laws of organization', that explain how individual pieces can successfully be perceived as a unified whole.[3]

1. Proximity: Elements close together are more likely to be seen as a singular unit.

2. Similarity: We group items together based on shared characteristics like colour, size, shape or orientation.

3. Proximity and Similarity combined: Using both of these systems in tandem can either strengthen or weaken perceived groupings.

4. Common Fate: Elements moving (or appearing to move) in the same direction form a group.

5. Prägnanz: This law is the most general of the eight and says that when presented with a set of ambiguous elements people will always prefer to interpret them in the simplest way.

6. Einstellung (Set): Rhythm, repetition and pattern create groupings.

7. Good Continuation and Closure: Continuity means that we are more likely to perceive continuous smooth flowing lines, while closure suggests that

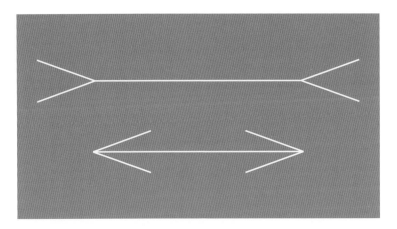

← In this illusion the horizontal lines, although the same length, appear to vary due to their endings.

← In this illusion we see a triangle and a star, when there are only individual circles with triangles cut out of them. Our brains perceive the whole and make sense of them to form a more familiar shape.

← Known as the Rubin Vase, this famous illusion demonstrates the figure-ground distinction of Gestalt psychology. Whether you see a vase or two faces can be influenced by design choices.

STEREO
RS 821 SD

Command records

PROVOCATIVE PERCUSSION VOL. III

© 1961 GRAND AWARD RECORD CO. INC. NEW YORK. N. Y.

Further Reading →

Rudolf Arnheim, *Visual Thinking* (University of California Press, 1969)

Max Bill, *Architecture Words 5: FORM, FUNCTION, BEAUTY = GESTALT* (Architectural Association Publications, 2010)

Donis A. Dondis, *A Primer of Visual Literacy* (MIT Press, 1973)

Above: *Provocative Percussion Vol.III*, album cover, Josef Albers, 1961.

Opposite Left: Chapter opener illustration for *Engagées* by Charlotte Daubet, Malika Favre, 2021.

Opposite Right: Cover design for *Co-Art: Artists on Creative Collaboration* by Ellen Mara De Wachter (Phaidon) designed by A Practice for Everyday Life, 2017.

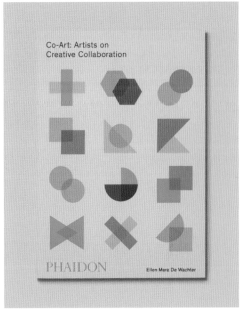

Co-Art: Artists on
Creative Collaboration

PHAIDON   Ellen Mara De Wachter

elements that form enclosed spaces are
perceived as a group, and that the human
brain will even fill in any gaps in
the search for a 'complete shape'.
Enclosure within a shape (e.g. circles
within a square box) also creates a
logical grouping.

8. Past Experience: We understand certain
elements to be related based on past
exposure and cultural conditioning.

Although gestalt theory can be
difficult to understand thanks to the
complex psychological and linguistic
jargon used by writers like Wertheimer,
it influenced graphic design throughout
the 20th century. This was particularly
true during postwar modernism, when many
practitioners sought a scientific basis
to rationalize their work.

Colour Theory

'Colours are forces, radiant energies that affect us positively or negatively, whether we are aware of it or not.'
Johannes Itten, *The Elements of Colour*[4]

Throughout history we have sought to understand colour, both scientifically and emotionally. Followers of the ancient philosopher Aristotle (384–322 BCE) are thought to have been the first to articulate theories about colour, proposing that all exist between white and black and involve mixtures of the four elements – fire, air, water and earth. It was not until Sir Isaac Newton's (1642–1726/27) treatise *Opticks* (1704) that a scientific explanation of colour was finally proposed, Newton observed light passing through a prism and correctly identified that white light was made up of all the different colour hues found within the colour spectrum of red, orange, yellow, green, blue, indigo and violet. He proposed that every colour could be made by the correct combination of these rainbow hues, even white — previously thought of as the absence of colour.

While Newton's experiments proved much of what we now understand about the properties of light, arguments about the nature of colour continued among later thinkers. Johann Wolfgang von Goethe (1749–1832), in his *Theory of Colours* (1810), was less interested in scientific facts than in the psychology of colours and our experiences of them. Goethe developed a colour wheel where he labelled hues with the 'allegorical, symbolic, mystic' qualities he associated with them: yellow is good, red is beautiful, orange is noble, green is useful, blue is common and mean, while purple is needless. Although not rooted in data, Goethe was right that colours have psychological associations: some shared and rooted in nature and common experience; others cultural, personal or mysterious. These ideas would inspire many artists searching for a logical rationale behind colour choices, beyond relying on a subjective visual preference. Although Goethe, a noted poet and writer, took a more mystical approach to the psychology of colour, later colour theorists were more interested in classification, and the identification of binaries like warm versus cool, bright versus dull or active versus passive.

Much of the debate around colour came from a seeming contradiction: white light was apparently made from all the other colours combined, yet by combining paint in all the colours you would get something dark, near black. The reason behind this is that there are two ways of making colour – additive and subtractive methods. In additive systems, colours are created by mixing different amounts of light: black is no light, white is pure light, and every other colour is made through different combinations of red, green and blue light. Screen-based systems are additive and use the RGB colour mode; when they are turned off they are black and when turned on they 'light' up. Subtractive colours begin as white, but through the use of a physical blocker (such as pigments, dyes or inks) colours are created due to the absorption of portions of the white light that illuminates the object, changing what is reflected back at the viewer. Printing is a subtractive process, as it

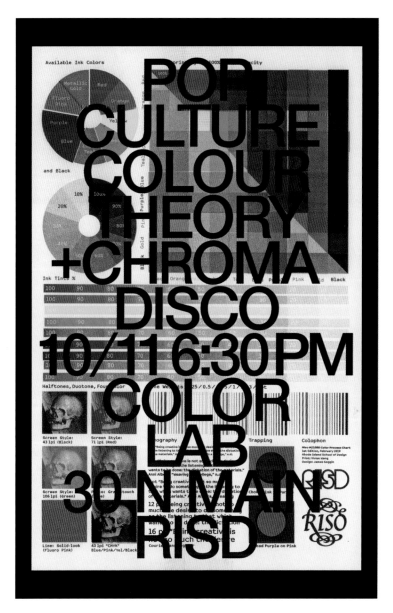

Above: Poster for 'Pop Culture Colour Theory', Rhode Island
School of Design, Providence, James Goggin (Practise), 2019.
Black Riso text layer printed over James Goggin & Vivian Wang,
Riso MZ1090 Color Process Chart, RISD, 2018. Ten-colour Risograph
poster, printed by Vivian Wang.

relies on the reflection (not projection) of light: more ink means darker colours. Full-colour printing relies on a white background, on which CMYK (cyan, magenta, yellow and black) inks are combined to produce any required shade, with white itself only achieved through the absence of ink. The addition of black in the four-colour printing process (signified by K for 'key') creates a truer black and is more economical than overlaying three coloured inks.

The invention of colour printing is credited to Jacob Christoph Le Blon (1667–1741), through the use of different 'plates' in primary colours. It arose via the work of Newton and other scientists who identified that, through the combination of two of the three primary colours, secondary colours such as orange, green and purple could be created. The right combination of the three primaries could create almost any hue. However, there are bright colours that are achievable on RGB screens but cannot ever be matched by a printed CMYK four-colour process. Colours unachievable by combining CMYK inks, known as 'special colours', are made using pigments and come ready-mixed from colour library companies such as Pantone.

In the 20th century the most important thinkers on colour were at the Bauhaus (see pages 26–31): Johannes Itten (1888–1967), Paul Klee (1879–1940), Wassily Kandinsky (1866–1944) and Josef Albers (1888–1976). Kandinsky, who had considered the psychological associations of colour in *Concerning the Spiritual in Art* (1911), proposed that there was an inherent affinity between colours and forms. Famously, he argued that a triangle should be yellow (a sharp

colour); a circle should be blue (a deep and peaceful colour); while a square should be red (an active and purposeful colour). These shape and colour pairings became emblematic of the Bauhaus, although not everyone agreed with his ideas. Itten, a Swiss painter and follower of Mazdaznan (a mystical neo-Zoroastrian religion), developed and taught the preliminary course that all Bauhaus students had to attend upon joining the school to learn basic fundamentals. Colour theory was a key part of this, and Itten was interested in the subjective nature of colour, as well as the science behind our perception of it. He developed a 12-colour wheel and suggested ways to find harmonious pairings within it: as 'dyads' – two colours directly opposite each other on the wheel; three-colour 'triads' formed by an equilateral triangle overlaid on the wheel or by an isosceles triangle which picked the two colours either side of the colour directly opposite the point of the triangle; and four-colour 'tetrads' made with squares or rectangles on top of the wheel with each corner picking out a colour. Itten, who compiled his colour theories into his 1961 book *The Art of Colour*, also proposed seven kinds of contrast that impact how we judge colours against each other; 'contrast of hue, light–dark contrast, cold–warm contrast, complementary contrast, simultaneous contrast, contrast of saturation, and contrast of extension'.[5]

Albers, who had studied under Itten and built on his former teacher's theories, stressed how our perception of colour is influenced primarily by the colours around it. In his 1963 book *Interaction of Colour*, Albers states

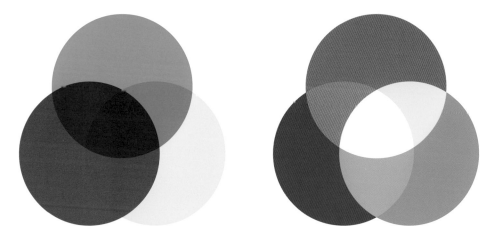

Above: On the left is the CMY colour space, an example of a subtractive colour system. On the right is the RGB colour space used by screens, an example of an 'additive' system based on the projection of light.

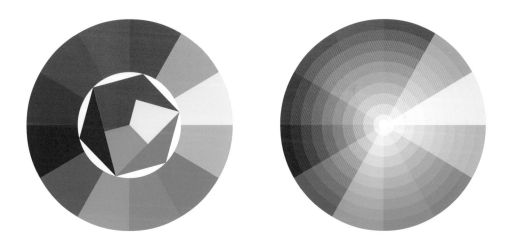

Above: On the left is a colour wheel (after Johannes Itten) created with CMY ink. These 'primary' colours for printing are shown in the central triangle, with 'secondary' colours in the middle hexagon made from the combination of two 'primary' colours at full strength, and a twelve-colour rainbow created in the outer circle with six extra 'tertiary' colours. The illustration on the right shows the same twelve-colour rainbow with 'tints' decreasing in increments.

that 'in order to use colour effectively
it is necessary to recognize that colour
deceives continually', and used extensive
illustrations to prove that context
changes how colours appear to us, placing
'practice' before 'theory'.[6]

Albers was always keen to stress that
experience of colour is personal – an
important point. As graphic designers, we
can choose colours based on preference
or instinct, but there is also the option
(often prompted by commercial contexts)
to justify our choices using science,
psychology or associative rationalization.
While some of the associations of
colour are rooted in shared tangible
experiences of the natural world, many
others are culturally specific and not
fixed or universal, and others still
are purely personal and subjective.
We also have to remember that people have
different abilities to see colour, with
the most common 'colour blindness', or
colour vision deficiency (CVD), being
an inability to differentiate between
red and green. A complete lack of colour
perception (achromatopsia) is found in
roughly one in 30,000 people.

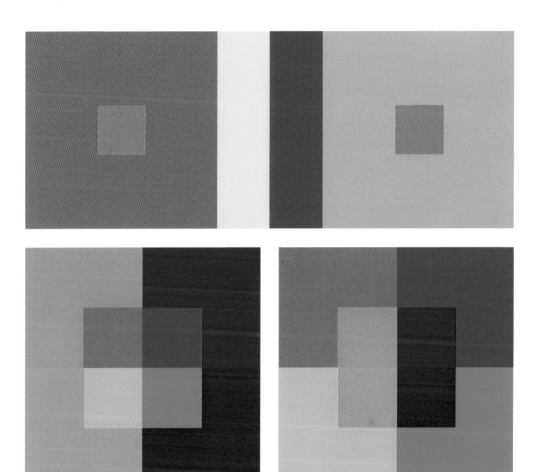

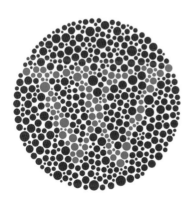

Above: Examples (as used by Josef Albers) of how context can change the appearance of colour.

Left: The Ishihara test used to identify red-green colour blindness. Someone with the condition would be unable to make out the green 'W'.

Further Reading →

Sean Adams, *The Designer's Dictionary of Colour* (Abrams, 2017)
Josef Albers, *Interaction of Colour* (1963)
Eddie Opara & John Cantwell, *Color Works* (Rockport, 2014)

Logo

The term 'logo' originated as an abbreviation of either 'logotype', 'logogram' or 'logograph', all of which mean a mark or drawing representing a word. Logotype remains a term in graphic design, meaning a typographic logo that spells out the company's full name (also known as a 'wordmark'). A logo implies a symbol - something that graphically represents a word (usually a company's or organization's name) non-verbally - although some logos combine symbols with text. 'Brandmark' and 'trademark' have also been used to mean the same thing, but logo has become the dominant term, although it is just one aspect of what is generally called 'branding'. A brand originally referred to a mark burned onto the skin of livestock to identify ownership.

Besides cattle brands, other historic examples of logo-like symbols (vital when literacy was rare) include emblems, mascots, coats of arms, crests, hallmarks, monograms (made from combing two or more letters) and makers' marks. Producers have long aimed to identify their goods, differentiating them from their competitors, but the modern conception of a logo arose after the Industrial Revolution - the transition to mechanized factory production that began in the late 18th century - as advertising and packaging became more sophisticated and consumerism grew. Legislation such as trademarking and copyright laws became particularly important in protecting companies' logos from being copied or faked. Many early logos were based on a company founder's signature, but symbols were also explored: the first trademark in the United Kingdom was for Bass Brewery, which in 1876 registered the red triangle it had long applied to its beer barrels.

Modernism's preoccupation with reducing complexity down to a simple essence, would be influential on the development of the logo design discipline. The latter half of the 20th century - generally considered the 'golden age' of logo design - coincided with the height of modernist influence. Logos were just one aspect of the comprehensive 'corporate identity' programmes developed by modernist designers, albeit the most visible. In contemporary branding, there has been a shift away from emphasis on a singular logo, with designers instead aiming to create flexible systems and immersive 'brand worlds'. Yet logos continue to fascinate, garnering much praise and critique. Logo symbols generally fall into one or more of a few categories - abstract shapes, pictorial, monogrammatic (using one or more letters or numbers) or emblems (using traditional forms found in heraldry such as shields and badges).

Top Row (L→R): United Airlines, Saul Bass & Associates (1974), Schwitter Klischees, Karl Gerstner (1962).

Middle Row (L→R): British Steel, David Gentleman (1969); Glasgow Airport, Margaret Calvert (1965).

Bottom Row (L→R): Deutsche Bank, Anton Stankowski (1974); Swiss Federal Railways, Hans Hartmann (1972).

Further Reading →

David Airey, *Logo Design Love* (Peachpit, 2014)
Stephen Bateman and Angus Hyland, *Symbol* (Laurence King, 2014)
Michael Evamy, *Logo* (Laurence King, 2021)

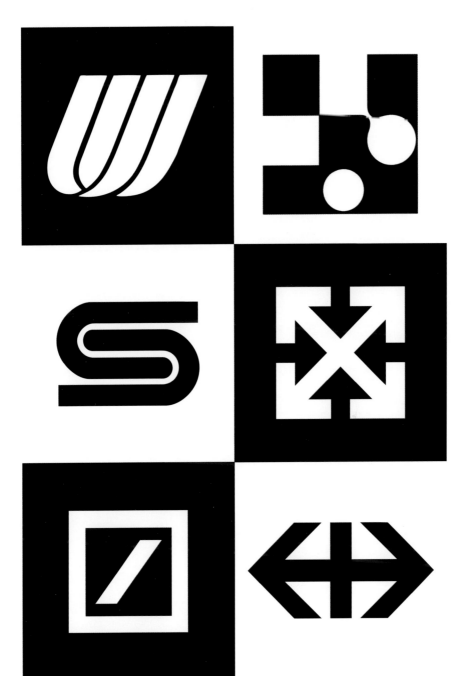

Ornament

Ornamentation is a significant point of debate in design history: a key early principle of modernism was a total opposition to its use. In 1908 Austrian architect Adolf Loos (1870–1933) declared in his essay 'Ornament and Crime' that the 'evolution of culture is synonymous with the removal of ornament from utilitarian objects'.[7] For Loos and his fellow proto-modernists, ornament was wasteful and created products that were replaced when they went out of fashion, rather than when they stopped functioning. The turn against ornament, it was hoped, would be part of a more efficient, rational world; it was as much a social cause as an aesthetic one.

The definition of ornament – 'a thing used or serving to make something look more attractive but usually having no practical purpose' – is perhaps clearer in other areas of design, such as architecture or product design, than in graphic design, where visual appeal is frequently tied up with the purpose of the communication, especially in a commercial context. While few would argue that a purely functional pieces of design like road signs or medicine instruction booklets are suitable places for ornament's beautifying presence, in our hyper-capitalist economy attracting eyes is often more important than clarity.

For modernists, ornamentation was shunned, giving their work a purity and strong visual impact. However, it came back with a vengeance once culture turned towards postmodernism. Ornament, it was argued, was a main carrier of meaning in graphic design and deserved to be a serious consideration in any piece of visual communication. Postmodern practitioners also considered the gendered and racial context of the anti-ornament tendency, noting that ornament had long been associated negatively with femininity and women's 'irrational' tendencies, as well as with peoples and cultures that did not fit into the narrow confines of white Eurocentric modernism. In her 2003 essay 'Toward a Definition of the DecoRational', American designer Denise Gonzales Crisp notes that the 'rationalist aesthetic as theorized and practiced by Mid-Century Modernists is not only of a different time, but of a different place, a different gender, a different ethos'.[8] Digital technology, and its seemingly infinite options and techniques, has seen ornament become an intrinsic aspect of contemporary graphic design and a major area of experimentation.

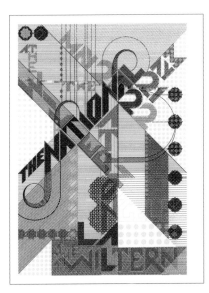

Above Left: 'The National' poster, Marian Bantjes, 2010.

Above Right: Rebrand of the Crane Paper Company, COLLINS, 2020.

Below Right: Book design for *The Beauty Book*, Sagmeister & Walsh, Phaidon, 2018.

Below Left: 'Vlow! Festival' poster, Studio Feixen, 2016.

Further Reading →
Jessica Helfand, *Design: The Invention of Desire* (Yale University Press, 2016)
Owen Jones, *The Grammar of Ornament* (1856)

Defaults

'Default' is a word with many meanings, but in a design context it usually refers to an approach presented automatically. Although there were cases where design could be 'default' in the pre-digital age (e.g. if a printer had only one typeface), interest in the idea of 'default design' mostly arose with the personal computer. Software is programmed to have a preordained setting that users are presented with by default before they make a conscious decision to specify an alternative. Default can also mean a customary or standard process, something reverted to by choice.

Though a contentious term, 'default graphic design' has come to signify particular limitations the designer has consciously chosen to embrace (rather than coming from necessity), such as primarily using black and white, using typefaces that are preloaded on all computers at preset point sizes, using images without manipulation, keeping layouts as basic as possible - e.g. having everything centred - and eschewing guiding principles like typographic hierarchy. In web design, there has been a trend for 'brutalist' websites which are stripped back, functional and don't rely on complex special effects.

Modernism was, for some designers, an attempt to find a new 'default' for visual communication - a rational, efficient way of working suitable for the modern age. Later, the stylistic excesses of postmodern graphics led to many designers feeling exhausted by endless possibilities, as well as uneasy with design trends' connection with rampant capitalism, to which the exploration of constraints or utilitarianism was a rebellion. In a 2003 interview in *Emigre*, American designer and writer Rob Giampietro (b. 1978) discussed 'default systems in graphic design', which he considered 'critiques of the conditions of their own making' that offer 'a release from the breathless pace at which design now runs'.[9]

In branding, there have been attempts at an 'unbranding' approach - the creation of identities that stand out by rejecting normal rules about uniqueness and 'ownability', often in a way laced with irony. Embracing defaults can be seen as one symptom of a wider rejection of the aims or methods of dominant graphic practice. As a term, default has negative connotations (to default on a loan means failing to pay it), implying a lack of thought or care. In reality, a lot of graphic design that appears 'default', comes from a position of criticality, involving experiments in standardisation, a self-referential interest in work that reveals the manner of its own creation, a reckoning with the legacy of modernism, focus on intellectual rather than aesthetic questions, or a mixture of the above.

RICHARD VENLET

TITLE	00
WORKS	50
PERIOD	11 08 90
	21 11 02
FORMAT	27,6 X
	21,6 CM
AUTHORS	3
ILL.	207
PAGES	232
ISBN	90-72828
	27-5
COPIES	1300
PRICE	30.00 €

Left: Book cover for *Richard Venlet: 00*, Mevis & Van Deursen, 2002.

Below & Bottom: VICELAND graphic identity, Crotel, 2017.

Vernacular

Vernacular is a term that comes from discussions of language, where it can mean a 'mode of expression that occurs in ordinary speech rather than formal writing'.[10] It began to be used in a design context in discussions of architecture, thanks to such influential books as Bernard Rudofsky's *Architecture without Architects* (1964) and *Learning from Las Vegas* by Robert Venturi, Denise Scott Brown and Steven Izenour (1972). Vernacular design is broad, but refers to examples of visual communication that are amateurish, everyday, non-corporate, unsophisticated, crudely made, anonymous or awkward. Vernacular can also be used to refer to regionally specific design styles.

While examples of vernacular graphic design, by their very definition, are not produced by design agencies or likely to get featured in glossy magazines, they often have an unpretentious charm of their own that cannot be matched by slicker, corporate graphic design. Vernacular graphics can be filled with personality, and the originality that comes from a disregard for conventional design rules. For this reason, many designers have seen vernacular graphics as a rich source of visual inspiration, and it is not uncommon for designers to collect examples that have caught their eye. Thanks to the rise of free digital software that makes it easier than ever for people with no formal design training to achieve a professional look, vernacular examples of graphic design are becoming rarer, which only adds to their appeal, making them stand out even more.

Taking inspiration from the vernacular would be particularly associated with

Above: 'Fire Sale' poster, Junki Hong / FISK, 2017.

Opposite Above: Outwest tyepface, Ed Fella for Emigre fonts, 1993.

Opposite Below: Newspaper advert for Masticar food festival Buenos Aires, Yani Guille & Co., 2016.

Avalon Emerson + Ben UFO

Friday Dec 3
BROOKLYN
Knockdown Center
Lighting by Nitemind

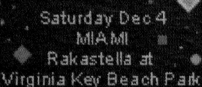

Saturday Dec 4
MIAMI
Rakastella at
Virginia Key Beach Park

Friday Dec 17
SAN FRANCISCO
DJ Dials Presents
at 1015 Folsom

Saturday Dec 18
LOS ANGELES
Making Time at
Don Quixote

the postmodern era (see pages 56-63). The *everyday* became a rich source for those seeking to challenge high modernism's elitism and the conservative status quo. Particularly vocal about the virtues of the vernacular was Tibor Kalman (1949-99), who referenced everyday sources in much of his work. Writing with Karrie Jacobs in 1990, Kalman declared: 'The vernacular is designed as if design were a regular thing to do, and not the sacred mission of an elite professional class. It's design that hasn't been ordered and purified by the methods of trained practitioners. It's communication without the strategy, marketing, or the proprietary quantitative research. And that's what's good about it.'[11]

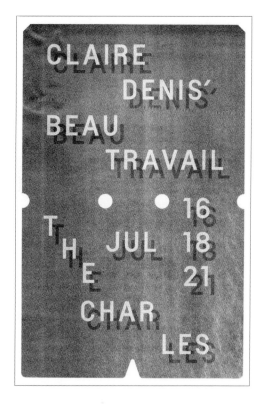

Above: 'Beau Travail at The Charles' theatre risograph poster, Shiva Nallaperumal, 2022.

Opposite: 'Avalon Emerson + Ben UFO' tour poster, Noah Baker, 2021.

Further Reading →
Nick Deakin & James Dyer, *Graphic Events: A Realist Account of Graphic Design* (Onomatopee, 2022)
Peter Hall, *Tibor Kalman: Perverse Optimist* (Princeton Architectural Press, 2000)

Propaganda

Referring to any piece of media designed
to influence public opinion in the
furtherance of an agenda (usually a
political or social one), propaganda is
mostly associated with either wartime or
oppressive regimes. Propaganda as a form
of visual communication usually implies
manipulation, through bias, selective
information or outright falsehoods.
Propaganda is not objective: it often
provokes emotional, irrational responses.

Particularly influential on the
phenomenon of propaganda was Edward
Bernays (1891–1995), a nephew of
psychoanalyst Sigmund Freud (1856–1939).
In his 1928 book *Propaganda* Bernays, who
is also credited with pioneering the
field of public relations, writes that
'whether in the sphere of politics or
business, in our social conduct or our
ethical thinking, we are dominated by
the relatively small number of persons
who understand the mental processes and
social patterns of the masses. It is
they who pull the wires which control
the public mind.'[12] Bernays articulated
the huge impact that mass media and
modern advertising were having on public
consciousness. Global propaganda itself
had emerged earlier, during World War I,
particularly through posters. Every major
country involved in the war developed
similar techniques in their printed
attempts to encourage men to enlist
in the armed services and influence
the behaviour of those staying behind.
Techniques included caricaturing the
enemy, inciting patriotism, using shame
and peer pressure, reinforcing the
justness of the cause, and presenting
idealized visions of home.

Bernays saw propaganda as a vital
component of a democratic society, but
it would become associated with the
totalitarian regimes that arose in the
interwar period, which sought to use
modern media to control their citizens.
By the time of the Cold War, propaganda
in the West had become more sophisticated
and in general aimed to be less obvious,
not even appearing to be propaganda. This
has been termed 'soft power' – getting
people to want the outcome you want
through covert co-option, not blatant
coercion. Graphic design itself became
an example of American 'soft power'
propaganda when the United States
Information Agency organized 'Graphic Arts
USA', an exhibition that toured Soviet
cities during 1963–4, featuring leading
examples of American graphic art, with
the ulterior motive of showing how much
commercial and artistic freedom existed
under capitalism.

Above Left: 'Women of Britain say "Go!"' British poster, Parliamentary Recruiting Committee, E.P. Kealey, 1915.

Above Right: 'Subscribe to War Bonds!' German poster, Lucian Bernhard, 1917.

Below Right: 'First Call' US poster, James Montgomery Flagg, c.1917.

Below Left: 'War Until Victory' Russian poster, 1917.

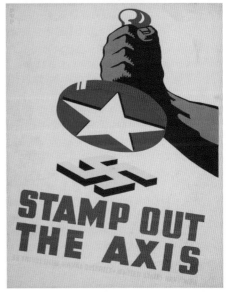

Above Left: 'Free from Misery', US Office of the Coordinator of Inter-American Affairs poster, Alexey Brodovitch, 1942.

Above Right: 'He's Watching You' poster, Glenn Grohe, 1942.

Below Right: 'Stamp out the Axis' poster for the Thirteenth Naval District, United States Navy W.P.A., Phil von Phul, 1941.

Opposite: 'Destroy This Mad Brute' US poster, San Francisco Army Recruiting District, Harry R. Hopps, 1917.

Further Reading →

Steven Heller, *Iron Fists: Branding the 20th-Century Totalitarian State* (Phaidon, 2008)

Margaret Timmers (ed.), *The Power of the Poster* (V&A Publications, 1999)

Design Politics

'Every human artefact, whether painting, poem, chair, or rubbish bin – evokes and invokes the inescapable totality of a culture, and the hidden assumptions which condition cultural priorities.' Norman Potter, *What is a Designer?* (1969)[13]

Graphic design can be overtly political – serving party campaigns or grassroots activism – but all graphic design is, in itself, political. Like all media and communication, whether knowingly or not, design either conforms to the existing socio-political order or challenges it. As the Austrian-American designer Victor Papanek (1923–98) explained, in 'an age of mass production when everything must be planned and designed, design has become the most powerful tool with which man shapes his tools and environments (and, by extension, society and himself).'[14]

The modernist dream of apolitical, objective neutrality has been challenged by postmodernism and the sustained growth in social justice movements, which have brought attention to power dynamics and cultural biases. Modernist neutrality came from a particular demographic – white, European, male, educated, middle and upper class – a reflection of who held power; their idea of what constituted 'neutral', therefore, was far from it. Even defining graphic design is a task with political implications, involving the judgements of those who have traditionally been in privileged positions to make such calls, with inherent biases and motivation to uphold the status quo. As pointed out by French theorist Roland Barthes (1950–80), dominant ideologies present their systems as natural, rather than as what they are – elaborate constructions.

In a 1970 essay, US philosopher Susan Sontag (1933–2004) explored the role of design within capitalism: 'What keeps posters multiplying in the urban areas of the capitalist world is their commercial utility in selling particular products and, beyond that, in perpetuating a social climate in which it is normative to buy.'[15] This idea was built upon by French philosopher Jean-François Lyotard (1924–88), who wrote that designers' work 'brings commodities into circulation. It promotes them. Whether it is cultural and of public or social interest, or of private use and interest is a difference forever futile once culture has become part of the market and the public is privatised'.[16] A figure astutely aware of the connection between graphics and politics was Dutch graphic designer Jan van Toorn (1932–2020), who wrote that design 'traditionally views its own action as serving the public interest, but which is engaged at the same time in the private interests of clients and media […] accepting the world image of the established order as the context for its own action.'[17]

Above Left: Make Amazon Pay poster for Progressive International, Michael Oswell, 2020.

Above Right: 'Raymond Loewy Genius' exhibition poster, Grapus, 1987.

Below: 'Every Poster is a Political Poster', Other Forms, 2017.

Further Reading →

Ruben Pater, *Caps Lock: How Capitalism Took Hold of Graphic Design, and How to Escape from It* (Valiz, 2021)

Ruben Pater, *The Politics of Design: A (Not So) Global Design Manual for Visual Communication* (BIS, 2016)

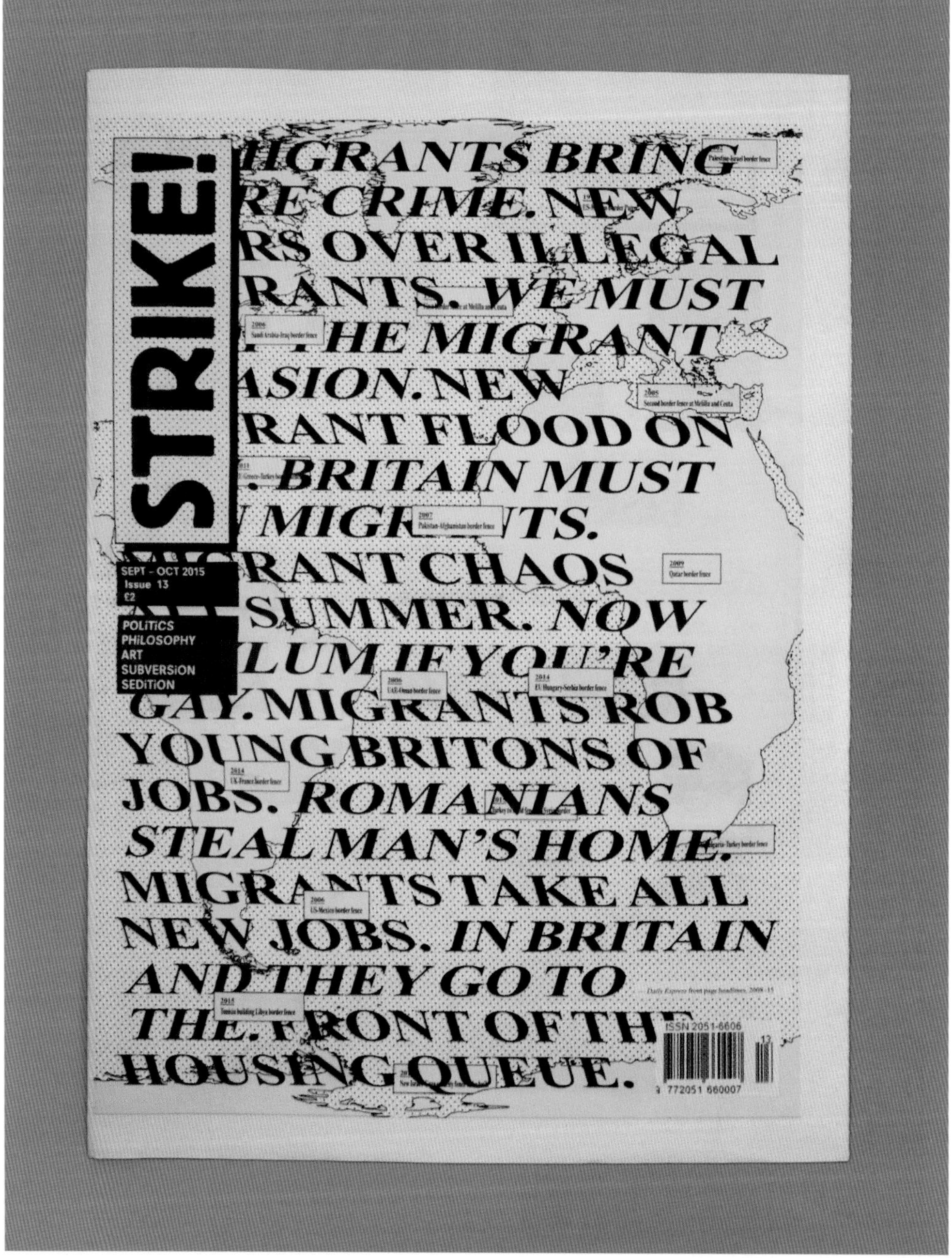

STRIKE!

SEPT - OCT 2015
Issue 13
£2

POLITICS
PHiLOSOPHY
ART
SUBVERSION
SEDiTiON

MIGRANTS BRING
RE CRIME. NEW
RS OVER ILLEGAL
RANTS. WE MUST
HE MIGRANT
ASION. NEW
RANT FLOOD ON
BRITAIN MUST
MIGR TS.
RANT CHAOS
SUMMER. NOW
LUM IF YOU'RE
GAY. MIGRANTS ROB
YOUNG BRITONS OF
JOBS. ROMANIANS
STEAL MAN'S HOME.
MIGRANTS TAKE ALL
NEW JOBS. IN BRITAIN
AND THEY GO TO
THE FRONT OF THE
HOUSING QUEUE.

Daily Express front page headlines, 2008-15

ISSN 2051-6606

3 772051 660007

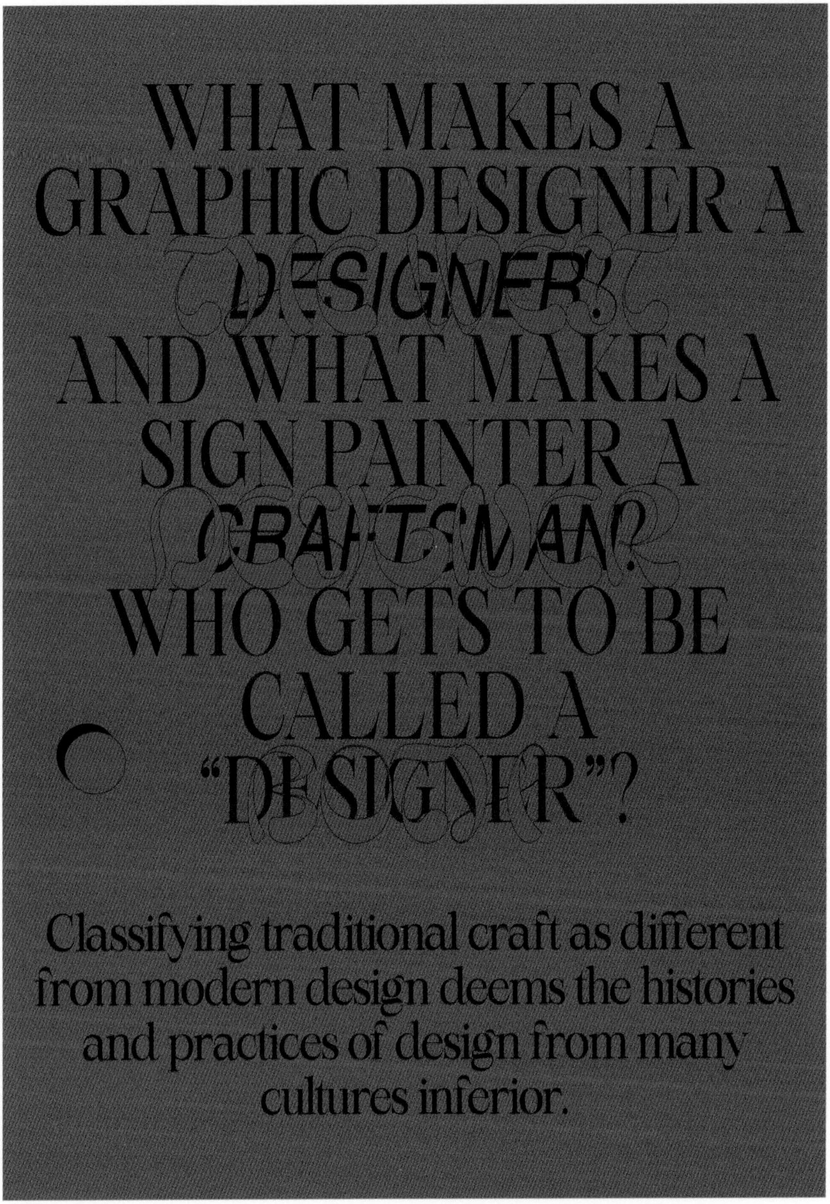

WHAT MAKES A
GRAPHIC DESIGNER A
DESIGNER?
AND WHAT MAKES A
SIGN PAINTER A
CRAFTSMAN?
WHO GETS TO BE
CALLED A
"DESIGNER"?

Classifying traditional craft as different
from modern design deems the histories
and practices of design from many
cultures inferior.

Above: 'Reclaiming Cultural Identity through Graphic Design' poster,
Dionne Pajarillaga, 2021

Opposite: *Strike!* magazine cover, Barnbrook, 2015.

Ethics

Successfully used, graphic design can help to sell products, spread messages, influence minds and change behaviour. As individual graphic designers, we must ask ourselves whether there are contexts in which we would not want our skills to be put to use. In some cases – for instance tobacco advertising – laws have been put in place to stop the promotion of a harmful product. But more often it is up to designers themselves to decide where they draw the line ethically, and what they feel comfortable using their expertise on. As graphic designer and activist Lucienne Roberts (b.1962) puts it: 'Every decision we make as designers has an ethical dimension, requiring us all to "balance the forces" in our own small way as responsible individuals.'[18] Designers play a role, big or small, in wider systems and are complicit through involvement.

Many of the early 20th-century avant-garde movements were concerned with how art and design could be used in useful, productive, ethical ways, often with a political dimension. By the mid-century, many graphic designers had become subsumed by consumerism, although not all were comfortable with this state of affairs and the morally dubious techniques employed in advertising and promotions. The sixties saw a watershed moment: Ken Garland's (1929–2021) 1964 manifesto 'First Things First'. Co-signed by 21 other British designers, Garland's text was a plea for designers to use their skills responsibly for 'worthwhile purposes' and to reverse their priorities towards 'more useful and more lasting forms of communication'.

Garland, an outspoken designer who often used his skills for causes he believed in, influenced a new generation. However, he had foreseen the direction the industry was heading in and had little power to change the kind of jobs available to design graduates, which have always been concentrated in corporate and advertising fields. The manifesto would be republished and renewed for the new millennium in 1999, with 33 signatories declaring that 'unprecedented environmental, social and cultural crises demand our attention' and critiquing uncontested consumerism.[19] Another, environmentally focused, version was published online in 2020, coinciding with the 50th anniversary of Earth Day.

The term 'citizen designer' has become popular as a label for designers who contribute their skills in a meaningful, responsible way, using their 'visual language training to address societal issues, either within or in addition to their professional design practice'.[20] When it comes to ethical design, recent discourse has also made sure to point out that having the agency to turn down work or challenge employers is a privilege.

first things first

A manifesto

A manifesto

We, the undersigned, are graphic designers, photographers and students who have been brought up in a world in which the techniques and apparatus of advertising have persistently been presented to us as the most lucrative, effective and desirable means of using our talents. We have been bombarded with publications devoted to this belief, applauding the work of those who have flogged their skill and imagination to sell such things as:

cat food, stomach powders, detergent, hair restorer, striped toothpaste, aftershave lotion, beforeshave lotion, slimming diets, fattening diets, deodorants, fizzy water, cigarettes, roll-ons, pull-ons and slip-ons.

By far the greatest time and effort of those working in the advertising industry are wasted on these trivial purposes, which contribute little or nothing to our national prosperity.

In common with an increasing number of the general public, we have reached a saturation point at which the high pitched scream of consumer selling is no more than sheer noise. We think that there are other things more worth using our skill and experience on. There are signs for streets and buildings, books and periodicals, catalogues, instructional manuals, industrial photography, educational aids, films, television features, scientific and industrial publications and all the other media through which we promote our trade, our education, our culture and our greater awareness of the world.

We do not advocate the abolition of high pressure consumer advertising: this is not feasible. Nor do we want to take any of the fun out of life. But we are proposing a reversal of priorities in favour of the more useful and more lasting forms of communication. We hope that our society will tire of gimmick merchants, status salesmen and hidden persuaders, and that the prior call on our skills will be for worthwhile purposes. With this in mind, we propose to share our experience and opinions, and to make them available to colleagues, students and others who may be interested.

Edward Wright
Geoffrey White
William Slack
Caroline Rawlence
Ian McLaren
Sam Lambert
Ivor Kamlish
Gerald Jones
Bernard Higton
Brian Grimbly
John Garner
Ken Garland
Anthony Froshaug
Robin Fior
Germano Facetti
Ivan Dodd
Harriet Crowder
Anthony Clift
Gerry Cinamon
Robert Chapman
Ray Carpenter
Ken Briggs

Published by Ken Garland.
Printed by Goodwin Press Ltd. London N4

WORK HARD & BE NICE TO PEOPLE

Above: 'First Things First' manifesto, published and designed by Ken Garland, 1964.

Left: 'Work Hard & Be Nice To People' letterpress poster, Anthony Burrill, 2004.

Further Reading →

Steven Heller & Veronique Vienne, *Citizen Designer* (Allworth Press, 2018)

Elizabeth Resnick (ed.), *Developing Citizen Designers* (Bloomsbury, 2021)

Lucienne Roberts, *Good: An Introduction to Ethics in Graphic Design* (Bloomsbury, 2020)

Gender

'For the contributions of women in graphic design to be discovered and understood, their different experiences and roles within the patriarchal and capitalist framework they share with men, and their choices and experiences within a female framework, must be acknowledged and explored.' Martha Scotford (1994).[21]

Graphic design has, like society, been historically male-dominated. Of course, there were examples of women working in the 20th century who showed that gender was no limit on ability, but in a patriarchal world their roles were often marginalised, downplayed or ignored.

Here are just two examples. Cipe Pineles (1908-91), a talented magazine art director and illustrator was proposed for the prestigious Art Directors Club of New York by her mentor, Mehemed Fehmy Agha (1896-1978), for ten years straight. However, she became a member – the first woman in its 28-year history – only in 1948 when the club wished to induct her husband, William Golden (1911-59), who pointed out that his wife was more qualified. Pineles, whose work was further marginalized by being primarily for women's magazines, later became the first female inducted to the Art Directors Club Hall of Fame in 1975. It would take 15 years for another woman to join her.

Also in the mid-century era, we have the example of Elaine Lustig Cohen, who worked for her husband Alvin Lustig, first in an administrative role, then, as Alvin's eyesight deteriorated, as a more hands-on assistant, but he still made all creative decisions, even once blind. Elaine, who described her role as that of an 'office slave', took on all her husband's clients when he died at 40, soon proving she was every bit as talented in her own right.

For designers, the role of gender has many facets: graphic design can be used powerfully in the fight for gender equality (e.g. in the work of groups such as the See Red Women's Workshop or the Guerrilla Girls), but graphic design can also be complicit in the communication of sexist messages and imagery. As an industry, design remains overwhelmingly male-dominated, with women often still facing discrimination, overt sexism, the 'glass ceiling' and gendered labour. Gender equality in design would mean truly equal opportunities and not having gender dictate the style of work, or type of client or project that a designer is expected to do. Gendered language comes into this, and graphic design is particularly susceptible to 'gendering' more generally, with particular styles being described as 'masculine' or 'feminine' based on stereotypical, 'binary' ideas of gender.

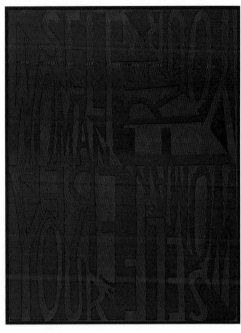

Above Left: 'The State and Sexist Advertising Cause Illness - Don't Let These Men Invade Your Homes', See Red Women's Workshop, 1974.

Above Right: *Woman Free Yourself* print, Faith Ringgold, 1971.

Below: *Women against violence against women*, print, Ann Aiken, c.1975.

Further Reading →

Extra Bold: A Feminist, Inclusive, Anti-racist, Nonbinary Field Guide for Graphic Designers (Princeton Architectural Press, 2021)

Anne Massey, *Women in Design* (Thames & Hudson, 2022)

THE ADVANTAGES OF BEING A WOMAN ARTIST:

Working without the pressure of success
Not having to be in shows with men
Having an escape from the art world in your 4 free-lance jobs
Knowing your career might pick up after you're eighty
Being reassured that whatever kind of art you make it will be labeled feminine
Not being stuck in a tenured teaching position
Seeing your ideas live on in the work of others
Having the opportunity to choose between career and motherhood
Not having to choke on those big cigars or paint in Italian suits
Having more time to work when your mate dumps you for someone younger
Being included in revised versions of art history
Not having to undergo the embarrassment of being called a genius
Getting your picture in the art magazines wearing a gorilla suit

A PUBLIC SERVICE MESSAGE FROM **GUERRILLA GIRLS** CONSCIENCE OF THE ART WORLD

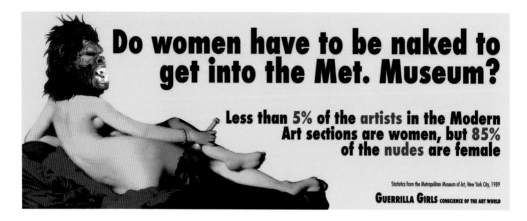

Do women have to be naked to get into the Met. Museum?

Less than 5% of the artists in the Modern Art sections are women, but 85% of the nudes are female

Statistics from the Metropolitan Museum of Art, New York City, 1989

GUERRILLA GIRLS CONSCIENCE OF THE ART WORLD

Top: 'The Advantages of Being a Woman Artist' poster, Guerrilla Girls, 1988.
Above: 'Do Women Have to Be Naked to Get into the Met. Museum?' poster, Guerrilla Girls, 1989.

Above: *Riposte* magazine, Shaz Madani Studio, 2019.

Left: *The Xenofeminist Manifesto* by Laboria Cuboniks, book cover by Chloe Scheffe, 2018.

Below: Illustration for For All Womankind, Deva Pardue, 2016.

Race

In 'The Black Experience in Graphic Design', a 1968 article for *Print*, Dorothy Jackson concluded by saying: 'There is no such thing as "black design," only design by a black person. The problem — for everyone — is to get more black people into positions where they can make their own unique contribution as designers.'[22] The piece features input from five Black designers whose frustrations around the lack of opportunity, racism and tokenism (being hired to improve diversity rather than for ability) of the American design industry highlight issues that remain relevant. Although there have been some improvements in racial equality in Western societies generally since 1968, graphic design remains overwhelmingly white, with diversity often failing to reflect the ethnic makeup of the general population, an issue that intersects with factors such as class, gender and nationality.

Rather than the best-case scenario being that more individuals identifying as Black, indigenous and people of colour (BIPOC) are allowed into the industry by white gatekeepers, there are increasing calls to 'decolonize' graphic design. This would mean decentring and challenging the predominantly white, Eurocentric, Western values, standards and conventions that have dominated design, creating a more pluralistic and inclusive idea of graphic design that values different backgrounds and perspectives, not homogeneity.

Many racial discrepancies can be traced back to modernism, whose denigration of ornament had racial undertones (particularly evident in Adolf Loos's outright racist 'Ornament and Crime' essay) and which, in seeking to enforce aesthetic standards, had a colonial mindset.

In the wake of the Black Lives Matter (BLM) movement, discussions of race have never been so mainstream, and in the design industry there has also been dialogue about the difference between 'performative' allyship, done to get good 'optics', and action that actually makes a difference. Most of the powerful designs from the Civil Rights era (such as the work of Emory Douglas [b. 1943]) came from Black-led protest movements, rather than the white American design industry. However, as Bobby C. Martin Jr pointed out in 2020, historically 'many of the jobs promoting Black culture were awarded to White designers. Now I'm left to wonder how many of the recent ads showing support for the Black Lives Matter movement were created by Black designers or Black-owned agencies?'[23]

Having more diverse workforces would make 'racial justice' content less hypocritical, and would hopefully also lead to advertising and design agencies being more sensitive and less likely to repeat the racial stereotypes and harmful missteps that litter the history of our media. Post-BLM there have already been improvements, such as the dropping of racialized product mascots like 'Uncle Ben' and 'Aunt Jemima' which perpetuated stereotypes dating back to slavery, but much remains to be done and urgently.

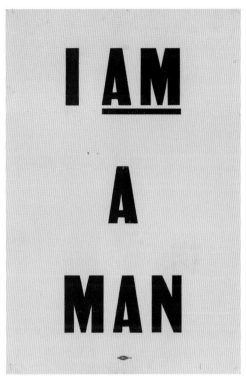

Above Left: *Harlem: A Forum of Negro Life* Issue 1 cover, illustrated and designed by Aaron Douglas, 1928.

Above Right: 'I AM A MAN' placard from the Memphis Sanitation Workers' Strike, 1968.

Below: 'Revolution in our Lifetime' Poster for the Black Panther Party, Emory Douglas, c.1970.

Further Reading →

BIPOC Design History, bipocdesignhistory.com
Peter Claver Fine, *The Design of Race* (Bloomsbury, 2021)
Kelly Walters, *Black, Brown + Latinx Design Educators* (Princeton Architectural Press, 2021)

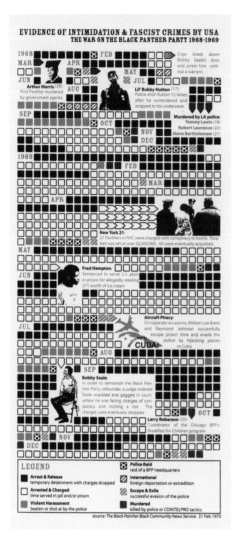

Above Left: 'Evidence of Intimidation & Fascist Crimes by USA: The War on the Black Panther Party 1968-1969', poster, Michael Hoerger, 2010.

Above Right: Letterpress poster, Amos Paul Kennedy Jr, 2020.

Right: Placard used on the March on Washington for Jobs and Freedom, 1963.

Above: Black Outdoor Art Project, Jahnavi Inniss, 2020.

Below Left: *Lakȟóta + Dakȟóta Visual Essay*, Sadie Red Wing, 2016.

Below Right: 'To Be Known and Heard: Systemic Racism and Princeton University' virtual exhibition, Isometric Studio, 2021.

Sexuality

Graphic design has long been dominated by, and tailored to, cisgender heterosexual people, but design has also played a major part in the history of LGBTQ+ (an abbreviation for lesbian, gay, bisexual, transgender and queer, with the plus acknowledging that there are many further gender identities and sexual orientations) movements that have fought for rights, acceptance and equality throughout the last two centuries. As noted by the authors of *Extra Bold*, 'design and creativity have played powerful roles in movements to make gay sexuality and diverse gender identities visible and accepted within the broader culture. Artists have also sought to keep queerness queer, by resisting assimilation and embracing difference.'[24]

Much 'queer' design, like the term 'queer' itself (once a pejorative term for gay people - the word originally meant something strange or wrong), has been about embracing or reclaiming styles, symbols and language. A case in point is the pink triangle: once used by the Nazis as a badge to identify gay men in concentration camps, it was revived as a symbol of LGBT pride and protest against homophobia in the 1970s, and was used by the AIDS Coalition To Unleash Power (ACT UP) group in its iconic poster design - paired with the unflinching slogan 'Silence = Death' - that became a rallying cry for action during the AIDS crisis. ACT UP, and the AIDS activist artist collective Gran Fury that evolved from it, used sophisticated graphics in an attempt to 'compact complex messages into smooth one-liners'. The pink triangle was chosen because 'any single photographic image

would be exclusionary in terms of race, gender and class'. Much design in LGBTQ+ contexts has been about this kind of wide acceptance of diversity, as represented by the rainbow flag first designed by Gilbert Baker (1951-2017) in 1978, rather than binaries or prescription.[25]

Many queer designers have sought to champion aesthetic experimentation and excess, rather than wanting to be assimilated into 'mainstream' culture and its ideas of 'good taste'. This has included celebrating styles denigrated as vulgar, kitsch or camp - a characteristic that is hard to define but involves, as explored by Susan Sontag in her 1964 essay 'Notes on Camp', frivolity, naïveté, affect and theatrics. However, as with any minority in graphic design, equality also means the freedom to design however you want, rather than being expected to adopt a particular style or approach due to your identity.

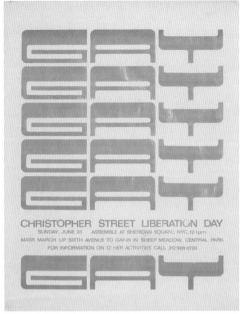

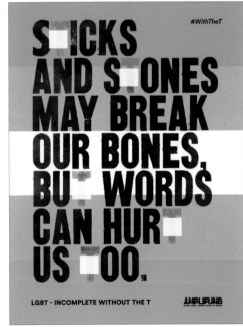

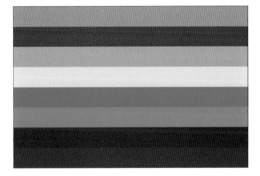

Above Left: 'Silence = Death' poster, ACT UP, 1987.

Above Right: Poster for Christopher Street Liberation Day, 1970.

Below Right: LGBT rainbow flag, Gilbert Baker, 1978.

Below Left: '*LGBT: Incomplete without the T*' campaign poster, Grey London, 2018.

Further Reading →

Andy Campbell, *Queer X Design: 50 Years of Signs, Symbols, Banners, Logos, and Graphic Art of LGBTQ* (Running Press, 2019)

Appropriation

Emerging from late 20th-century post-colonial academic spheres, 'cultural appropriation' is defined as 'members of a majority group adopting cultural elements of a minority group in an exploitative, disrespectful, or stereotypical way'.[26] Cultural appropriation involves power dynamics; it can only be done to historically marginalized or oppressed groups, and by people who are in a privileged position of greater power.

For designers, accustomed to finding inspiration everywhere, it is important to understand what, in the 21st century, is no longer socially acceptable. Appropriation in a graphics context usually is not intentionally malicious; it often comes from a misguided attempt at appreciation or homage. In general, more sensitivity, thought and deeper research can help designers to avoid the exploitation or misappropriation that can be harmful, unsuitable or offensive. Common pitfalls facing graphic designers when dealing with minority cultures include exoticizing (seeing unfamiliar visual culture as superficially more exciting), stereotyping, and harmfully representing entire cultures through a few limited and superficial decorative motifs. Designers also need to be careful not to 'Westernise' the traditional designs of marginalized groups they do not belong to. This only further adds to the 'othering' and perception of inferiority or 'primitivism' that has long been an effect of colonialism. Quoted in a 2020 article, the Native American graphic designer Sadie Red Wing advises that 'taking consideration of traditional cultures in design practices is having the designer defend their design choices without the simple answer: "because it looks cool".'[27] For designers and illustrators depicting people, care must be taken to avoid caricature, a problem that has come to the fore recently around sports team mascots that use harmful stereotypes.

In typography, font websites are littered with tags that 'enforce stereotypes about cultures that are marginalised as "tribal," "folk," or "ethnic."'[28] Stereotypography is a term used to describe the 'stereotyping of cultures through typefaces associated with them', something with a history dating back to 19th-century wood type.[29] There is a historically entrenched tendency to use cruder typefaces for design work related to 'ethnic' content, as well as to create Latin typefaces that clumsily imitate the forms and styles of non-Latin writing systems, reducing sophisticated alphabets to clunky stereotypes.

abcdefghijklmn
opqrstuvwxyz

abcdefghijklmn
opqrstuvwxyz

abcdefghijklm
opqrstuvwxyz

Above: Examples of 'stereotypography': Wonton (Image CLub, 1995); Linotype MhaiThaipe (1997), and Linotype Pide Nashi (1997).

Left: Washington Redskins logo. The team changed its name to Washington Commanders in 2020, while dropping the Native American mascot.

Design as Art

Trying to define the difference between art and design is challenging. Distinctions between art and design are usually related to 'function': most arguments have it that design must serve a practical purpose, whereas art needs no reason to exist. This is complicated by the 'conceptual' turn in art: when artists in the 1960s began to create work that was about the idea and process, not finished objects. Elsewhere, artists like Andy Warhol (1928-1987) - who had begun his career as a commercial illustrator - and his 'Factory' upset the notion that a work of art is created by an individual.

The influence of conceptual art, and ideas around 'authorship' led to many designers questioning their 'servile' role, blurring the boundaries between art and design further. In the modernist era there were designers who painted, such as Swiss stalwarts Max Bill (1908-94) and Richard Paul Lohse (1902-88) (see page 38). Although ideas developed across disciplines, for these practitioners there was usually a clear distinction between 'art' and 'design'. Not all such polymaths saw it thus, however. Among them was Bruno Munari (1907-98), who in *Design as Art* (1966) presciently wrote that by seeking to 'destroy the myth of the Great Artist, of the enormously costly Masterpiece, of the one and only unique divine thing', the 'traditional artist is being transformed into the designer'.[30]

In the wake of postmodernism, trying to distinguish between 'art' and 'design' is increasingly futile, a question of semantics and intent rather than observable characteristics. A better question is: can you use graphic design to create art? Historically, examples show that you can: many Dada artists (see page 23) used typography and created publications (as would the Fluxus movement in the sixties and seventies); the concrete poets printed text-based artworks, while many have used the 'artist's book' as a medium, famously Ed Ruscha (b. 1937) and Dieter Roth (1930-98).

There are artists who use experience in graphic design to their advantage, notably Barbara Kruger (b. 1945), and groups (e.g. Metahaven) that do not allow the distinction between art and design to interfere in their work. There are also graphic designers who count artists as collaborators: Fraser Muggeridge studio, for example, regularly works with Fiona Banner (b. 1966) and Jeremy Deller (b. 1966), alongside more conventional clients.

Further Reading →
Benoît Buquet, *Art and Graphic Design* (Yale University Press, 2021)
Alex Coles (ed.), *Design and Art* (Whitechapel Gallery, 2007)

story, *n.* **1.** *Archaic.* **a.** A connected narration of past events. **b.** A history. **2. a.** An account of some incident. **b.** A report; statement. **c.** An anecdote, esp. an amusing one. **3.** In literature: **a.** A narrative in ⬛⬛⬛ r verse; a tale; esp. ⬛⬛⬛ narrative less elabo ⬛⬛⬛ vel. **b.** The plot of a narrative. **4.** *colloq.* A fib; a lie. **5.** *U.S. Journalism.* Any news article. — *v.t.;* 1. *archaic.* To narrate or describe in story. 2. To adorn with a story, or scene from history, etc.

Top + Above: Jeremy Deller, Warning Graphic Content, The Modern Institute, Glasgow, November 2021–January 2022. Design by Fraser Muggeridge Studio.

Left: *Untitled [Printed Matter Matters],* Barbara Kruger, 1989. Kruger worked at Condé Nast magazines before working with text and images as an artist.

Designer as Author

Although connected to the idea of graphic designers as writers, the 'authorship' in 'designer as author' goes deeper than writing. 'Author' has historically implied ownership, authenticity and authority. In the post-World War II era many branches of critical philosophy challenged traditional notions of the author as the sole arbiter of meaning. In line with postmodern currents, the 'dethroning' of the author was rooted in subjectivity and interpretation.

Particularly influential on postmodern ideas of authorship was Roland Barthes' 1967 essay 'The Death of the Author'. Barthes declared that; 'We know now that a text is not a line of words releasing a single "theological" meaning (the "message" of the Author-God) but a multi-dimensional space in which a variety of writings, none of them original, blend and clash. The text is a tissue of quotations drawn from the innumerable centres of culture.'[31] Barthes pointed to a modern notion of authorship: meaning was interpreted by readers, rather than imposed by authors.

What, then, does this have to do with graphic design? The designer's role was traditionally that of a service provider, optimally presenting content the designer has been given. A designer setting a book would not interpret the text; their role was an anonymous one, simply to make sure it was as easy to read as possible. As the American typographic expert Beatrice Warde (1900-69) wrote in her 1932 essay 'The Crystal Goblet, or Printing Should Be Invisible': 'Type well used is invisible as type, just as the perfect talking voice is the unnoticed vehicle for the transmission of words.'[32] Inherent in what

Warde wrote is the concept of authorship; the designer can, through their choices, aid or disrupt how a text is read and how its meaning is perceived. Designers are responsible for an extra layer - the interface between author and reader. Even using Warde's estimation of good typography - well-ordered, serif type - as an example, the designer is still a kind of co-author, imbuing authority and prestige by shaping text in a way that conformed to traditional rules.

For modernist designers, the goals of objectivity, rationalism and functionalism meant that they were even further from authorship. The content came first and the designer's subservient job was to present it neutrally. By the 1960s new technology and ideas impacted designers. Especially important was the Canadian theorist Marshall McLuhan (1911-80), particularly his contention that 'The medium is the message', by which he meant that the content of a piece of media does not arise from just what it says, but how it says it. Taking a leaf from McLuhan, it could be argued that the content of a design cannot be separated from the design itself.

It was one of McLuhan's books that would present a new type of book design in which the designer is credited as an author. *The Medium is the Massage* (1967), designed by Quentin Fiore, took an 'integrated' approach to the presentation of text and image, with the two working in tandem across double-page spreads

Opposite: *The Art of Looking Sideways* by Alan Fletcher (2001). Conceived, written and designed by British graphic designer and Pentagram co-founder Alan Fletcher, this book explored a plethora of subjects related to creativity through an eclectic approach that playfully integrated text and image.

Words and pictures on how to make twinkles in the eye and colours agree in the dark. Thoughts on mindscaping, moonlighting and daydreams. Have you seen a purple cow? When less can be more than enough. The art of looking sideways. To gaze is to think. Are you left-eyed? Living out loud. Buy junk, sell antiques. The Golden Mean. Standing ideas on their heads. To look is to listen. Insights on the mind's eye. Every status has its symbol. 'Do androids dream of electric sheep?' Why feel blue? Triumphs of imagination such as the person you love is 71.8% water. Do not adjust your mind, there's a fault in reality. Teach yourself ignorance. The belly-button problem.

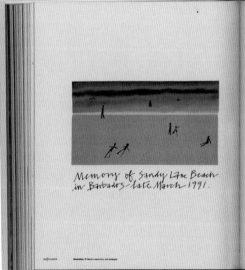

Memory of Sandy Lane Beach in Barbados late March 1991.

and over pages. In the book, McLuhan writes: 'All media work us over completely. They are so pervasive in their personal, political, economic, aesthetic, psychological, moral, ethical, and social consequences that they leave no part of us untouched, unaffected, unaltered.'[33] The design, illustrating McLuhan's point about medium and message, takes more inspiration from the moving images of film and television than traditional book design. New media changes old media, and the designer, even by a process as simple as the pairing of text and image, becomes a co-author, changing how the reader understands and interprets the text.

Another example of an integrated approach is the book *Ways of Seeing* (1972) written by John Berger (1926–2017) and designed by Richard Hollis (b. 1934). Published as an adaptation of a television documentary series, the book's design uses image within text, aiming to match Berger's on-screen narration. Hollis's approach was influenced by the book designs of French filmmaker Chris Marker (1921–2012), particularly *Commentaires* (1961) in which he presented his scripts alongside stills, translating film into print. Film provides a useful analogy: the role of 'designer as author' has

Above: *Dot Dot Dot* magazines, Issues 1–11 designed and edited by Peter Biľak and Stuart Bertolotti-Bailey, Issues 12–20 designed and edited by Stuart Bertolotti-Bailey and David Reinfurt, 2000–2010.

been likened to that of a director; though they may not write the script, the film director shapes the audience's experience.

Postmodernism saw many designers – motivated by a desire to find agency away from the primarily service-oriented role of the designer under modern consumer capitalism – take an interpretive or critical role, or choosing to work with self-generated content. However, for some, this showed that designers self-consciously lacked confidence in their practice. The most important discussion of 'The Designer as Author' was Michael Rock's (b. 1959) 1996 essay of the same name in *Eye*. Rock explored the idea of graphic authorship, at a time when it was becoming a buzzword, concluding that:

> An examination of the designer-as-author could help us to rethink process, expand design methods and elaborate our historical frame to incorporate all forms of graphic discourse. But while theories of graphic authorship may change the way work is made, the primary concern of both the viewer and the critic is not *who* made it, but rather *what* it does and *how* it does it.[34]

Rock wrote a follow-up in 2009, as he felt the essay had been 'read as a call for designers to generate content: in effect, to become designers and authors, not designers as authors.' Rock was keen to stress that, while he thought more designers writing was positive, he wanted to challenge the widely held notion in design theory and academia that 'developing content is more essential than shaping it, that good content is the measure of good design'. Instead, he argued that 'the manipulation of form' – the mainstay of graphic design – can be 'transformative' and that worthwhile graphic design is not dependent on quality content, self-authored or otherwise.[35]

Authorship is a complex issue, but has helped bring attention to what is called an 'expanded practice', whereby designers are engaged in related tasks alongside their role as a graphic designer, be it as writer, editor, publisher, artist, curator, activist, researcher, critic or entrepreneur, to give a few examples. Since designers gain an intimate knowledge of content, it is unsurprising some gravitate towards trying their hand at roles they have closely observed their clients and collaborators do.

Further Reading →
Michael Rock, *Multiple Signatures: On Designers, Authors, Readers and Users* (Rizzoli, 2013)

Chapter 3:
Practice

Grids

'Working with the grid system means
submitting to laws of universal validity.
The use of the grid system implies
the will to systematize, to clarify
the will to penetrate to the essentials,
to concentrate
the will to cultivate objectivity instead
of subjectivity
the will to rationalise the creative and
technical production processes
the will to integrate elements of colour,
form and material
the will to achieve architectural dominion
over surface and space'

Josef Müller-Brockmann,
Grid Systems in Graphic Design **(1968)**[1]

Opposite Left: Poster design for Pratt Institute, Studio Ghazaal Vojdani, 2015.

Opposite Right: 'Wim Crouwel: A Graphic Odyssey' poster for exhibition at the Design Museum, London, Philippe Apeloig, 2011.

Previous Spread: Detail from a book cover, Tom Etherington, 2022.

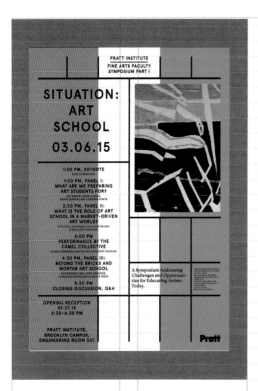

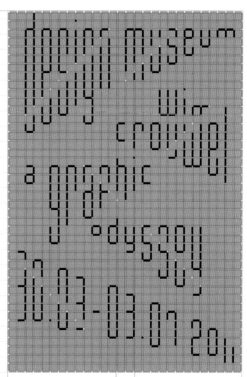

Graphic design is the organization of visual material. Faced with this task, most people favour order over chaos and look to create a system to best present their given content within the required confines. Grids, created with straight lines and predominantly right angles, allow designers to build a system for arranging content in a rational and ordered way, and can establish rules that maintain consistency across projects and applications. While embracing instinct can offer freedom and energy to designers, in most areas of graphic design some kind of organizational principle is required. This is particularly true when the extent of a project grows, for instance, a book or website with hundreds of pages.

Grids serve two purposes: making the designer's role easier and more logical, while also making the information simpler for viewers to digest.

The desire for order and pattern is built into human nature. Historically, medieval scribes would draw out evenly spaced lines on which to write. With the mechanization of typography, the grid became even more fundamental: metal type worked on a modular system, with letters cast in rectangular units, set in straight lines and locked into a rectangular frame, and metal blocks used to create even spacing. It was a process that strongly favoured straight lines and right angles. Efficiency and standardization were guiding principles of the Industrial Revolution, taken up by modernist designers in the 20th century to shift their discipline towards logical objectivity.

Swiss graphic designers (see pages 38-41), such as Josef Müller-Brockmann (1914-96), Karl Gerstner (1930-2017) and Emil Ruder (1914-70) became ardent advocates for grid systems, seeing them as part of a drive to create a more rational society. Swiss designers spread their gospel, with Dutch designer Wim Crouwel (1928-2019) a key convert, earning the nickname Mr Gridnik. Gerstner was particularly interested in the mathematical logic of the nascent world of computer programming, but ironically it would be the computer, combined with postmodernism, that was a catalyst for designers to challenge the hegemony of the grid, which some saw as a tool of conformity and control. However, due to the square pixel grid – the fundamental building block of digital design – escaping the grid on a screen was an impossibility.

Digital design programs have made it easier than ever to create grids; straight lines and right angles are the default setting. Even if you attempt to design without a grid, many programmes will encourage the alignment of elements through their user interface (UI) design, and may automatically even out spacing. While grids can appear limiting, it is worth remembering that they are as simple or complicated as they need to be, and should serve their function as an aid rather than an obstacle.

The main types of grids are: even vertical 'columns' with consistent spaces between (known as gutters); a 'baseline' grid of equidistant horizontal lines; a 'modular' grid made of regularly sized squares or rectangles with even spacing around them; an 'all-over' grid where the entire page is broken into consistent units, and a 'hierarchical grid' designed to break up content according to its importance. Often, designers will use a combination of these types of grids.

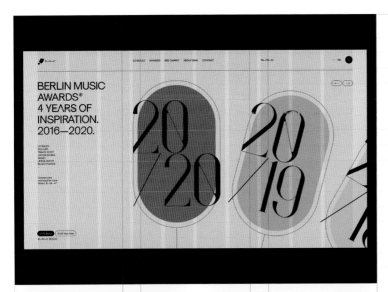

Above: Berlin Music Awards website concept (with ten-column grid visible), Obys, 2020.

Below: Graphic identity and poster designs by Jeremy Jansen and Edwin van Gelder, 2016-2017.

Further Reading →

Allen Hurlburt, *The Grid: A Modular System for the Design and Production of Newspapers, Magazines, and Books* (Van Nostrand Reinhold, 1983)

Josef Müller-Brockmann, *Grid Systems in Graphic Design* (Verlag Niggli, 2015)

Timothy Samara, *Making and Breaking the Grid* (Rockport Publishers, 2017)

Hierarchy

A system in which things are <u>ARRANGED</u> ACCORDING TO THEIR <u>IMPORTANCE</u> OR <u>STATUS</u>, hierarchy is vital to graphic designers, impacting how their audience will receive the information they are presenting.

A lack of hierarchy can lead to key information being missed, or cause confusion in the viewer's mind about what order they should be reading a piece of design.

The luxury of attention cannot be taken for granted; failure to guide eyes through an obvious process can mean that information fails to be delivered. There are also cases where hierarchy can be a matter of safety, for instance on road signs that must be read at speed.

Designers can create hierarchy in many ways, the most obvious being scale. Generally speaking, we 'read' a piece of design in size order, taking in the largest elements first. However, the strategic use of white space can sometimes emphasize the importance of a smaller element, as can graphic devices such as →arrows←, circling or <u>underlines</u> that signify importance. At very large sizes, however, there is the risk of something becoming a background, seeming less important than smaller elements that come to the foreground.

Colour can use be used to pick out important elements: brighter colours jump forward - so long as there is enough contrast - while a single colour will be seen first on a design that is otherwise black and white.

In typography, hierarchy can be created not just through font size but also through weight: **bold text implies importance**, UPPERCASE STANDS OUT, *italics, too,* and <u>underlines</u>. However, as with size and colour, hierarchy relies on varying levels — try to make all text stand out and nothing will. The mixing of different fonts can also create hierarchy:

a heavy sans-serif is often used for headlines, whereas the regular weight of a neutral typeface is likely to be used for body text.

When reading, we start at the top and work downwards, scanning horizontally as we go. Developments in eye tracking have confirmed this, and in highly commercial areas of design, such as packaging, this technology is already being used to ensure designs are 'read' as desired.

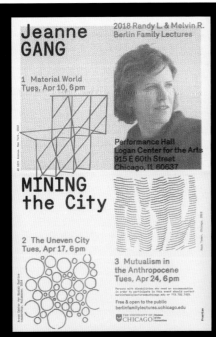

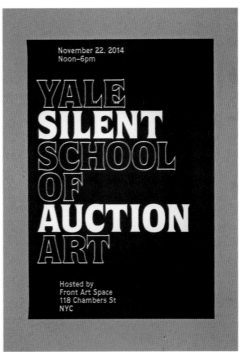

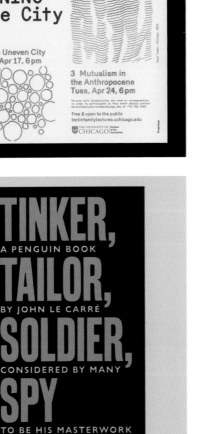

Above Left: 'Jeanne Gang: Mining the City' University of Chicago, Division of the Humanities, four-colour Risograph poster, James Goggin (Practise), 2018. Printed by Perfectly Acceptable Press.

Above Right: Yale 'Silent Auction' poster, Yotam Hadar, 2014.

Below: *Tinker, Tailor, Soldier, Spy* book cover, design by David Pearson, copywriting by Nick Asbury, 2020. Art direction by Jim Stoddart, Penguin.

Proportion

Defined as the 'harmonious relation of parts to each other or to the whole', proportion has been an important concept throughout history. From the writings of ancient Roman architect Vitruvius (c. 80-70 BCE - after c. 15 BCE), which would go on to inspire Leonardo da Vinci's (1452-1519) Vitruvian Man, to Le Corbusier's (1887-1965) Modular Man, the search for visual harmony through proportion has fascinated many. Studying proportions in the natural world and attempting to apply them in human creations was once connected to belief in a divine creator, but did not stop with the rise of science and secularism. Discoveries such as Charles Darwin's (1809-82) theory of evolution fuelled the continued search for a hidden, universal mathematical order.

In the 13th century Italian mathematician Fibonacci (c.1170-c.1240-50) identified a numerical sequence, whereby the next figure is found by adding up the two numbers before it. When turned into a two-dimensional form, this creates a smooth spiral that has been identified in natural forms like shells and fern fronds. A connected proportion is the golden ratio, first discussed by the ancient Greeks and labelled the 'divine proportion' in 1509: its numerical value is approximately 1.618, found by adding 1 and $\sqrt{5}$, and then dividing by 2. A golden rectangle whose sides are in the golden ratio will retain its proportions if a square the size of its shortest side is removed. Although a golden rectangle is visually harmonious, modern paper sizes set by the International Organization for Standardization (ISO) - A4, A3 and so on - have a ratio of 1.414, as each smaller format is half the size of the previous one.

For graphic designers, the lure of using a mathematical rationale to justify or inform their creative decisions has been strong, particularly in modernism. However, proportion has a deep history. In book design, page construction was long based on theories of harmony, with the text block being proportional to the overall page, often at two-thirds its size. This method, which also involved inner and upper margins being half the size of outer and bottom ones (2:4 horizontally and 3:6 vertically), became known as the Van de Graaf canon of page construction. It has been found throughout medieval manuscripts and was reproduced by book designers like Jan Tschichold (1902-74) and Jost Hochuli (b. 1933).

Some designers find ideas of proportion like the golden ratio helpful, but many find them arbitrary or post-rationalizations. Mathematics rarely holds all the answers, and we must also trust our eyes and minds.

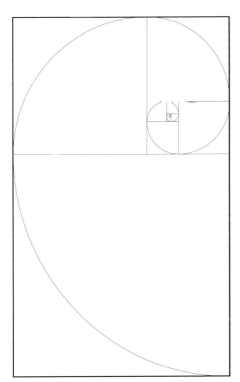

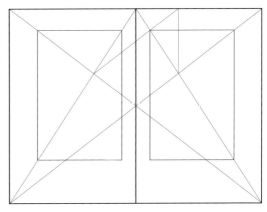

Above Left: The Fibonacci spiral, named after Italian mathematician Leonardo Bonacci, known as Fibonacci.

Above Right: The classical, Van de Graaf canon approach to page design, shown on an octavo (6x9) format. The text block is two-thirds the size of the overall page.

Below: Guidelines for Union AI, Order, 2022.

Style

'"Too much style" helps us conceal that nagging inkling we have that our own work may be out of style, and "no substance" convinces us that our potentially dated work is somehow more meaningful, rendering style irrelevant. Sometimes, it is even true.'
Paula Scher, 1989[2]

Questions of style – Should designers develop a unique one? Can any style even be considered unique today? Is it possible not to have a style? Is it OK not to stick to one alone? Who gets to say what is a style? – have dominated and divided graphic designers throughout the history of the discipline. Any discussion of style in graphic design is impossible without considering related topics, such as fashion or taste, or considering the social, cultural and political contexts in which we work.

Style is a word whose meaning is open to interpretation: in some cases, style refers to a distinctive *way* of doing something; in others it refers only to appearance. A stylish object is one that is well designed or particularly attractive – highly subjective terms. To be *in* style means to be fashionable. In graphic design 'style' has often been taboo, with different camps having varied reasons for trying to move the discipline away from questions of visual style. For modernists, style was a kind of unnecessary ornament, far too subjective to be a worthwhile pursuit. The designers at Unimark International – the modernist agency founded by, among others, Massimo Vignelli (1931–2014) – wore lab coats, to signify they were more scientists than artists.

Writing in *Emigre* in 2004, Jeffery Keedy (b. 1957) noted: 'Modernism made the issue of style much easier for designers to deal with, since it gave them a style that they could pretend was not a style. But technology, multiculturalism, globalism, postmodernism, and the "democratization of taste" are demanding a more sophisticated response. Digital technology has made it clear that graphic design is not just about the technical production of objects and information.'[3]

Style is always easier with hindsight: from the perspective of a historian, it is much simpler to rationalize visual looks. For designers, the spectre of 'style over substance' looms large and has driven focuses on realms like problem solving, communication, method or business. But style is inescapable – it is a vital aspect of visual culture – and designers ignore it at their peril. As Susan Sontag (1933–2004) wrote in 1965, 'antipathy to "style" is always an antipathy to a given style. There are no style-less works of art, only works of art belonging to different, more or less complex stylistic traditions and conventions'.[4]

Writing in 1991, American graphic designer Saul Bass (1920–96) noted: 'We all need to remember, or perhaps learn, that substance is more significant than style.'[5] For designers like Bass and Paul Rand (1946–96), who found success working in their own distinctive styles, this kind of rhetoric was understandable: by the end of their careers they were keen for their work not to be reduced to aesthetics. Yet their critiques of postmodern graphic design made similar assertions about the division between style and substance: that era's stylistic

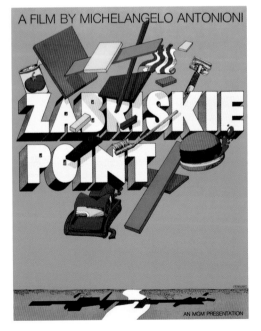

Above Left: American Dance Festival poster, George Tscherny, 1962.

Above Right: 'Flims' poster, Hans Handschin, c.1935.

Below Left: Film poster, Milton Glaser, 1970.

experimentation came from many complex positions, reflecting global changes. Even many postmodern designers were keen to distance themselves from 'style', seeing it as a distraction. Austrian Stefan Sagmeister (b. 1962) hung a sign declaring 'style = fart' in his studio, and the phrase was included in his most iconic work – a 1993 AIGA lecture poster that featured a photograph of the designer's nude torso onto which text had been carved with a scalpel. Sagmeister, however, later disowned this assertion, writing: 'It was the headline of a theory that style and stylistic questions are just hot air and meaningless. I discovered that this is simply not true. Through experience I found that if you have content that is worthwhile, the proper expression of that content, in terms of form and style, is actually very important. It can be a very useful tool to communicate that content.'[6]

For designers today, style can be a trap. Get noticed for working in a particular way that proves successful, and clients will come to you wanting more of the same. Imitators will also undoubtedly pop up, and the 'mood board' culture of commercial design can reduce the work of others to a grab-bag of styles to copy or take 'inspiration' from. Meanwhile, as the number of graphic designers grows bigger and the world smaller, especially thanks to social media, standing out without a distinctive style can be hard. Style is as thorny an issue as ever (connected to the problem of originality) but not one that designers can avoid. In a special 2014 issue on 'Style' the editors of *Varoom* magazine concluded: 'When "style" stops being a thing that we should aspire to

or own, or imitate, or something that's timely and on-trend, of the moment, when style becomes a mechanism for changing us, for changing a way of making, that's when "style" gets creative'.[7]

Further Reading →
Seymour Chwast & Steven Heller, *Graphic Style: From Victorian to Hipster* (Abrams, 2018)
Steven Heller, *Graphic Style Lab* (Rockport, 2015)

Above Left: Poster, David Rudnick, 2016.

Above Right: Album cover, Hassan Rahim/1201AM, 2017

Below Right: Album cover, Bráulio Amado, 2018.

Below Left: Film festival identity, Studio Moross, 2020.

Problem Solving

'*Our* thesis is that any one visual problem has an infinite number of solutions; that many of them are valid; that solutions ought to derive from the subject matter; that the designer should therefore have no preconceived graphic style.'
Alan Fletcher / Colin Forbes / Bob Gill, *Graphic design visual comparisons* (1963)

Alan Fletcher (1931-2006), Colin Forbes (1928-2022) and Bob Gill (1931-2021), who came together to form the agency that later became Pentagram, put forward this thesis on graphic design as a discipline whose primary focus should be 'problem solving'. This position came as a kind of middle-ground approach between the 'anonymous' designers who subscribed to the most rational modernist dogma, and the earlier role of the 'commercial artist' who worked in a distinctive, consistent personal style. Gill put problem solving at the heart of his career, writing in 2013: 'If you want your lives and your work to be interesting, don't just do layouts - but think about the brief and come up with an opinion that will inform your design approach. If you're designing a logo for a dry cleaners, don't sit at your computer, go to a dry cleaners!'[8]

While the kind of problems Gill had in mind are the projects that designers usually enjoy the most, not all aspects of graphic design are so creative. A clever idea is not always the end goal; graphic design can also be about figuring out how best to display information and achieve clarity. Not all the problems facing a graphic designer are conceptual ones; they can be formal or technical. Josef Müller-Brockmann, a proponent of modernism, had a very different portfolio from Gill, yet titled his 1961 opus on design *The Graphic Artist and His Design Problems*. In the book he writes:

'The withdrawal of the personality of the designer behind the idea, the themes, the enterprise, or the product is what the best minds are all striving to achieve.'[9] For Brockmann, the problems were around finding systematic approaches appropriate for a modern technological world.

For many designers and theorists, the focus on problem solving in graphic design is seen as egotistical; most jobs involve finding solutions to issues, and there is no monopoly on creativity. Not all problems can be solved by design, particularly wider structural ones. Victor Papanek (1923-98), in his book *Design for the Real World*, included a succinct diagram labelled 'The Design Problem'. This shows a pyramid at the top of which is a tiny triangle labelled 'the designer's share'; below it the rest of the pyramid is labelled 'the real problem'.[10]

20% off
Martin
RentaCa

Although our rates are low for a start, we'll give a 20% discount to all airline staff. Choose from 20 different models–Mini to Triumph 2000. You can even have caravans or minibuses. We'll collect or deliver your car free at the Airport. Our depot is only a few minutes away. Pick up one of our price lists and see how easy car hire can be, or give us a ring at Colnbrook 2282 (dial XM4 from London).

Further Reading →
Edward de Bono, *Lateral Thinking: A Textbook of Creativity* (Penguin, 2009)
Alan Fletcher, *The Art of Looking Sideways* (Phaidon, 2002)
Michael Johnson, *Problem Solved* (Phaidon, 2012)

Top: Press advertisement, Bob Gill, 1967.

Above Right: Poster for the Hughes Aircraft Company, designer unknown, 1965.

Below Right: Art Walk Piedmont identity design, Mucho, 2021.

Above: Office Games logo design, The Partners, 2008.

Graphic Wit

The impulse to do something clever - to pun, joke or riddle - through communication has always existed. In graphic design such an instinct has been labelled as an 'ideas-focused' or 'concept-driven' approach, in the sense that work that uses these kinds of techniques is functioning on a level beyond just the initial surface read. Visual wit requires the viewer be an active participant; there is something happening on an intellectual level, not just at an aesthetic or informational one. Although there is the risk that some viewers will miss the designer's intent or consider them 'gimmicks', the use of wit has long been popular in commercial areas of visual communication, particularly advertising, branding, packaging and book covers. The logic being that it encourages the viewer to look again, or look for longer, and that the payoff - solving the puzzle or getting the joke - creates a more memorable design.

Advocates for the use of visual wit argue that, unlike design which relies on aesthetic appeal, ideas-based designs have a timeless quality and an originality that comes from having figured out a solution unique to the specific creative problem. The most common technique of visual wit is the two-in-one image, achieved through the fusion of two separate elements or the hiding of one image within another, often through the use of negative space.

In 1959 Herb Lubalin (1918-81) declared that 'at the heart of American graphics is the idea, the concept. All else - photography, typography, illustration, design - is its handmaiden.'[11] While Americans like Bob Gill, George Lois (1931-2022) and Henry Wolf (1925-2005) were key proponents of ideas-driven graphics post-World War II, they were by no means alone. Many European poster artists in the first half of the 20th century had adopted similar techniques, such as Cassandre (1901-68), Raymond Savignac (1907-2002) and Abram Games (1914-96), whose motto was 'Maximum Meaning, Minimum Means'.

In sixties London, thanks to the influence of American ex-pats such as Bob Gill and Robert Brownjohn (1925-70), a generation of young graphic designers were taking up this intelligent yet playful approach in their commercial work, including Alan Fletcher, Colin Forbes and Derek Birdsall (b. 1934). The use of visual wit has remained popular since the sixties, particularly in the United States and Britain, but has its detractors, on both sides of the modernism/postmodernism debate, who consider it a contrived, repetitive or limiting approach, and terms like 'idea' and 'concept' too grandiose.

Above: American Library logo, The Click, 2021.

Below: Galt Toys catalogue cover, Ken Garland and Associates, 1969-70.

Above: *Revolt* book, Paul Belford Ltd, 2018.

Opposite Above Left: 'Security Leak' poster for IBM, Ken White, 1969.

Opposite Above Right: *Everything and Less* book cover, Ben Denzer, 2021.

Opposite Below: Logo for The British Hat Guild by Counter Studio, 2019.

Further Reading →

Gail Anderson & Steven Heller, *The Graphic Design Idea Book* (Laurence King, 2016)

Beryl McAlhone & David Stuart, *A Smile in the Mind* (Phaidon, 1998)

James Webb Young, *A Technique for Producing Ideas* (1965)

Pictograms

Pictograms, also known as icons, are a form of graphic pictorial communication rendered in a simple, consistent illustrative style. Icons can be representational, symbolic or, in some cases, ideographic (i.e. representing a concept). Icons are commonly found in contexts where transcendence of language is vital or quick understanding is a safety concern.

An important moment in the development of modern pictograms was the founding of Isotype (International System of Typographic Picture Education) in the 1920s by Austrian philosopher Otto Neurath (1882–1945). Neurath, working with his eventual wife Marie (1898–1996) and artist Gerd Arntz (1900–88), aimed to develop a 'picture language' that would aid visual learning, bringing life to data and making information more accessible. Arntz and Marie Neurath developed a distinctive and incredibly legible visual style for Isotype that used flat colour and consistent sizes, simplifying forms down to their absolute essence. Neurath – a lifelong socialist – hoped Isotype would transcend language and inform the masses effectively, transparently and accessibly.

The creation of icons often involves pushing the limits of simplicity – seeing what details can be lost while retaining clear, unambiguous meaning. Developing a new icon that does not rely on either representation or convention can be challenging, and success often comes through a process of usage and acceptance.

The need for originality can also be an added complication in icon design. A library of pictograms is often a common requirement for new brand identities, particularly in the digital realm. However, the best icons are often the simplest, which can be difficult to achieve in tandem with 'ownability'.

Some of the best-known pictograms have been for the Olympic Games, where icons represent each of the sports (and other general information) for a multilingual, international audience. The 1964 Tokyo Olympics were the first to use pictograms, with Masaru Katzumie (1909–83) and Yoshiro Yamashita using a systematic approach to their icons, with unifying features such as consistent line widths and body sizes. Around the same time, Jock Kinneir (1917–94) and Margaret Calvert (b. 1936) were completing their rationalization of British road signs, which included a library of simple symbols. For the 1968 Mexico Olympics, Lance Wyman's (b. 1937) pictograms focused on the equipment used. The Munich games in 1972 had an impeccably modernist approach thanks to a design team led by Otl Aicher, (1922–91) who created that year's influential pictograms using a diamond-based grid, resulting in consistent, dynamic angles.

Above Left: Cover of the *New York Times Magazine*, art directed by Annie Jen, illustrated by Francesco Muzzi / Story TK, 2021.

Above Right: Various Gerd Arntz pictograms designed for Isotype, c.1928–40.

Below: Mexico 68 Olympic pictograms, Lance Wyman, 1968.

Visual Language

'The same symbol can express many different ideas. It is potentially a highly versatile device. By juxtaposition, association, and analogy the designer is able to utilize its effectiveness to fulfil a specific function.'

Paul Rand, *Paul Rand: A Designer's Art* (1968)[12]

Visual elements that have widely understood, agreed-upon meanings and associations are key building blocks within graphic design. All visual materials, as explained by theorist Rudolf Arnheim (1904–2007), are processed cognitively as they are taken in optically. For designers, this fact can be utilized to great effect through an approach that reduces the number of elements within a design, highlights something specific, or changes context to focus viewer attention. Arnheim writes: 'The appearance of any item in the visual field was shown to depend on its place and function in the total structure and to be modified fundamentally by that influence. If a visual item is extricated from its context it becomes a different object.'[13]

One specific type of visual language, famously used by Paul Rand (1914–96) in his 1982 poster for IBM, is the rebus – a puzzle-like device where symbols replace either individual letters or parts of words. For instance, the letter 'h' followed by an ear would be read as the word 'hear'. Rebuses have historically been found as far back as medieval heraldry, but in the age of emoji the integration of images into text, as a replacement for words, is more prominent than ever.

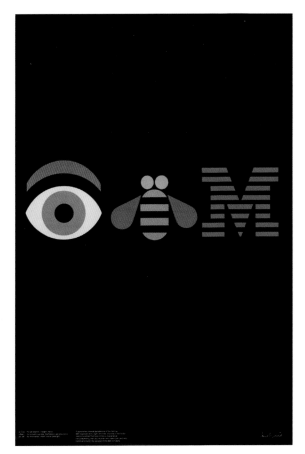

Above Left: Poster for IBM, Paul Rand, 1982
(The Eye Bee M rebus was first used in 1981).

Above Right: Poster for a Ladislav Sutnar exhibition,
Noel Martin, 1961. Born in the present-day Czech
Republic, Sutnar (1897-1976) was a pioneer of
modern information design.

Below: '1776' poster, Michael David Brown Inc.,
c.1970.

Further Reading →

Connie Malamed, *Visual Language for Graphic Designers* (Rockport, 2011)
Philip Thompson & Peter Davenport, *The Dictionary of Visual Language* (Penguin, 1982)

Chance & Accident

'Chance is beloved of Art, and Art of Chance'
Aristotle, quoting Agathon, *Nicomachean Ethics* (c.349 BCE)

Graphic design can be a rigid discipline, often focused on precision and logic, yet there are aspects that are far more free or spontaneous, where the aim is to create something intriguing or complex, rather than striving for perfection. Inspiration can come from unexpected sources, and designers are often said to be magpie-like, taking in the world around them, and soaking up ideas and visual stimuli like a sponge. In *A Designer's Art* (1968), Paul Rand writes:

> The artist is a collector.
> He accumulates things with the
> same enthusiasm that a little boy
> stuffs his pockets. The scrap heap
> and the museum are embraced with
> equal curiosity [...] Why one thing
> and not another is part of the
> mystery, but he is omnivorous.
> The artist takes note of that
> which jolts him into visual
> awareness.[14]

For many graphic designers, somewhat ironically perhaps, the most visually exciting stimuli are often those that happen by chance; these can be the things that really stop you in your tracks. To this end, designers will often reference these occurrences - things that are broken, processes gone wrong, strange juxtapositions, accidental compositions, random objects and so on - in work that is very much intentional. However, many designers instead choose to embrace a lack of control, aiming to introduce true chance into their work. This can come from different approaches. Particularly today, where perfection is so achievable digitally, many designers have turned to older techniques in search of charming imperfections.

Not all techniques that embrace chance and accident are traditional. In our 'post-digital' age, many designers are playing with coding to force computer errors and unpredictability, or using artificial intelligence to take creative decisions out of individual control.

SEPTEMBER 2 98 MESEROLE AV. BROOKLYN
GOOD ROOM: *Lloyd's* BAD ROOM:
Birthday ANALOG SOUL
  SUPER FAMILY
FEAT (SAHEER UMAR
LLOYD & FRIENDS & JAMAL DIXON)

Above: Poster (left), for
Good Room, Bráulio Amado,
2022. Source image (right).

Below: 'Beautiful world,
where are you?' Liverpool
Biennial 2018 catalogue
cover by Sara De Bondt
and Mark El-khatib with
Paul Elliman.

Further Reading →

Anna Gerber, *All Messed Up:
Unpredictable Graphics*
(Laurence King, 2004)

James F. O'Brien, *Design by
Accident: Accidental Effects
for Artists and Designers*
(Dover, 1969)

Laurie Rosenwald, *How to Make
Mistakes on Purpose: Bring Chaos
to Your Order* (Hachette Go, 2021)

Illustration

The word 'illustration' evolved from the Latin *illustro*, which had a dual meaning: to illuminate and to elucidate. Illustrations can illuminate something, making it more appealing, or they can explain, making visual that which would otherwise remain hidden.

An illustration is a pictorial visual communication – an image that serves a particular function in a specific context. The technical skills and tools involved in art and illustration are often the same, and an individual may well be highly capable of doing both. However, illustration is defined by intent or context, or both. As the authors of *The History of Illustration* write: 'The "what" (subject) and "how" (medium) of an image are not the defining factors; rather, the "why" (purpose) determines whether a work of art is illustration.'[15] A work of art does not inherently require any justification; to classify as illustration there must be purpose to its creation or application, be it explanation, persuasion, documentation, storytelling or even decoration. In this sense, given that graphic design is similarly defined by communication, any piece of art utilized by a graphic designer can become an illustration.

Historically, illustration was often done by fine artists who dabbled in commercial fields, either out of financial necessity or for a creative challenge. Prior to the invention of photography, illustration tended to be realistic; it was the only option for visual reportage or documentation. However, the technological limitations of pre-photographic mechanical reproduction

did push illustrators to particular techniques, such as engraving or woodcutting, that resulted in a certain level of stylistic interpretation within a representational approach. As with all visual areas, some illustrators developed unique approaches or styles, particularly among the 20th century's various avant-gardes. The widespread availability of photography by mid-century had a huge impact on illustration's function. As Lucienne Roberts writes: 'The ability of photography to represent the real reinvigorated illustration as an imaginative, conceptual and expressive medium for ideas.'[16]

Distinguishing graphic design from illustration can be vague; many graphic designers have also been illustrators, and vice versa. The introduction of typography is perhaps one potential point whereby

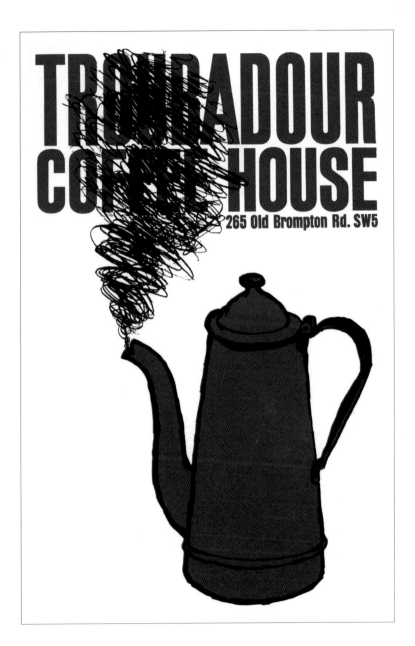

Above: 'Troubadour Coffee House' poster, Bob Gill, Fletcher/Forbes/
Gill, 1961.

Opposite: Motta press advertisement, artist unknown, c.1963.

Illustration **153**

an illustration becomes part of a larger piece of graphic design. Rather than seeing them as two necessarily distinct disciplines, it may be more appropriate to think of illustration as something that can be used by graphic designers in their creative process. Writing in 1964, Bob Gill and John Lewis declared that they were 'unequivocally against the teaching of illustration as a subject in our art schools' curriculum', adding that 'the training an illustrator needs, is what might be called a training in the practise of the graphic arts'.[17] Not all graphic design involves illustration, and not all illustration needs to become part of a graphic design, but in many examples it is impossible to disentangle an illustration from its context within a graphic design. This was very true in the mid-century era when prominent designers such as Alvin Lustig, Paul Rand, Lora Lamm (b. 1928), Bob Gill and Leo Lionni (1910–99) used illustration often. Many graphic designers during the fifties would dabble in children's book illustration, often writing them, too. Some of the best-selling author-illustrators of children's books in the 20th century – Eric Carle (1929–2021), Dick Bruna (1927–2017) and Eric Hill (1927–2014) – started as graphic designers. Perhaps the best-known example of the porous distinction between graphic design and illustration were the creatives at New York City–based Push Pin Studios (e.g. Milton Glaser, Seymour Chwast, John Alcorn, Reynold Ruffins and Edward Sorel). Push Pin utilized illustration as a key part of a distinctive graphic output in the fifties and sixties that employed eclectic styles.

Although illustration has primarily been associated with the creation of images by hand, in the digital age its definition has expanded to include work created on a computer. The distinction between photography and illustration is also not binary: collage can be considered an approach to illustration that uses photography, while many contemporary illustrators work by making three-dimensional creations and then photographing them. Today many graphic designers work with commissioned illustrations, but some continue to prefer to create images themselves. The boundaries remain blurred. For instance, in the United States, most book cover designers also create editorial illustrations for magazines and newspapers, utilizing the same approaches across both disciplines.

Opposite Above: Blume packaging illustrated by Jean Jullien, designed by Studio South, 2021.

Opposite Below Right: *Vanity Fair* cover, Javier Jaén, 2022.

Opposite Below Left: Poster for Rock the Mountain, Lebassis, 2020.

Further Reading →
Susan Doyle, Jaleen Grove & Whitney Sherman, *History of Illustration* (Bloomsbury, 2018)
Martin Salisbury, *Drawing for Illustration* (Thames & Hudson, 2021)
Lawrence Zeegen, *The Fundamentals of Illustration* (Bloomsbury, 2017)

Illustration **155**

Photography

The invention of photography in the 19th century did not have an immediate effect on graphic design, mostly due to its overall complexity and lack of colour. Even as colour photography developed, 'commercial art' was still dominated by illustrative techniques. Designers such as Cassandre, Joseph Binder (1899-1972) and Edward McKnight Kauffer (1890-1954) had prolific careers in which the use of photography was rare, relying instead on airbrush techniques when aiming for realism.

It was the more outright modernist designers who were among the first to embrace the creative potential of photography, particularly those at the Bauhaus, such as Herbert Bayer (1900-85) and György Kepes (1906-2001). The technological aspect of photography, and its capacity for 'objectivity' – a machine eye capturing rather than interpreting – promised a 'new vision' for the 20th century. László Moholy-Nagy (1995-1946), with his wife, Lucia Moholy (1894-1989), introduced techniques such as double exposure, photomontage and photograms to students, also encouraging exploration of unconventional perspectives. Russian Constructivists, such as Alexander Rodchenko (1891-1956) and El Lissitzky (1890-1941), were taking similar approaches to photography as well as moving film, the latter best illustrated by Dziga Vertov (1896-1954). Surrealist photographers were influential, too, particularly Man Ray (1890-1976), who had pioneered creative photograms — images made without a camera in the dark room, through exposed photographic paper.

Not all designers at the Bauhaus saw photography as applicable in their graphic work. For some it was a separate creative outlet, but Moholy-Nagy was adamant its use in visual communication was vital. In his 1923 essay 'The New Typography', Moholy-Nagy declared that 'Through an expert use of the camera, and of all photographic techniques, such as retouching, blocking, superimposition, distortion, enlargement, etc., in combination with the liberated typographical line, the effectiveness of posters can be immensely enlarged'.[18]

A key designer who took up the Bauhaus's photographic mantle in graphic design was Herbert Matter (1907-1984), a talented Swiss photographer and designer who used colour exceptionally, most notably in his posters for the Swiss Tourist Office in the 1930s, which utilized dynamic angles, bold perspectives, photomontage and juxtapositions of scales. Matter achieved his work, particularly the colour, through his mastery of darkroom techniques and manual retouching. Moving to the United States in 1936, Matter connected with Alexey Brodovitch (1898-1971), art director of *Harper's Bazaar*, who would use him as a photographer. Brodovitch along with the likes of Mehemed Fehmy Agha (1896-1978), Alexander Liberman (1912-99) and Cipe Pineles (1908-91), would revolutionize magazine design through the introduction of colour photography, commissioning leading names like Edward Steichen (1879-1973), Richard Avedon (1923-2004), Lisette Model (1901-83) and Irving Penn (1917-2009). One of the most interesting examples of photographic graphic design from this era was Horst P. Horst's (1906-99) June

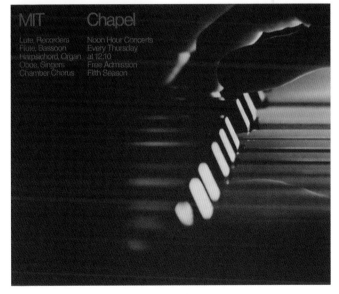

Above Left: 'Migränin calms pain and refreshes' poster, Hans Hillman, 1960.

Above Centre: IBM poster, Ken White, 1975.

Above Right: *Design 232* magazine cover, Keith Cunningham, 1968.

Below Right: 'MIT Chapel' poster, Dietmar R. Winkler, c.1965–1970.

Below Left: *Smash Song Hits* by Rodgers and Hart record cover, Alex Steinweiss, 1939.

1940 cover for *Vogue*, which featured a typographic masthead created out of hand-coloured photographs of posing models.

While the new generation of 'art director' graphic designers tended to rely on freelance photographers, there were still many in the mid-century who, like Matter, wanted to take photographs themselves for their design work. Examples of such creative polymaths include Lillian Bassman (1917–2012) and William Klein (1926–2022). The fashion magazines of the thirties to fifties tended to prefer photography inspired by Surrealism, which had the power to surprise and attract in equal measure. By the 1960s photography had become more conceptual and creative in design and advertising, particularly in the United States, as seen in the work of George Lois or Helmut Krone (1925–2006), who used images to witty, sophisticated ends.

Graphic designers associated with the Swiss and International Typographic Styles preferred a more objective approach to photography (they favoured them as an anonymous alternative to illustration). This often remained in black and white, or occasionally a single colour, which better suited their preference for flat colour backgrounds. Modernism's concern with efficient and economical production techniques also meant photographs were often halftone, with visible dots. Writing in 1966, Ken Garland (1929–2021) advised that to 'attempt the practice of graphic design without a working knowledge of the basic principles of photography is rather like attempting to be a doctor without any training in anatomy: just possible but not to be recommended either to the practitioner or to their prospective client.'[19]

The widespread availability of computers, design software and digital cameras in the new millennium would change the relationship between photography and graphic design for ever, making it easier for designers to either take their own photographs or find images to use in their work (e.g. stock photography). Digital photography has made the 'in-camera' approach to graphic design popular, whereby compositions are made as 3D constructions and then captured photographically – a technique Moholy-Nagy used in the 1920s.

Above: *Pit* magazine cover, design by Holly Catford, photograph and concept by Robert Billington, 2022.

Below: Album cover, design by Hingston Studio, photograph by Julia Noni, 2018.

Art Direction

D&AD, the organization founded in 1962 as Design and Art Direction, defines art directors as 'visual storytellers who create the overall style of a product'. It also adds that 'As an art director, you'll need to come up with the visual language for a project, articulate your ideas to your team, and then execute your creative vision to make the finished product – be it a film, ad, magazine or book cover'.[20] For graphic designers, art direction usually means overseeing or directing a creative collaborator working in a different field, such as an illustrator, photographer, artist or typographer, whose work will be an element used by the designer in their project. Some graphic designers prefer to be self-sufficient generalists, but for most there are times when it is best to call on a specialist to bring a vision to fruition.

In a book on art direction Steven Heller (b. 1950) writes: 'Educationally speaking, art direction is a curious phenomenon. Even though I've never seen a class devoted to it, it is a huge profession. Every magazine, newspaper, book publisher, record company, advertising agency, etc., employs art directors. But how do you become one?'[21] It is a good question; often graphic designers learn art direction out of necessity, falling into it because they find themselves in a role that involves a lot of overseeing, leaving little time for them to execute creative work themselves.

In the world of advertising, the job title of art director is somewhat different from other areas of graphic design. Advertising has long been dominated by creative teams: duos made up of a copywriter (who writes the words) and art director (who makes the visuals). Historically, copywriters were seen as the concept generators and were more likely to climb the agency ladder, while art directors did the grunt work, but this has changed much in recent decades.

In terms of job titles, art director can be confused with creative director, a term that implies the overseeing of other graphic designers, and seniority or importance within an organization. The difference between these two roles is mostly semantic, with much crossover. Art direction is generally considered more hands-on, while creative direction is more strategic and managerial, but both involve providing briefs and feedback to other creatives.

Further Reading →
Steven Brower, *Inside Art Direction* (Bloomsbury, 2019)
Steven Heller & Veronique Vienne, *Art Direction Explained, At Last!* (Laurence King, 2009)

Above Left: Packaging and brand identity for food storage brand Inka, designed and art directed by Elizabeth Goodspeed, photography by Ian Shiver, 2020.

Above Right: *Brain* magazine cover image, Wade & Leta, 2020.

Below: 'V&A Fashioning Masculinities' exhibition posters, designed and art directed by Hingston Studio, 2022.

Abstraction

A word with many related but differing meanings, the pertinent definition of 'abstract' is: 'relating to or denoting art that does not attempt to represent external reality, but rather seeks to achieve its effect using shapes, colours, and textures'.[22] For graphic designers, abstract visual material means non-objective; pure abstraction does not aim to provide a depiction of an identifiable thing (person, object, animal, etc.). Something described as semi-abstract has a recognizable subject matter that the artist or designer has created a highly stylized version of, to the extent that it is not a realistic rendering, but rather gestures to something existing. For instance, the poster at top right by Dietmar Winkler (b. 1938), a German-born designer who worked for the Massachusetts Institute of Technology (MIT), appears to be abstract; the composition contains simple geometric shapes - stripes of differing widths and a pair of curved triangles. However, the text reveals that the poster is for an organ and trumpet concert, the stripes alluding to the pipes of an organ, and the triangles referencing trumpet shapes. The result is arguably more memorable than something either purely representational or fully abstract.

Abstraction can be about creating something visually intriguing, particularly when designing for a topic which itself lacks any real-life things to use as easy signposts to the subject matter. Through the choices made within abstraction - such as about which colour, shapes or textures to use - designers can evoke the right mood or feeling, sparking associations in the viewer's consciousness and leaving room for interpretation. Semi-abstraction can be a kind of puzzle, encouraging the deciphering of meaning within something that initially appears decorative.

Abstraction has been found in the 'applied arts' for millennia, but it came into Western 'fine art' in the early 20th century through artists such as Wassily Kandinsky (1866–1944), Hilma af Klint (1862–1944) and Sonia Delaunay (1885–1979), for some the journey went via semi-abstraction (e.g. the Cubists), but by 1915 Kazimir Malevich (1879–1935) and Piet Mondrian (1872–1944) were creating work completely free from reference to the external word. Kandinsky wanted visual art to be more like music – which had 'devoted itself not to the reproduction of natural phenomena, but rather to the expression of the artist's soul' – embracing emotion and spirit rather than merely trying to replicate what we see around us.[23] The rise of photography, for many modernists at least, made abstract graphics more worthwhile than 'representational' illustration.

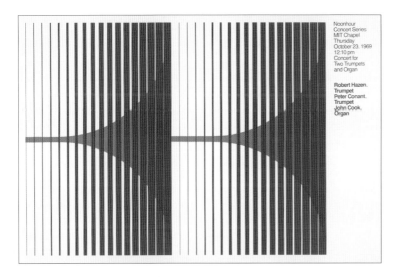

Above: 'MIT' poster, Dietmar R. Winkler, 1969.

Below Right: 'Harvard GSD' poster, The Rodina, 2018.

Below Left: *Mold* magazine Issue 2 cover, Eric Hu with Matthew Tsang, 2017.

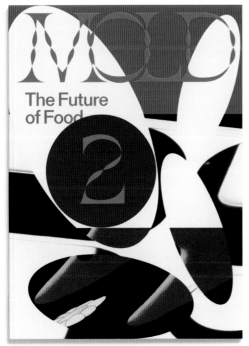

Collage

Used for both the finished work and the method used to make it, collage is a type of montage, traditionally created with an assemblage of paper materials that are arranged and stuck down. Also known as photomontage or découpage, collage involves the combination of found elements, cut or ripped from their source, and combined to create a new composition rich in juxtaposition.

Collage has long been an easy way to create without the need for expensive equipment; many average Victorians collaged scrapbooks or homemade greeting cards. Some of the first creatives to explore collage formally were the Dadaists (see page 23). Hannah Höch (1889–1978), Raoul Hausmann (1886–1971) and Kurt Schwitters (1887–1948) used collage to combine ephemera, found photographs and assorted typography to express political dissent and satirize bourgeois society (whose magazines provided source material). The political power of collage, shown by John Heartfield (1891–1968) in his works militating against fascism, would be utilized in the 20th century and beyond, as seen in the work of the artist Peter Kennard (b. 1949), who has designed for many pacifist and environmental organizations.

Collage would be explored by most 20th-century avant-garde movements, such as in the work of the Constructivists Alexander Rodchenko (1891–1956) and Gustav Klutsis (1895–1938), the Surrealists – who saw it as a chance for free expression of the unconscious – and Bauhauslers like Moholy-Nagy and György Kepes (1906–2001). The avant-gardes influenced post-World War II graphic designers, who found collage an expedient and engaging way to create images, particularly in new fields such as record and paperback book covers, before 'straight' photography became dominant. Many key post-war names, such as Alan Fletcher, Ivan Chermayeff (1932–2017) and Bruno Munari favoured collage, particularly using ripped paper, for commercial clients, but also used it in their personal artistic work.

Collage also proved popular with postmodernism: it suited the blending of 'high' and 'low' culture, appropriation and parody. Collage was perfect for the punk movement's DIY spirit and rough aesthetic. Ransom note-style typography, used in Jamie Reid's (b. 1947) designs for the Sex Pistols, epitomized punk's attitude. Software, particularly Photoshop, has made image combination a mostly digital affair today, but the physicality of collage remains appealing, and it is still a popular technique in graphic design.

Above Left: *The Emigrants* book cover, Peter Mendelsund, 2016.

Above Right: *Domus* magazine cover, William Klein, 1960.

Below: Album cover, Ivan Chermayeff, 1959.

Further Reading →

DR.ME, *Cut That Out: Contemporary Collage within Graphic Design* (Thames & Hudson, 2016)

Accessibility

Recognition of the importance of accessibility and a drive to reduce the number of people excluded from an activity have been growing steadily in contemporary society. Accessibility has become an important consideration for designers across disciplines. An aim is to create 'universal design', defined as 'the design of products and environments to be usable to the greatest extent possible by people of all ages and abilities.'[24]

For graphic designers, the main considerations concern people with reduced vision, visual impairment and colour blindness, or visual cognitive difficulties, which can be caused by conditions like autism and dyslexia. Some ways in which designers can improve accessibility are by: making sure colour contrast is high; eschewing the use of colour alone to convey meaning; being careful with colour schemes (not relying on red and green, or pairings of saturated bright colours); having a clear informational hierarchy; and choosing highly legible typefaces (larger x-heights help). There are tools available that allow designers to preview their work for different colour blindness types, or analyse contrast levels, as well as accessibility consultants who can be brought in to give an expert perspective. The larger the potential audience, the more urgent it is to consider these questions. In digital contexts, designers have further considerations, such as screen-reader users, and differing dexterity levels for interactive elements that need to be clicked or navigated.

Accessibility in graphic design is integral in more user-centric areas, yet borders on taboo in others – particularly those where freedom of personal preference and stylistic expression is a creative or commercial imperative. The fear, perhaps, is that any form of prescriptive direction on accessibility terms – for instance, adherence to particular typefaces or colours – will lead to homogeneity. However, graphic design has always evolved with society, changing to fit new technologies and contexts. Undoubtedly, improving accessibility is just another frontier to cross, but we have to be realistic and accept that it will require research, time, money and a widespread will to evolve. As the authors of the influential 1998 book *The Universal Design File* write: 'It is unlikely that any product or environment could ever be used by everyone under all conditions. Because of this, it may be more appropriate to consider universal design a process, rather than an achievement.'[25]

ELEMENT BREAKDOWN

1 Head Position
Head is forward to indicate the forward motion of the person through space. Here the person is the "driver" or decision maker about her mobility.

2 Arm Angle
Arm is pointing backward to suggest the dynamic mobility of a chair user, regardless of whether or not she uses her arms. Depicting the body in motion represents the symbolically active status of navigating the world.

3 Wheel Cutouts
By including white angled knockouts the symbol presents the wheel as being in motion. Knockouts work for creating stencils and having just one version of the logo keeps things more consistent and allows viewers to more clearly understand intended message.

4 Limb Rendition
The figure depicted in this icon is consistent with other body icons found in the ISO 7001 - DOT Pictograms. A different portrayal of the body would clash with these established and widely used icons and could lead to confusion.

5 Leg Position
The leg has been moved forward to allow for more space between it and the wheel which allows for better readability and cleaner application of icon as a stencil.

Above: Soap Co. packaging, Paul Belford Ltd, 2015.

Below: 'International Symbol of Access' redesign, The Accessible Icon Project, Tim Ferguson Sauder, Sara Hendren and Brian Glenney, 2011. This symbol aimed to combat the passivity of the established ISA symbol.

Protest

The struggles of the subjugated, marginalized and under-represented in society often starts with the fight for a voice in an unjust system. From placards and banners held at protests, to posters and graffiti hastily put on walls, painted murals, or stickers and badges that can be attached to almost anything – the visual means available to protest movements can be incredibly powerful. Often, the right design can crystallize a cause, providing a visual shorthand for an issue, raising public awareness.

The communication techniques of the powerful can be turned against themselves, as in the Situationist idea of *détournement* (subverting existing messages to reveal the ideologies hidden within) or in comic parody. However, the design of protest is usually oppositional to the establishment approach – cruder, more direct and less concerned with graphical niceties. The visual history of protest has been dominated by typography; especially big, bold sans-serifs that unapologetically shout their messages. Graphics are often reduced to simple symbols that can easily be applied to anything – for instance the raised fist, the peace symbol or the black-and-red flags of anti-fascism. Colour schemes are often relied upon, such as the Suffragettes' green, white and purple, or the Pan-African movement's red, black and green. Sometimes a single colour can symbolize an entire protest, such as the 2004 Orange Revolution in Ukraine.

Photographic imagery can be particularly uncompromising when used for protest, with designers unafraid to use powerful, even upsetting, visuals to open eyes. Skulls, mushroom clouds, missiles, blood and death have all been used throughout history. A particularly famous example was The Art Workers Coalition's 1968 anti-Vietnam War poster, which showed a photograph of the Mỹ Lai Massacre, overlaid with red text reading 'Q. And babies? A. And babies.' which came from an interview with a US soldier who participated in the atrocity.

Often, protest movements require means and methods that are more extreme than would be used in conventional settings. Despite this, the aesthetics of protest have been as easily appropriated by capitalism as any other distinctive approach, leading to many contemporary movements being slicker with their graphics – taking a branded approach to coordinated campaigns to benefit from the same advantages as the multinational companies they are protesting.

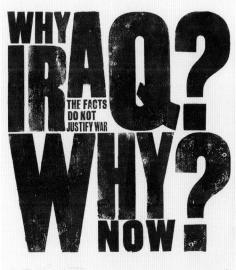

Above Left: 'No Draft, No War, No Nukes' poster, designer unknown, c.1969–75.

Above Right: 'Why Iraq Why Now?', Alan Kitching, 2003. Commissioned by Mark Porter at the *Guardian*.

Below Right: 'Honor King: End Racism!' wearable placard, Allied Printing Trades Council, 1968.

Below Left: 'Votes for Women' banner, Allied Printing Trades Council, c.1897–1919.

Above Left: *Atomkraft? Nej tak* (Nuclear Power? No Thanks) badge, Anne Lund, 1975.

Above Right: Black Power badge, CORE (Congress of Racial Equality), c.1966.

Right: Anti-Nazi League badge, David King, 1978.

Below Right: *Antifaschistische Aktion* (Anti-fascist Action) badge, Bernd Langer, c.1980.

Below Left: Votes for Women pin, Women's Freedom League, c.1907.

Above Left: 'NO' Stop the War Coalition poster, David Gentleman, 2003.

Above Right: 'american sampler', Corita Kent, 1968–9.

Below: Anti-Apartheid Movement poster, David King, 1985.

Further Reading →

Milton Glaser & Mirko Ilić, *The Design of Dissent* (Rockport, 2017)

Liz McQuiston, *Visual Impact: Creative Dissent in the 21st Century* (Phaidon, 2015)

Silas Munro, *Strikethrough: Typographic Messages of Protest* (Letterform Archive, 2022)

Rick Poynor, *David King: Designer, Activist, Visual Historian* (Yale University Press, 2020).

The Environment

Graphic designers living in the 'Anthropocene Epoch', where human activity has had a significant impact on Earth's ecosystem, have a responsibility to consider ecology. For designers, environmental issues are twofold: How can we make our work more sustainable and less damaging? And how can our skills raise awareness of climate change, highlight evidence and combat disinformation? Although graphic designers do not all share the same views – we are as likely to be as apathetic about the environment as anyone else – the nature of a designer's work can bring ecology into focus.

The Environmental Movement came to the fore around the late sixties amid the hippie generation. Although it does not mention environmental issues directly, Ken Garland's influential 'First Things First' manifesto (1964) illustrates that designers were becoming concerned about their role in rampant consumerism, and considering ways that graphic design might be used on 'things more worth using our skills and experience on [...] through which we promote our trade, our education, our culture and greater awareness of the world'.[26] A more explicit text was US journalist Vance Packard's (1914-96) *The Waste Makers,* which, very presciently for 1960, warned about the dangers of unchecked consumerism and railed against 'planned obsolescence' (products designed to have artificially short lifespans), pointing the finger at the advertising industry for encouraging people to buy more than they need. Designer Victor Papanek (1923-98) would continue this thinking in *Design for the Real World,*

which featured a chapter linking design to ecological damage. Papanek writes that; 'If design is ecologically responsive, then it is also revolutionary [...]. If design is to be ecologically responsible, it must be independent of concern for the gross national product (no matter how gross that may be). Over and over I want to stress that in pollution, the designer is more heavily implicated than most.'[27]

An early event in the ecological movement was the 1970 founding of Earth Day, envisioned as a chance to raise awareness of the need for environmental protection. The inaugural year featured posters by Yukihisa Isobe (b. 1935), Robert Rauschenberg (1925-2008) and Robert Leydenfrost (1925-87), who created a bleak photomontage of Earth wearing a gas mask. In later years posters would be designed by Peter Max (b. 1937), Milton Glaser, Seymour Chwast and Paul Rand. The year 1970 also saw the debut of the internationally used symbol for recycling, created by Gary Anderson (b. 1947), who won an open competition set by the Container Corporation of America.

Posters and placards have remained areas where designers use their work to raise awareness of climate change but, as with any protest movement, some of the most effective have been produced urgently by DIY means, not professionals. Recently, as the crisis worsens and politicians continue to do little, imagery and design have become less cutesy, and more direct. A good example is the work of the group Extinction Rebellion, which uses an hourglass symbol as its logo, and bold, typographic designs. As public awareness of ecology has grown, many companies have engaged in what is termed 'greenwashing', falsely attempting to appear more

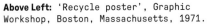

Above Left: 'Recycle poster', Graphic Workshop, Boston, Massachusetts, 1971.

Above Right: Poster and symbol for the first Earth Day, Yukihisa Isobe, 1970.

Below Right: 'Only One Earth' poster, Hirokatsu Hijikata, 1994.

Below Left: Recycling symbol designed by Gary Anderson, winner of a competition set by the Container Corporation of America, 1970.

environmentally friendly through their marketing, PR or graphic design, which often involves the use of the colour green itself as well as natural imagery.

From a practical perspective, graphic designers have to be mindful of ecology when choosing clients or employers, considering how complicit they are in helping harmful industries and looking to be eco-friendly in their work. Obvious ways can be found by designers working in print: materials can be recycled or recyclable, and ethically sourced papers can be obtained, as can natural (not synthetic) materials and printers and producers who are carbon-neutral. In the packaging sector, the push towards reducing needless material, and promoting reusable and refillable packs rather than disposables, must be continued. Often, the trade-off between luxury finishes and fancy materials, and environmentally friendly ones is something print designers need to reckon with, but responsibility also falls on manufacturers, who need to improve their processes, too.

Digital designers must also consider their environmental impact, as, sadly, digital design is no more inherently sustainable than print, for example in terms of its use of electricity. Designers can look to improve energy efficiency by reducing the amount they store online in power-intensive data centres.

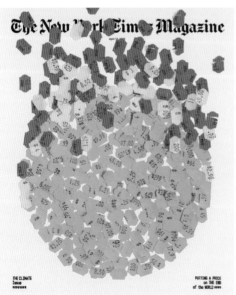

Above Left: Poster for Extinction Rebellion, Anthony Burrill, 2019.

Above Right: #NODAPL linocut poster, Leila Abdelrazaq, 2016.

Below: *The New York Times Magazine* cover, Pablo Delcan, 2019.

Further Reading →

Joanna Boehnert, *Design, Ecology, Politics: Towards the Ecocene* (Bloomsbury, 2021)

Peter Claver Fine, *Sustainable Graphic Design* (Bloomsbury, 2016)

Victor Papanek, *The Green Imperative* (Thames & Hudson, 2021)

Clichés

'While the cliché is a derogatory word in literary circles, the visual cliché is essential in the world of graphic communicators. The visual cliché can immediately give life to an idea. It gives clear meaning to what could be an abstraction.' **George Lois**[28]

A cliché usually means something – such as a phrase, idea or image – that is overused or unoriginal. Clichés are often described as trite, predictable, meaningless or banal. While in forms of entertainment such as a film or video game the déjà-vu effect of a cliché can be annoying, in visual communication using something people are familiar with is often effective. This is not to say that there are not many visual tropes that are overused to the point of exhaustion, but for graphic designers the deployment of a cliché is more about context and usage, rather than something to be avoided completely.

Philip Thompson, in *The Dictionary of Graphic Images*, writes clichés 'persist because they contain an essential truth that appeals to our collective sense of myth and form [...]. It is the international and trans-cultural acceptance of the visual cliché that is its greatest virtue. It enables the designer to breathe new life into a dried husk knowing that the basic symbolism is within common experience.'[29]

The term 'cliché' was originally the French for the printing term 'stereotype', a durable printing plate made from a cast of set metal type. Clichés remain related to stereotypes, which have more negative or harmful connotations, meaning something generalized or misconceived (often leading to prejudice). Graphic designers may choose to use a clichéd image in a satirical or ironic way to knowingly highlight stereotypes. Usually, this is done safely in the knowledge that the intended audience gets the joke.

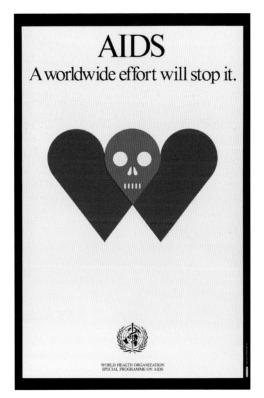

Above Left: 'AIDS: A Worldwide Effort Will Stop It.' poster, Milton Glaser, 1987.

Above Right: *Projekt 150* magazine cover, Hubert Hilscher, 1983.

Below: 'Give' poster for International Red Cross, Matthew Liebowitz, c.1952.

Retro

'Retro' refers to something which is inspired by, or imitative of, a style from the not-too-distant past. We tend to consider the latter half of the 20th century as being retro. Art Nouveau and Art Deco (from the 1900s and 1920s, respectively) are perhaps still considered retro, at a push. Go too far back and something ceases to be retro, instead becoming simply old-fashioned. A decade would have been stylistically diverse, but retro tends to rely on stereotyping: ten years of fashions get reduced to tropes – a few characteristics and mannerisms usually drawn from 'pop culture'.

While there are times when designers aim to create something that looks authentically old, for instance prop designers for a historical film, retro graphic design is more about taking obvious inspiration from the past in the creation of something otherwise new and contemporary. Retro design can come from a place of homage, nostalgia or irony, and a designer can dial up or down how retro they want their work to be.

Sometimes it may just be the case that certain colour combinations or typefaces give a piece of design a generally retro feel, without the designer aiming for any particular era; this can be done unconsciously or accidentally. In some cases, retro might be a reason not to develop a particular design if it isn't appropriate for the context. As with any fashion, retro influences come in cycles, with particular decades inspiring designers for short periods. There is always a space between an era ending and it becoming retro and ripe for plunder, but the time frame seems to be shrinking as the influence of the internet makes trends shorter lived. Retro graphic design can easily veer into becoming 'kitsch' – something 'in poor taste because of excessive garishness or sentimentality, but sometimes appreciated in an ironic or knowing way'.[30]

Modernist graphic designers sought to end the use of the previous era's styles in their work – to work so rationally as to not even create a 'style' – but ironically modernist graphic design would simply become another moment in history for later generations to borrow from, reducing a method to stylistic tropes. Although retro graphic design came to the fore during postmodernism, when many designers turned to past styles, there are earlier examples, such as the revival of the use of Victorian typefaces in fifties Britain or the eclectic work of Push Pin Studios in sixties New York.

Opposite: *The Smudge* Volume 2, Issue 7, cover design by Clay Hickson, 2018.

Further Reading →
Simon Reynolds, *Retromania: Pop Culture's Addiction to its Own Past* (Faber & Faber, 2012)
Tony Seddon, *Greetings from Retro Design: Vintage Graphics Decade by Decade* (Thames & Hudson, 2015)

July
2018

Volume 2
Issue 7

Pastiche

While 'retro' is defined by taking inspiration from a selected bygone era's general style, 'pastiche' refers to a similar process done in a more specific way to either the work of one person or a particular piece of work. Pastiche has to be done knowingly; the reference is meant to be blatant. Pastiche is like 'parody', although the latter generally comes from a place of either mockery, humour or critique, and requires the viewer to understand the reference to generate the correct satirical or comic response. Pastiche can come from a positive place, for instance as homage, and can still be effective if the audience is unaware of the source.

The distinction between pastiche and 'sampling' is less clear cut, but probably lies in the amount of an original work that is referenced. A sample may involve taking a bit from an older work, in the creation of something new. Pastiche, in contrast, borrows from a work in its entirety; take away the original piece and you are left with nothing. In this way, to again borrow musical terms, a pastiche is more like a 'remix' or 'cover' than a song that samples parts from a previous song as one element of something otherwise new.

To count as pastiche, a designer must recreate the referenced work themselves. The style can be roughly the same (or entirely different) but it must be a new interpretation or twist on the original. An exact copy obviously cannot be considered as something new, but the boundary between pastiche and appropriation (borrowing without permission) and plagiarism (outright copying) is hotly debated, and from a legal copyright perspective, very complex and geographically varied. A successful pastiche usually finds the right balance between transformative changes to the original and making sure the reference remains clear, while also being respectful to the context of the work being pastiched.

Both pastiche and parody became important characteristics of postmodern culture, in which, for many, 'originality' ceased to be a key motivation, partly out of a feeling that the eclectic experimentation of the 20th century had exhausted possibilities. As the American literary critic Frederic Jameson wrote: 'In a world in which stylistic innovation is no longer possible, all that is left is to imitate dead styles, to speak through the masks and with the voices of the styles in the imaginary museum.'[31]

this sunday, april 25 1993
noon sharp / $5

at macondo cultural center
hollywood, california

bikini

with not for the lack of trying
plus lather and canopy

Above Left: Book cover, designed by Gail Anderson and Joe Newton, illustrated by David Cowles, 2013. After Milton Glaser's *Dylan* poster, 1967.

Above Right: 'Bikini Kill' poster, Mike Joyce, 2013. After Josef Müller-Brockmann's *Der Film* poster, 1960.

Below: Book cover, Tyler Comrie, 2020. After Filippo Tommaso Marinetti's *Zang Tumb Tumb* cover, 1914 (see p.22).

Trompe-l'œil

A French term meaning 'trick of the eye', 'trompe-l'œil' usually refers to the mimicking of three-dimensionality and depth in a flat, two-dimensional artwork. However, it can also be used as a catch-all term for any optical illusion. As a technique, it has been around for centuries, appearing first in paintings, where artists aimed to create such realistic renderings that viewers could not distinguish between reality and illusion. In painting the adoption of one-point perspective was a kind of trompe-l'œil. Surrealism would push optical illusion further, but it was the advent of abstraction that had the most bearing on graphic design, as artists explored how flat shapes could be used to achieve eye-catching visual effects.

This reached its height with the Optical (Op) art movement, a term coined in the 1960s but with roots in Neo-impressionism, Cubism, Futurism and the Bauhaus. Op artists, such as Bridget Riley (b. 1931) and Victor Vasarely (1906–97), often worked in black and white for maximum visual impact, creating abstract shapes and patterns that appear to pulse, move or come in and out of the flat canvas, in a way that can be disorienting. As expressed in the catalogue to MoMA's 1965 movement-defining *The Responsive Eye* exhibition, Op aimed not for 'beauty of form, tasteful relationships, nor equilibrium in the old sense but the activation of vision'.[32]

Op artists were partly inspired by printing techniques that were familiar to graphic designers. There was a symbiotic relationship between Op art and graphic design, best illustrated by the artist and graphic designer Franco Grignani (1908–99). One of Italy's leading post-war designers, Grignani used optical illusion techniques in his painting but was equally adept at applying them on covers, posters and trademarks for clients such as Penguin, Pirelli and Woolmark.

Optical illusion in graphic design was popular in the sixties and continued to be in the seventies thanks to psychedelia, but it remains a technique that designers can use to incredible effect, as it is almost guaranteed to gain the viewers' attention. Trompe-l'œil can be used beyond just flat printed graphics. There is a way of doing it in physical space whereby an image is visible only from a particular spot due to perspective – an 'anamorphic' technique popularized by Swiss artist Felice Varini (b. 1952) that also works for typography and graphics and which can be captured on camera.

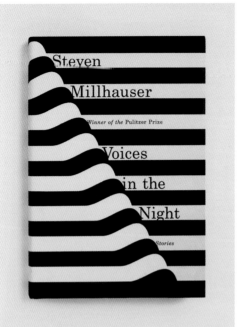

Above Left: Book cover, Janet Hansen, 2015.

Above Right: *'Das Plakat'* exhibition poster, Fons Hickmann/M23, 2020.

Below Right: Pirelli printed advert, Alan Fletcher (Fletcher/Forbes/Gill), 1962.

Below Left: Press advertisement for an exhibition of textiles, Franco Grignani, 1957.

Type as Image

'What is typophoto? Typography is communication composed in type. Photography is the visual presentation of what can be optically apprehended. Typophoto is the visually most exact rendering of communication.'

László Moholy-Nagy,

***Painting, Photography, Film* (1925)[33]**

The invention of moveable type and the printing press caused a division between text and image; previously the same hand had frequently created both. In some logographic written languages that use symbols to represent a complete word (as opposed to systems that use alphabets representing sounds) the distinction between image and text is less clear. The blurring of the boundaries between text and image has long been an interest of scribes, artists and designers in all cultures. From Islamic calligraphy and the illuminated initials of medieval manuscripts, to Dadaist collage (see page 23), the calligrams of Guillaume Apollinaire (see page 23), and post–World War II concrete poetry, creating image out of text, and text out of image, has been a source of inspiration throughout the history of visual communication.

The invention of photography, which caused further distinctions between text and image (in comparison to illustration), also created new possibilities in combining typography and image. These new opportunities were something that was particularly exploited by interwar modernist designers, such as Herbert Matter and László Moholy-Nagy, the latter coining the term 'typophoto' to describe the technique in 1925. The post–World War II turn towards conceptual, ideas-based graphic design made use of the possibilities of phototypesetting to distort and manipulate text into expressive compositions, as seen in the work of Americans such as Robert Brownjohn, Bob Gill and Louis Danziger (b. 1923).

From integrating text into a picture digitally, to turning typography into an illustrative, expressive image, 'type as image' remains popular in contemporary graphic design, particularly in advertising, editorial and book cover design. Leading British book designer David Pearson (b. 1978) even named his studio Type as Image, in honour of this favoured technique.

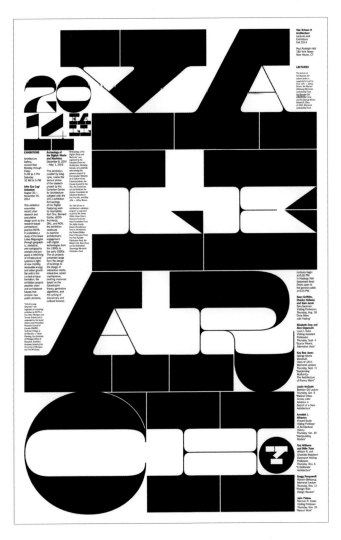

Above Left: Poster for Yale School of Architecture, Jessica Svendsen and Michael Bierut, Pentagram, 2014.

Above Right: *Fascism: History and Theory* book cover, David Pearson, 2020.

Below: Planet Displays press advertisement, Bob Gill, 1965.

Further Reading →

Ivan Chermayeff & Tom Geismar, *Watching Words Move* (Chronicle Books, 2016)

[Robert] Massin, *Letter and Image* (Studio Vista, 1970)

JONATHAN SWIFT

A TALE OF A

TUB

'It is a fatal MISCARRIAGE,

SO ILL TO ORDER AFFAIRS,

as to pass for a

FOOL

IN ONE COMPANY,

when in another you might be treated as a

PHILOSOPHER'

Penguin Books .... Great Ideas

Chapter 4:
Typography

Typographic Lexicon

Typography has its own complex set of terms and jargon, some of which have become well known in the digital age, while others remain mysterious to the uninitiated. What follows is a glossary of some key terms.

TYPEFACE: Typeface refers to a designed set of alphanumeric characters, which can be in different weights and styles while remaining consistent. Helvetica, for instance, is a typeface - the overarching name that refers to all the different weights and styles.

FONT: Often used interchangeably with 'typeface' in the digital age, font refers to a specific style of a typeface. Helvetica is a typeface; Helvetica Bold Italic is a font. In the days of metal type, an individual font was also defined by its size. One way to distinguish between typeface and font is that the typeface is the overall design, while the font is what designers use.

FAMILY: While the typeface is the design of the characters, family refers to the collection of fonts in different weights and styles that share a name. Again 'typeface' and 'family' have become synonymous in the digital age, although family tends to imply that a typeface contains different weights and styles. A super-family is one that contains an extensive variety of styles, weights and widths. 'Type system' is sometimes used

as a term to refer to a collection of related families that cross categories - for instance a serif and a sans-serif.

WEIGHT: Weight refers to the heaviness of the strokes in a font and is one of the common distinguishing features between fonts within a family. Fonts with thinner strokes are usually labelled as light, with the thinnest known as extra-light or hairline. At the heavier end of the scale comes bold, extra bold, black and extra-black. The term 'black' comes from the fact that the thicker the strokes get the blacker the overall visual effect is of the printed black text. 'Heavy' is sometimes used in place of bold. In the middle there is a variety of terms, such as regular, standard or normal. Medium is often used as a mid-point in weight between regular and bold, while 'book' can serve the same function between light and regular. To avoid confusion, some type designers have favoured the inclusion of numbers to designate weights. Font widths, which run from condensed to extended, usually come in the same weights as the 'regular' width.

GLYPH: Glyphs are the individual characters of a font, whether that be a number, letter or symbol. It is used rather than 'character', as a font may have multiple glyphs of the same character. These extra glyphs for the same character are known as 'alternates'.

CASE: Uppercase refers to capital letters, while lowercase refers to the small letters. These terms come from the pre-digital era when physical cases of type were divided, with capitals

Previous Spread: Book cover for *A Tale of A Tub* by Jonathan Swift, Penguin Great Ideas, David Pearson, 2004.

kept on top and small letters below. Case can also refer to the use of capitals: capitalizing the first letter of every word is 'title case', while the use of capitals to signify the start of sentences is 'sentence case'.

ITALIC: Italic refers to type that is slanted forwards, based on traditional handwriting styles, and often used for emphasis or to differentiate between text, for instance the title of a book. Italic fonts tend to be narrower than their 'roman' (meaning non-italic or upright) counterparts. Some fonts, especially sans-serifs, have 'obliques' where the letters are mechanically sloped, rather than 'true italics' where letters are redesigned in slanted versions and often change entirely.

BASELINE: The baseline is the line on which glyphs sit, although only those with flat bases sit exactly on it; curved elements cross the line slightly.

X-HEIGHT: The x-height is the distance between the baseline and the top of a lowercase x. The x is chosen as it is usually straight at the top and bottom, but many lowercase letters share the same height, such as v, w and z. Again, curved-topped letters such as a, c, e, m, n, o, r and s may cross the x-height line (often known as the mean line or mid-line) slightly. The term 'cap-height' is used for the height of capital letters. The x-height is a key identifying characteristic that varies greatly across typefaces: higher x-heights make typefaces appear bigger even if their cap-height is the same as a typeface with a smaller x-height.

Higher x-heights make typefaces more legible at smaller sizes.

ASCENDER: Ascenders are the parts of a lowercase letter that extend above the x-height.

DESCENDER: Descenders are the parts of a lowercase letter that drop below the baseline. Some have specific names – for example the 'tail' – which is the lower part of a y – or the 'loop' – which is the bottom of a g.

COUNTER: Counters are the enclosed or partially enclosed negative space found within many letters. Some have specific names – for example the 'eye', which is the top part of the lowercase e. Aperture refers to the entrance to counters that are not fully enclosed.

DOUBLE-STOREY: Double-storey is used to describe a lowercase a or g that has two counters rather than just one. Gill Sans for instance has a double-storey a, while Futura's a is single-storey.

SWASH: A swash is an ornamental addition to a glyph. Sometimes this means an extension or embellishment of an existing part of a letter – for example the leg of a K, or an outright addition of an extra element. Swashes are most commonly found on cursive and script fonts, where they imitate elaborate old handwriting styles, but sometimes appear on serifs, particularly in italic.

LIGATURE: A ligature is when two characters are connected and united into a single glyph. In most cases, they exist where two adjacent characters would bump into each other or be very tight, so ligatures help solve spacing issues. Common ligature pairings include fi, fl and ff. Some fonts may have three-letter ligatures. 'Gadzook' refers to a ligature where the join is not part of either letter originally, the most common being a loop between c and t (ᶜt) or s and t (ſt). The ampersand symbol (&) is based on a ligature between e and t, from the Latin *et*, meaning 'and'.

TITTLE: Tittle is a term for the dot found at the top of i and j characters, which usually floats above the x-height and is separate from the rest of the letter.

FIGURES: Figures are the number characters within a font and come in multiple varieties designed for different uses. Lining figures are numbers that all sit on the baseline and are usually the same size as the cap-height. Old-style figures have different heights, some of which match the cap-height, with others that hang below the baseline. Both types come in two varieties: proportional – where the numbers have different widths and fit nicely together – and tabular – where the numbers are monospaced and consistent widths (ideal for use in tables).

DINGBATS: Historically these typographical symbols or ornament were often used for section breaks in books, or to create ornamental borders. Entire dingbat fonts that contain just useful or ornamental symbols, not letters or numbers are available.

KERNING: Kerning refers to the space between letters. Font designers create kerning pairs to make sure the space between letters appear optically even; otherwise designers have to do this manually to avoid setting that is too loose or tight. Kerning is different from tracking, which designers use to increase or decrease the spacing between entire sequences of characters in one go.

MONOSPACE: A monospaced font is one where the characters all have the same width, ignoring usual proportions, and have even spacing rather than needing kerning pairs. Typewriter fonts are usually monospaced, and are popular in the digital age for computer code.

SMALL CAPS: Small caps (SC) are capital letters that are roughly as tall as the x-height. While this can be achieved digitally by reducing the size of capital letters, a true SC font is designed so that the weight and proportion are consistent with lowercase letters. Petite caps are designed to be exactly the same as the x-height and can be used for 'unicase' setting where uppercase and lowercase letters are all the same height.

POINT SIZE: Points are the unit of measurement in typography. A point is 1/12 of a pica - another typographical unit, which is 1/6 of an inch, making a point 1/72 of an inch. In physical type, the point size referred to the height of the metal rectangle in which the letter sat, rather than the height of the letter itself. This convention has continued digitally, where each glyph sits in an invisible box known as the 'em square'. Due to factors like cap height and x-height, fonts appear to be different sizes when set at the same point size.

LEADING: Leading refers to the vertical space between lines of type, historically achieved by inserting lead strips between lines of metal type. It is measured from baseline to baseline and is also known as 'line spacing'.

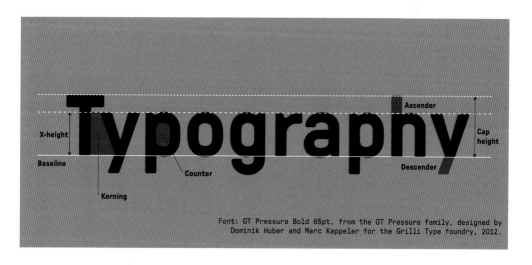

Font: GT Pressura Bold 65pt, from the GT Pressura family, designed by
Dominik Huber and Marc Kappeler for the Grilli Type foundry, 2012.

Typographic Origins

'The written character is and remains the basis of every typographical activity. It is not a creation of our century. The written character goes far back in time, spanning the vast distance from early hieroglyphics to the abstract written symbols of today and involving many contradictions.' Emil Ruder, *Typography: A Manual of Design* (1967)[1]

Typography as a discipline (distinct from writing) began with the invention of 'moveable' type that allowed text to be mechanically produced by a printing press. However, it is intrinsically linked to the longer history of writing systems and language itself. The earliest forms of writing, devised to provide a permanent and transferable equivalent of verbal communication, were pictogram-based – simplified pictures of things represented the word for the thing itself. What differentiated ancient 'pictographic' writing from 'drawings' was the simplification of form, shared and agreed upon meanings and the development of additional 'ideograms' – arbitrary symbols which represent an idea or concept rather than a physical object. Overall, for a writing system to flourish, any ambiguity had to be removed; writing had to be widely understood.

Perhaps the best-known example of pictogram-based writing is ancient Egyptian hieroglyphics, but even that system used a combination of pictograms, ideograms, symbols for entire words (logographs), single-consonant characters, phonetic (sound-based) elements and determinatives that marked the semantic category of a word to avoid ambiguity. What first looks like a primitive system was highly complex and evolved into simplified cursive systems. First the Hieratic script, then the Demotic, which were both more alphabetic than their

predecessor, using signs representing individual phonemes (the smallest unit of speech). Another early writing form was cuneiform, from the ancient Middle East, which evolved from a pictographic proto-writing into one that used mostly syllabograms (signs for whole syllables) in a system that employed wedge-shaped strokes that were created by a stylus.

How truly alphabetic writing systems (ones that used only a standardized set of letters for phonemes – no pictograms, ideograms or syllabograms) developed is not fully known, but it is widely accepted that the first was in a Semitic language, developed around the Sinai Peninsula and Canaan, just east of Egypt. What is known as the North Semitic alphabet had 22 letters, which represented only consonants, and was written right to left (as Hebrew and Arabic still are). This original alphabet soon spread to the Phoenicians of the Eastern Mediterranean by the 11th century BCE, evolving as it went, before eventually becoming the ancestor of the Greek alphabet, from which a great many European alphabets would derive their origins. Greeks eventually began to write left to right and developed vowel letters, but, as with most early writing systems, the ancient Greek alphabet comprised only capitals, did not use word spaces and had no punctuation. The Romans were surrounded by peoples using the Greek alphabet, and their Latin alphabet evolved

Above Left: Cuneiform tablet from Anatolia, c.20th–19th century BCE.

Below Left: Bronze military diploma fragment from the reign of Roman emperor Trajan, 113/14 CE.

Above Right: Bronze fragment of an inscription in Greek Doric script, c.490–480 BCE

Centre: Folio from a Qur'an manuscript in Kufic script, 8th–9th century CE.

Below Right: Demotic script from ancient Egypt, inscribed on the Rosetta Stone, 196 BCE.

Above Left: Reproduction of text from the Gutenberg Bible, originally printed in 1455.

Above Right: Dutch Psalter (Book of Psalms), scribed c.1400–1500.

Below Right: Italian edition of Ovid's *Metamorphoses*, Venice, printed in 1499.

Below Left: *Hypnerotomachia Poliphili*, Aldus Manutius, Venice, printed in 1499.

by taking some letters from the Greek and Etruscan, and creating a few of their own, to form a 23-letter alphabet. With the addition of J, U and W, the Latin alphabet became the one used by most of the languages of Western Europe.

In medieval Europe a lowercase style of writing, known as Carolingian minuscule, grew out of the uncial (an uppercase cursive style used by European scribes around 400–800 CE) and half-uncial (another, smaller uncial that had ascenders and descenders) scripts, and a desire for smaller letters that were quicker to write. The requirements of book scribes led to a further writing style, blackletter, whose heavy, narrow letters, as well as many joining ligatures, made writing faster and more space efficient – desirable as demand for books grew. It was blackletter type that was used by Johannes Gutenberg in 1439 on his Bible, the first to be mechanically produced with metal moveable type in Western Europe (although moveable type had been used in China c.1040 CE).

By the Renaissance, many printers felt blackletter was crude, and looked back for inspiration, settling on what is known variously as the humanist minuscule or antique, combining Latin capitals with a Carolingian lowercase. This style of typography – pioneered mostly in Venice by typographers such as Aldus Manutius (1449–1515), Nicolas Jenson (c.1420–80) and Francesco Griffo (1450–1518; cutter of the first italic typeface around 1500) – would be long-lived, remaining the conventional style for book typesetting in Latin-based languages today. It was also around this time that the Arabic numbers (using 0–9, a system with roots in India) began to replace Roman numerals.

It is important to note that innovations in paper production, which spread west from China through the Arabic world, arrived in Europe in time for the innovations of Johannes Gutenberg (c.1400–68), which required a smoother paper to be effective.

Further Reading →

John R. Biggs, *Letter-forms and Lettering* (Blandford, 1977)
Johanna Drucker, *Inventing the Alphabet* (University of Chicago Press, 2022)

Serifs

Serifs are the small strokes – often taking the form of flared lines or elegant, sharp flicks – that project from the terminals (ends) of larger strokes on some typefaces. Referred to variously historically as surripses, syrifs, cereps, ceriphs and surryphs, the question of what to call serifs came into focus once sans-serifs typefaces arrived in the 19th century and typographers needed an agreed-upon term to label what was missing. In Japan, the equivalent of serifs on Kanji and Kana letterforms are known as *uroko* (meaning 'fish scales') due to the way they transition from thick to thin towards a point.

There are many types of serif and categories of serif typefaces, but the main fundamental distinction is between adnate and abrupt serifs. Adnate serifs attach smoothly and more organically to the stem from which they come, sometimes this is also known as a bracketed serif, with the 'bracket' referring to the curved transition. Abrupt serifs (also known as unbracketed) are sudden, attaching directly to the main stroke with no transition or flow, often at a right angle. The shapes of serifs, and how they attach, are particularly key factors in the construction and categorization of the multitude of serif typefaces that developed in the wake of moveable type in Europe.

The origin of serifs stretches back beyond Gutenberg. Serif typefaces are also known as 'romans'. Serifs in the pre-printing era were a result of the hands that wrote them and the tools they used; some of the earliest writing implements were angled or pointed broad-nibbed pens, carved from bamboo or reeds (later feather quills), or animal-hair brushes. Such tools were flexible enough to allow for modulated strokes, with the angle they were held at, and the direction they were moving in, impacting variation between thick and thin. Pointed tools tended to result in fine lines at either end of strokes, with the tool moving horizontally with writing direction and then down through the letter; the origins of bracketed serifs can be found here. Carving is a very different process to writing, created slowly and forcefully with a chisel and mallet. Some of the earliest alphabetic inscriptions are Greek and generally lack serifs, although the method of inscription often resulted in flared, serif-like terminals.

In ancient Rome serifs would gradually become more pronounced. It was long thought that these small triangular serifs were a natural result of chisel shapes. However, historians of typography now agree that the inscriptions were first painted by a scribe using a flat brush held at an angle, like a broad-nibbed pen, with the carver following the outlines to create a permanent version. The monumental importance of such inscriptions, combined with the Roman passion for precise engineering, can explain why ornamental details developed that were not always found in general handwriting. Harmony, geometry and balance were important, and there are obvious comparisons between the serifed form of a carved letter I and the shape of a Roman column. The pinnacle of Latin inscriptional capitals is generally considered to be Trajan's Column (113 CE)

By the time of Gutenberg's 42-line Bible, it was blackletter scripts that dominated late-medieval Europe, and the

THE ARGUMENT.

LUCIUS Tarquinius (for his excessive pride surnàmed Superbus) after hee had caused his owne father in law Servius Tullius to be cruelly murd'red, and contrarie to the Romaine lawes and customes, not requiring or staying for the people's suffrages, had possessed himselfe of the kingdome: went accompanyed with his sonnes and other noble men of Rome, to besiege Ardea, during which siege, the principall men of the Army meeting one evening at the tent of Sextus Tarquinius the king's sonne, in their discourses after supper every one commended the vertues of his owne wife: among whom Colatinus extolled the incomparable chastity of his wife Lucretia. In that pleasant humor they all posted to Rome, & intending by theyr secret and sodaine arrivall to make triall of that which every one had before avouched, onely Colatinus finds his wife (though it were late in the night) spinning amongest her maides, the other ladies were all found dauncing and revelling, or in severall disports: whereupon the noble men yeelded Colatinus the victory, and his wife the fame. At that time Sextus Tarquinius being enflamed with Lucrece beauty, yet smoothering his passions for the present, departed with the rest backe to the campe:

Above Left: Photograph of an inscription on Trajan's Column, Roman, 113 CE.

Above Right: Serifs, marked in orange, on Times New Roman capitals.

Below Right: *Divina proportione*, Luca Pacioli, illustration by Leonardo da Vinci, 1509.

Below Left: William Morris's Golden Type, 1890, in a book printed by the Kelmscott Press.

Questa lettera .M. se caua del tondo e del suo quadro le gambe surtili uogliáo esser per mezo de le grosse comme la senistra del. A. le extreme gambe uogliano esser al quan to dentro al quadro le medie fra quelle e le intersecationi de li dianietri lor grosseze . grosse e surtili serefarescano a quel le del. A. cóme di sopra in figura aperto poi compren dere.

Fette Fraktur
Alte Schwabacher
Clemente Rotunda
English Textura
Old English

Blackletter

Garamond
Bembo
Poliphilus & *Blado*
Caslon
Janson

Humanist / Old-Style

Baskerville
Fournier
Bulmer
Times New Roman
Caledonia

Transitional

Didot
Bodoni
Walbaum
Modern No. 20
Century

Didone / Modern

Clarendon
Playbill
Calvert
Rockwell
Courier

Slab Serif

Albertus
ITC Elan
PL Latin
ITC Barcelona
Friz Quadrata

Glyphic

first moveable type used there was in the Textura style. Blackletter as a category had many varieties, such as Rotunda, Bastarda, Schwabacher and Fraktur. However, their forms all showed shared calligraphic origins, not least the serifs that, with their frequent angular diamond shapes, point to the use of a flat-ended pen in their drawing. The first metal typefaces were designed by punch-cutters, who manually carved the letters from which type was cast. Like Gutenberg, they mostly had backgrounds in metalsmithing, so achieving the fine details of serifs was possible. Blackletter fell out of favour in many parts of Europe by the Renaissance, a time when many creative fields were looking to ancient Rome for inspiration, particularly in Italy.

What would emerge was a style of serif typeface - now known as Humanist, Old-Style, Garalde or simply 'roman' - that combined the forms of Latin inscriptional capitals with the lowercase of the Carolingian scripts developed in the 8th century under Emperor Charlemagne (747–814). Renaissance punch-cutters applied some of the features of Roman capitals, such as modulated strokes, a slightly diagonal axis and angled wedge-shaped serifs, to lowercase letters that did not exist in Latin inscriptions. Notable early Old-Style typefaces include Garamond (Claude Garamont [c.1510–61], c.1540), Jenson (Nicolas Jenson, c.1470–80) and Caslon (William Caslon [1692/93–1766], 1722). Some of the most significant early roman typefaces came out of Venice and were the work of the cutter Francesco Griffo (1450–1518), working with printer Aldus Manutius (from which they get the name Aldine) in around 1495–1505. Typefaces later based on their work

together include Bembo (Monotype, 1929) and Poliphilus (Monotype, 1923) with its italic counterpart, Blado — based on Griffo's pioneering italic type (c.1501). The Arts and Crafts movement was a motive for some designers to turn backwards for typographic styles, and many new Old-Style typefaces were designed in the 19th and 20th centuries (although often based on Renaissance sources) such as William Morris's (1834–96) Golden Type (1890), Bruce Rogers's (1870–1957) Centaur (1914), Frank Hinman Pierpont's (1860–1937) Plantin (1913), Hermann Zapf's (1918–2015) Palatino (1948) and Jan Tschichold's (1902–74) Sabon (1967).

The next big development in serif typefaces would be associated with the Enlightenment era (when rationality and science dominated), which began in the late 17th century. These 'transitional' serifs moved a little further from their humanist, calligraphic origins towards something more analytical and structured, with upright stress in counters, more contrast between thick and thin, and straighter serifs with reduced bracketing. A key example is the *Romain du Roi* (King's Roman), a commission to develop a new typeface that only the French royal printer could use, put out by King Louis XIV (1638–1715) in 1692. The task was given to a committee of the Academy of Sciences, whose member Jacques Jaugeon (fl. 1690–1710) designed each letter precisely on a consistent grid of squares (8 × 8 for capitals, 8 × 9 for lowercase), with each square containing a smaller 6 × 6 grid. These were then engraved on copper by Louis Simmoneau (1645–1728) and then punch-cut by Philippe Grandjean (1666–1714). The finished *Romain du Roi* type would take decades but was hugely innovative, particularly its horizontal serifs.

The most famous transitional serif is Baskerville, designed by the British typefounder and printer John Baskerville (1707-75) in the 1750s. It is a very legible, well-spaced typeface with generous proportions, almost horizontal serifs, vertical axis and sharp contrast. Baskerville's technological innovations, alongside ongoing improvements in paper quality, made such fine details achievable. Transitional serifs have long been a favoured choice as text faces. Probably the world's most used typeface, Times New Roman, designed in 1932 for *The Times* newspaper by Monotype's Stanley Morrison (1889-1967), can be classified as transitional, as it used the proportions and forms of old-style Plantin, but was given more contrast and straight serifs.

By the late 18th century the developments of transitional types would reach their logical conclusion in 'modern' serifs, which had even higher contrast and abrupt hairline serifs that were completely flat at the top and bottom. In these typefaces, vertical strokes (which are perfectly upright) are thick and horizontals are very thin, while construction is very utilitarian. Modern serifs are sometimes known as 'Didone', a term that combines the surnames of the two most significant pioneers of this style and their eponymous typefaces – the French Didot (1784) and Italian Bodoni (1798), designed by Firmin Didot (1764-1836) and Giambattista Bodoni (1740-1813), respectively. Didone faces are generally not well suited to large amounts of text or small sizes, as their thick verticals can be distracting, and they lack the humanistic, optical qualities that made traditional serifs easier on the eye. Modern serifs are better at large sizes where their elegant forms can be appreciated. Through their usage by magazines such as *Harper's Bazaar* and *Vogue* and by brands like Armani and Dior, Didone became associated with fashion and luxury. However, they would also be used by designers – including Herb Lubalin (1918-81) and CBS television's Georg Olden (1920-75) – seeking distinctive typefaces to stand out in areas increasingly dominated by plain sans-serifs.

As poster advertising expanded in the 19th-century, font designers experimented with styles that would work best at big 'display' sizes. Among these was the 'fat face', which took contrast to bold extremes, pioneered by English founders Vincent Figgins (1766-1844) and Robert Thorne (1754-1820). Also developed were slab serifs, which were like Didones minus the contrast and with heavy, unbracketed square serifs, and the freakish reverse-contrast 'Italians' which flipped the stress of 'Moderns' with heavy horizontals and hairline verticals. By the mid-19th century, a more mannered approach to slab serifs developed, usually known as Clarendons after the typeface of the same name by Robert Besley (1794-1876) of London's Thorowgood Foundry, or sometimes as Ionics. Clarendons feature characteristics shared by earlier roman text faces; a large x-height, mild stroke contrast and bracketed serifs, but also have slab serifs, a generally heavy appearance and ball terminals on the ends of some letters. Clarendons

The quick brown fox jumps over the lazy dog. **В чащах юга жил бы цитрус? Да, но фальшивый экземпляр!** Ζαφείρι δέξου πάγκαλο, βαθῶν ψυχῆς τὸ σῆμα. 色は匂へど 散り ぬるを 我が世誰ぞ 常ならむ 有為の奥山 今日越えて 浅き夢見じ 酔ひもせず（ん）.

Above: Noto Serif; shown in Latin, Cyrillic, Greek and Japanese scripts. Noto Serif was originally known as Droid Serif and was designed by Steve Matteson (b. 1965) at Ascender Corporation in 2008 for Google.

came in a range of weights and widths, becoming an oft-used typeface for advertising as it was strong, but still eminently readable. Slab serifs remained popular in many contexts, and some solid examples were designed in the early 20th century, such as Rockwell (Monotype, 1934), Memphis (Rudolf Wolf [1895-1942], 1929), Beton (Heinrich Jost [1889-1964], 1929) and Stymie (Morris Fuller Benton [1872-1948], 1931), and beyond – Lubalin Graph (ITC, 1974), Calvert (Margaret Calvert [b. 1936], 1980) and Archer (Hoefler & Frere-Jones, 2001). Slab serifs are also associated with typewriters, as in the early 20th century these fonts were a perfect fit for the machines, due to their ability to be monospaced and how their prominent serifs made it easy

to distinguish letters at small sizes. Typewriter manufacturers had their own fonts, but foundries also released typewriter-style slab serifs such as Courier (Howard Kettler [1919-99], 1955) and ITC's American Typewriter (1974).

A final variety of serif fonts is 'glyphic'. These typefaces do not fit into the categories mentioned so far as they are based on engraving techniques rather than calligraphic traditions. They often have minimal serifs, and tapered stroke ends rather than conventional serifs, or uniformly triangular or wedge-shaped serifs. Typefaces with triangle-shaped serifs are usually known as 'Latins' due to the connection to ancient Roman inscriptions, which also explains why some glyphic fonts lack a lowercase.

MORT
AU ROI
VIVE LA
RÉPUBLIQUE

Freight Text Pro.
The quick brown fox
jumps over the lazy dog.
Ma la volpe, col suo
balzo, ha raggiunto il
quieto Fido. **Victor jagt**
zwölf Boxkämpfer quer
über den großen Sylter
Deich. *Voix ambiguë d'un*
cœur qui au zéphyr préfère
les jattes de kiwi. **Joshua**
Darden, 2005/2022.

GT Super Display Super Italic, 130 pt, Polish

Morfina

GT Super Display Super Italic, 65 pt, Polish

KONSTANTY WILLEMANN,
warszawiak, lecz syn

GT Super Display Super Italic, 40 pt, Polish

Jest cynikiem, lajdakiem i bon-vivan-
tem. Niewiernym mężem i złym ojcem.
Konstanty niechętnie bierze udział

Paulette
Jean-Jacques
Marie-Françoise
Pierre-Yves

⫸→ **Galaxy Stars** ←⫷

GEÓLOGOS ACHAM METEORITO *MAIS VELHO QUE A TERRA*

La plus jolie fleur du jardin

autrichien

½ *Papaye & Rhum*

LA LUNE RENVOIE LA LUMIÈRE DU SOLEIL. SON SPECTRE LUMINEUX EST PROCHE

ÉCLIPSE

→ *Orion, La Osa, las Pléyades (en Tauro) y El Boyero (Boötes)* ←

„Aber woher weißt du das?"

◆◆◇◇◇△⩍⩍○○●●◣⩍⫴⫴⫴⫴◆◆◇◇◇△⩍⩍○○

La Vía Láctea es una galaxia espiral donde se encuentra el sistema solar

JULES VERNE, 1865

Top Left: Injurial, Sandrine Nugue, 205TF, 2019.

Top Right: Freight Text Pro, Joshua Darden,
2005/2022.

Right: Bely, Roxane Gataud, 2016.

Above: Romain 20, Alice Savoie, 205TF, 2020.

Centre Left: GT Super, Noël Leu, 2018.

Despite the rise of sans-serifs, serif typefaces remain much used, particularly as text faces where their legibility outstrips that of sans-serifs, and new serif fonts continued to be designed in the 'cold-type' era and into the digital age, as designers find there are still interesting avenuoo to be explored. Historical serifs are constantly being revived, with tweaks and optimizations made to keep pace with technological developments and the requirements of digital screen usage. Typographic trends change rapidly, meaning graphic designers are always hungry for a serif that offers something exciting or new, or exceptionally good readability.

Further Reading →
Phil Baines, *Type and Typography*
(Laurence King, 2005)
Peter Dawson, *Type Directory*
(Thames & Hudson, 2019)
Ruari McLean, *Manual of Typography*
(Thames & Hudson, 1980)

Sans-serifs

The term 'sans-serif' refers to typefaces without serifs. Often considered more modern in look – many modernists felt serifs were needless ornaments and wanted typography to leave its calligraphic past behind– the first sans-serif typeface, London-based foundry Caslon's all-uppercase 'Two-Line English Egyptian' debuted in 1816.

Although Caslon used Egyptian for the first sans-serif type, the term (whose connection with Egypt the country is unclear) usually referred to a square slab serif with a consistent, heavy line width. The lack of variety in the line width of these slab serifs made it much more feasible for signwriters to drop the serifs entirely, a decision likely driven by a desire for novelty, and the attention that came with it. Rather than Egypt, the source of inspiration for early sans-serifs came from ancient Roman inscriptions, where the Latin capital letters were monoline, and geometric in construction and had barely visible serifs, especially from afar. Sans-serif lettering had become an occasional choice for architectural carved lettering by the early 19th century (although the English architect John Soane [1753-1837] was suggesting sans-serif, uppercase lettering for inscriptions as early as 1779) before being copied by sign painters and eventually becoming available as fonts.

Caslon's English Egyptian, although the first of its kind, was released with little fanfare and few examples of its use survive. Twelve years later, in 1828, Vincent Figgins (1766-1844) released his take on Caslon's innovation – the second serif-less typeface ever cut, coining the term 'sans-serif' to describe it. This '8 Line-Pica Sans-Serif' was heavier in weight than Caslon's sans, but similarly inelegant at times and uppercase only. It shared much with Figgins's Antique, the first slab-serif typeface. Figgins called his slab-serif 'Antique'. However, the same term was adopted in France to refer to sans-serifs, which in Germany were known as grotesks and in the United States as gothic (a term also often used to describe blackletter typefaces). Doric or grotesque also found usage in Britain, but it was Figgins's coinage, 'sans-serif', that became widely accepted.

Figgins's foundry would go on to release further sans-serif typefaces in a variety of sizes (including a condensed version in 1845), as did its rivals Caslon, which produced the first italic sans-serif in 1833, and Thorowgood, whose sans-serif Grotesque was the earliest to include lowercase letters upon its release in c.1834-5. In the mid-19th century sans-serifs remained an oddity, intended mainly for titling; they were bold display types, to be used in much the same way as other popular styles of the day, at eye-catching sizes on posters and playbills. The potential of sans-serifs as 'display' type developed through the creation of outlined, shadowed and reversed versions, and even an extremely refined typeface which achieved the illusion of dimensionality – Stephenson, Blake's 'Ten Lines Sans-Surryphs Ornamented' released around 1839.

By the second half of the 19th century sans-serif typefaces that were appropriate in weight and style for use as text fonts, not just headlines were finally emerging. It was German foundries, such as Bauer & Co.

Two line English Egyptian

W CASLON JUNR   LETTERFOUNDER

Two line nonpareil, Sans-serif

A LARGE, AND ELEGANT
ASSORTMENT, OF THE MOST
MODERN JOB LETTER.
ABCDEFGHIJKLMNOPQRSTUVWX

Seven line Grotesque

MENINGHURNE
mountainous

Above: William Caslon's Two Line English Egyptian, 1816, and Vincent Figgins's Two line nonpareil, Sans-serif, 1833.
Below: Thorowgood's Seven Lines Grotesque, 1834.

and Theinhardt, that made much progress on this front, releasing grotesk fonts that were lighter than the earlier English faces, had both cases and were available at text sizes. These innovations later spread back to Britain where, by the early 20th century, numbered grotesques from foundries like Stephenson Blake and Miller & Richard were being used for text applications, as was Caslon's Doric - even if purists maintained that sans-serifs were vulgar and less legible and would never be appropriate for use in book settings.

It was one of the last sans-serif releases of the 19th century that would lay the foundation for the future. Akzidenz-Grotesk, released in 1898 by the Berthold Type Foundry of Berlin, used proportions inspired by classic serifs like Walbaum and Didot to achieve a legible, neutral result. It helped that

ABCDEFGHIJKLMNOPQRSTUVWXYZ
abcdefghijklmnopqrstuvwxyz
&ÆŒ£1234567890.,;:-!?"()

Above: Akzidenz-Grotesk, Berthold Type Foundry, 1898.

it came in multiple widths and weights, and had corresponding 'oblique' cuts. Known as 'Standard' in the English-speaking world, Akzidenz-Grotesk (whose translation would be roughly 'jobbing sans-serif') was successful immediately. But thanks to its utilitarian, anonymous and unpretentious feel, it would become especially popular with modernist designers in Switzerland and Germany during the fifties, before the release of larger sans-serif families. In Britain, where Akzidenz was rare, designers looking to upset the traditional typographic status quo had to make do with the far more characterful Monotype Grotesque.

The early 20th century would see a slew of new sans-serif typefaces, such as the American designer Morris Fuller Benton's Franklin Gothic (1904–13) and News Gothic (1908), William Addison Dwiggins's (1880–1956) Metro (1929), Jakob Erbar's (1878–1935) Erbar Grotesk (1926) and Rudolf Koch's (1876–1934) Kabel (1927). Metro, Kabel and Erbar were examples of modernist principles being applied to type design: they were geometric in construction, taking the circle, square, triangle and straight lines as the building blocks for their forms. By far the most successful of the new geometric sans-serifs was Paul

Renner's (1878–1956) Futura (1927). With its low x-height and optical alterations that meant it was not truly geometric (the O for instance is slightly ovoid but looks like a perfect circle) or completely monoline, Futura was very readable yet still excitingly modern. Some of Renner's earlier experimental alternates for some letters never made it past the initial sketch phase, in much the same way that many of the radical sans-serif ideas coming from Bauhaus designers like Albers and Bayer were never released.

An alternative to the 19th-century grotesque or modernism-inspired geometric came in the form of 'humanist' sans-serifs, which were more closely connected to typography's handwritten past. These often shared characteristics and proportions with classical serifs, had 'true' italics and some contrast in their strokes. One of the earliest examples was calligrapher Edward Johnston's (1872–1944) Johnston Sans, commissioned in 1913 by Frank Pick for use on the London Underground railway system. Since it was not commercially available, an alternative came from one of Johnston's students, Eric Gill (1888–1940), whose Gill Sans was released by Monotype in 1927. Less obviously 'modern' than its competitors,

Above Left: Stephenson Blake Grotesque No.8, Elisha Pechey, 1863.

Above Right: Gill Sans Medium and Medium Italic, Eric Gill, 1928.

Gill Sans has never really found prominence outside Britain.

'Geometric' sans-serifs were, in theory, more modernist in principle, but fiercely modernist designers post-World War I tended to prefer the more utilitarian 20th-century grotesques in their work. Writing in 1928, Jan Tschichold declared that 'among all the types that are available, the so-called "Grotesque" is the only one in spiritual accordance with our time', adding that 'the sanserif types available today are not yet wholly satisfactory as all-purpose faces […] in particular the newest designs such as Erbar and Kabel, are inferior to the old anonymous sanserifs'.[2] Akzidenz Grotesk

was particularly popular among Swiss designers, who spread its fame across the world.

New sans-serif typefaces, often described as 'neo-grotesques' and produced in extended families with a range of weights and widths, soon reduced the reliance on Akzidenz. The best known is Helvetica, designed by Swiss typographers Max Miedinger (1910–80) and Eduard Hoffmann (1892–1980), and released by the Haas Type Foundry in 1957 as 'Neue Haas Grotesk'. Helvetica came from a desire for an extremely neutral typeface that could compete with Berthold's Akzidenz. Also released the same year, this time by French foundry Deberny & Peignot,

Above Left: Type specimen for Futura Light, typeface designed by Paul Renner, 1927.

Above Right: Cover of a type specimen from D. Stempel AG for Helvetica, the typeface designed by Max Miedinger and Eduard Hoffmann, released in 1957.

Below: Cover of a type specimen from Deberny & Peignot for Univers, designed by Bruno Pfäffli, Rémy Peignot and Adrian Frutiger, 1964. Univers, designed by Adrian Frutiger, 1957.

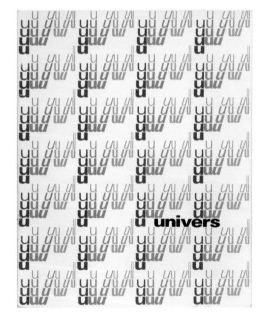

Further Reading →

Cees W. de Jong, *Sans Serif* (Thames & Hudson, 2006)

Petra Eisele (ed.), *Futura: The Book* (Laurence King, 2017)

Lars Müller, *Helvetica: Homage to a Typeface* (Lars Müller Publishers, 2005)

was Swiss typeface designer Adrian Frutiger's (1928–2015) Univers, which came in an impressive 27 styles, each numbered in a logical coding system. Univers's scientific qualities were accentuated by advertising which made use of periodic table-inspired layouts, and grids of letters showing how the typeface maintained consistency across its styles, weights and widths. Neo-grotesques became synonymous with the International Typographic Style (see pages 46–9) and dominated graphic design for the second half of the 20th century, particularly for use in signage and brand identities.

Although Helvetica and Univers would remain hugely popular, there were other trends and developments too. Heavy and condensed grotesques with large x-heights were in vogue at times, particularly as headline fonts. These included Walter Haettenschweile's (1933–2014) Schmalfette Grotesk (1954), Fred Lambert's Compacta (1963), Helvetica Inserat (1966) and Geoffrey Lee's (1929–2005) Impact (1965). Impact, thanks to its appearance as a default Microsoft font, is much used in the 21st century, but it was the development of phototype (see page 186) and dry-transfer lettering (e.g. Letraset) that helped propel these heavy, tightly kerned typefaces to popularity.

Other notable sans typefaces of the latter half of the 20th century include Hermann Zapf's Optima (1958), a humanist face inspired by Renaissance stone carvings, whose strokes fattened towards their ends, giving a visual effect similar to that of serifs. Following his success with Univers, Adrian Frutiger designed a humanist sans-serif –

Frutiger (1974) – and later a geometric, too – Avenir (1988) – which successfully applied humanistic principles to the genre. The best-known geometric sans-serif of the late 20th century was ITC Avant Garde Gothic, designed by Herb Lubalin and Tom Carnase (b. 1939) in 1970, but based on Lubalin's logo for *Avant Garde* magazine from 1968. Avant Garde is most notable for the variety of complex ligatures and alternate letters that appeared in its uppercase, allowing for extremely tight settings as seen in the original magazine masthead. Such tiny gaps between letters were again only possible thanks to the move from metal type to so-called 'cold type' (such as phototypesetting) – Avant Garde was never released as a 'cast' foundry font family.

Companies like PhotoLettering Inc., Letraset and ITC (co-founded by Lubalin, Edward Roundthaler and Aaron Burns) met the demand for more varied and expressive fonts as many designers grew bored of the ubiquity of typefaces like Helvetica. As well as releasing revivals of quirky 19th-century sans-serifs, these companies also gave designers the chance to design typefaces, which did not take as much up-front expense as had been the case in the days of 'hot metal'. Among these designers was Milton Glaser, whose Baby Teeth font was released in 1964 and found fame following its use on Glaser's iconic Bob Dylan poster in 1967. The digital revolution accelerated trends that had begun with phototypesetting – myriad revivals of old faces and a dizzying array of new fonts giving designers a vast selection to choose from. However, sans-serifs have remained more popular

26 good reasons to use AVANT GARDE GOTHIC BOOK

يعرف **قمر الدين** بأنه ألواح مجففة مصنوعة من لب ثمار المشمش، ويتميز بملمسه الناعم، وقوامه المطاطي، ومذاقه الحلو، حيث تتعرض العديد من الفواكه الموسمية للمعالجة للحفاظ على جودتها مدة طويلة.

COMMERCE
Referència

(DRUK MEDIUM, 100 PT)

TAUTOLOGY
Postulated

(DRUK MEDIUM ITALIC, 100 PT)

IBM Plex® is our new typeface.

Thin. *Thin Italic.*
Regular. *Italic.*
Bold. ***Bold Italic.***
Condensed Bold.
Mono Italic.

Above Left: ITC Avant Garde Gothic Book, designed by Herb Lubalin and Tom Carnase, 1970.

Above Right: Amareddine by Nadine Chahine/ Arabic Type, 2020.

Below Right: Specimen for Druk, typeface designed by Berton Hasebe for Commercial Type, 2014.

Below Left: IBM Plex®, font family designed for IBM by Mike Abbink and team, including Dutch foundry Bold Monday, 2017.

than serifs among graphic designers in many contexts, due to their modern feel and legibility. Geometric sans-serifs have been particularly popular in the last decade among technology companies aiming for a hi-tech but friendly feel. Many global brands have commissioned custom sans-serif typefaces of their own, due to a desire for ownership, the need for multi-language compatibility, and the rising cost of multi-user typeface licences.

Display Typefaces

'Display' is a loose category of typeface that covers anything that is not intended as a text type: they do not need to work for setting blocks of text or at small sizes, but rather are intended for headline use (limited amounts of text at larger scales). This gives display typefaces more licence to have features that would cause legibility problems at smaller sizes. Attention-grabbing qualities are often more important than clarity. Neither exclusively sans-serif nor serif, display fonts are not necessarily ornamental or decorative, but all ornamental or decorative fonts are display typefaces by their nature. Often, the lack of lowercase indicates a display font. Similarly, the availability of very few glyphs beyond a basic alphabet signals that the typeface is not suitable for extended texts.

Traditionally, a definition of 'display' related to point size. The English type designer Walter Tracy (1914–95) held that anything over 14 points is a 'display size', adding that 'when used about the design of type it means a face other than a traditional text face, a type of highly-developed individuality, or an inlined or shadowed version of a basic face, intended for publicity use'.[3] Tracy, a type designer at Linotype for three decades, provides a helpful maxim to explain the difference between text and display types: 'Text types when enlarged can be used for headings; display types, if reduced, cannot be used for text setting.'[4] Large type families occasionally feature a 'display cut' alongside the weights and widths of text faces, and usually this means

that some of the finer details are lost at the smaller 'optical' sizes. In some rare cases, such as Paul Renner's Futura, the display version of a typeface may be very different from its namesakes, but usually related in some way. Some typefaces may come in weights that, due to being very bold (e.g. Gill Sans Kayo) or light, are intended for display, but are not labelled as such. The same rule holds for widths: condensation or extension, when taken to extremes, can make a typeface no longer appropriate for text use, but ideal for display sizes where it can have more impact and be more space efficient.

Display faces have incorporated a huge range of features, ornaments, effects and construction methods, many of which are borrowed from sign painting, lettering or stone-carving traditions. Almost every potential embellishment and approach has been experimented with, but some crop up repeatedly across different historical display typefaces. Most common is the addition of extra details or decorations to a more standard typeface, such as a drop shadow, an inline, an outline, engraving effects, shading, or ornamental flourishes within the letters. Often, these are designed to imitate three-dimensionality or achieve a more eye-catching result. There is also the removal of parts of letters, to create a distressed look or a stencil cut; many modernist type designers arrived at a stencil effect through the use of basic geometric elements.

Going to extremes was another approach taken by designers creating display typefaces. During the 19th century, in the age of the playbill and bill poster, foundries were locked in

a battle to outdo each other, whether it was extreme weights (e.g. fat face), extreme contrast, extreme serifs (e.g. slab serifs) or extreme widths, particularly condensation which resulted in tall thin letters. Perhaps the most outlandish of this era were 'reverse contrast' typefaces, sometimes known as 'Italians' after the first of its kind, Caslon Italian (1821). These typefaces flipped the conventions of contrast, resulting in a weird but impactful effect. Many typefaces became 'display' through their construction, such as 'Tuscans', which feature bi- or trifurcated split serifs, or through the additions of extra spurs, often in the vertical centre of the glyphs or on serifs. Many display faces bring to mind the 19th century – often these are known as 'Circus' or 'Western' typefaces due to their particular historical associations.

During the early 20th century display typefaces evolved, following the Art Nouveau trend and becoming organic and flowing, then changing with Art Deco into something more refined and streamlined; Cassandre's Bifur (Deberny & Peignot, 1929) is perhaps the best example of the latter. Modernism would rebel against the aesthetic extremes of display typefaces and outlaw ornament. But by the sixties, hastened by the development of phototypesetting as the constraints of metal type fell away, many designers returned to the exuberance of display typography and looked to the 19th century for inspiration. The majority of postmodern typefaces, pushing legibility as they often did, could be classed as display faces. The advent of cheap font design software has caused the number of display fonts to grow exponentially, with a huge number freely available online, although the quality of such fonts varies.

Further Reading →

Paul McNeil, *The Visual History of Type* (Laurence King, 2017)

Jan Tolenaar, *Type: A Visual History of Typefaces & Graphic Styles, volume 1: 1628–1900* (Taschen, 2022)

LOCATION
CASLON ITALIAN REGULAR, 55 PT

REQUIRED
CASLON ITALIAN ITALIC, 55 PT

CRESTERII
CASLON ITALIAN CONTRA, 55 PT

WENIGER
CASLON ITALIAN REGULAR, 55 PT

SURFACED
CASLON ITALIAN ITALIC, 55 PT (ALTERNATE R)

GEOLOGICS
CASLON ITALIAN CONTRA, 55 PT

HUGTAKID
CASLON ITALIAN REGULAR, 55 PT

NATIINAG
CASLON ITALIAN ITALIC, 55 PT (SWASH A N)

TALUQDAR
CASLON ITALIAN CONTRA, 55 PT (ALTERNATE Q R)

EPICYCLIC
CASLON ITALIAN REGULAR, 55 PT

TRADE GOTHIC DISPLAY
TRADE GOTHIC DISPLAY
TRADE GOTHIC DISPLAY
TRADE GOTHIC DISPLAY

Above Left: Specimen for Caslon Italian, a typeface revival by Paul Barnes, Tim Ripper and Christian Schwartz for Commercial Classics, 2019.

Above Right: Trade Gothic Display, designed by Lynne Yun for Monotype, 2017.

Below Right: Display Typeface specimens, 1856.

Previous Spread: Author's own examples of display typefaces.

FOUR-LINE PICA ORNAMENTED.— No. 27.
MERRIMACK. 3456

FOUR-LINE PICA ORNAMENTED.— No. 28.
PETERSBURGH. 8901

DOUBLE PARAGON ORNAMENTED.— No. 23.
GLIMMERING STARLIGHT

DOUBLE PARAGON ORNAMENTED.— No. 24.
SHOOTING STARS. $407

TWO-LINE GREAT PRIMER ORNAMENTED.— No. 30.
FRENCH TRIMMING

TWO-LINE GREAT PRIMER ORNAMENTED.— No. 31.
CHOICE FRUITS. 137

TWO-LINE ENGLISH ORNAMENTED.— No. 29.
FORESHADOWING. $576,421

TWO-LINE PICA ORNAMENTED.— No. 33.
NORTH CHELMSFORD. 7586

JOHN K. ROGERS & CO.   BOSTON TYPE FOUNDRY.   SPRING LANE, BOSTON.

Scripts

Scripts are fonts designed to mimic writing done by hand. There are various categories within this, to cover the different ways people have written throughout history. The majority of fonts found in this category feature connecting elements that approximate joined-up writing and are slightly rightward sloping. Many script fonts trace their roots to the pre-typographic era when scribes were trained in particular writing styles, such as the uncial script, Carolingian minuscule (see page 197) or chancery hand (so called as it was developed as the official handwriting for ecclesiastical, legal, business and diplomatic records produced for medieval chancellors), to maintain the consistency and legibility of books and important documents. As book production and literacy grew in the second half of the Middle Ages, a new writing style developed in Northern Europe called blackletter. This was heavy, angular and compact, allowing more words per page. Although blackletter and its many subcategories are upright and not joined up (except for occasional ligature pairs), they are still considered script fonts as they derive from a handwriting style. The earliest printing typefaces in Europe were blackletter (see pages 197–201), and they remained popular in many countries, particularly Germany, Elsewhere, however, the antiqua style (which synthesized Latin capitals with Carolingian lowercase) replaced them.

Moveable type did not replace handwriting in many areas, and calligraphic handwriting styles, particularly cursive ones, continued to develop through the work of various engravers and writing masters. Notable styles included copperplate, English round hand and Spencerian scripts. These 'hands' were held up as the ideal for writing and were elegant, ornate and slanted. Their flourishes, fine strokes and joined-up nature made it near impossible for a cast-metal typeface to replicate them. One of the few early metal types based on handwriting was Claude Garamont's *Grecs du Roi*, developed in the mid-16th century. This was a Greek script based on the writing style of a Cretan scribe, but the variety of ligatures involved was costly and time-intensive for printers.

The end of the era of metal type, thanks to the invention of phototypesetting and eventually digital technology, led to a boom in the design of script typefaces, as connected letters suddenly became achievable. Popular in the mid-century era, some early successful script faces were Brush Script designed by Robert E. Smith (1910–unknown) for American Type Founders in 1942, and Mistral designed by Roger Excoffon (1910–83) for French type foundry Fonderie Olive in 1953. Both are examples of the 'casual script' category of fonts, which are energetic and characterful, often based on sign-painting techniques and look as if drawn with a brush. The other main category, 'formal scripts', are based on the 'hands' of 17th- and 18th-century writing masters who used a quill or metal nibbed pen to achieve stroke contrast and elegant swashes. These tend to be favoured in applications that require gravitas, such as formal invitations or official certificates.

Whistler

Les Signes du Zodiaque

Hazelnuts

Rainbow Kale

Starburst

Happy Birthday!

Giraffe

Carta Nueva Display

Carta Nueva Large

Carta Nueva Medium

Carta Nueva Deck

Carta Nueva Small

Mistral

Roger Excoffon

Fonderie Olive

1953 AaBbCcDd

EeFfGgHhIiJjKkLl

MmNnOoPpQqRr

SsTtUuVvWwXxYyZz

123456789!?*

Snell Roundhand

The quick brown
fox jumps over
the lazy dog?!

Above Left: Girard Script, House Industries, 2009.

Above Right: Carta Nueva by My-Lan Thuong for Sharp Type, 2020.

Below Right: Snell Roundhand, Matthew Carter, 1965.

Below Left: Mistral by Roger Excoffon for Fonderie Olive, 1953.

Further Reading →

Alfred Fairbank, *A Book of Scripts* (King Penguin, 1949)

Geum-Hee Hong, *Script Fonts* (Laurence King, 2016)

19

LEARNING.

The Design of Learning, is either to render a Man an agreeable Companion to himself, and teach him to support Solitude with Pleasure; or, if he is not born to an Estate, to supply that Defect, and furnish him with the Means of getting one.

Look cautious round, your Genius nicely know,
And mark how far its utmost Stretch will go.

Nobility, Riches, State, and Supremacy can procure us a customary Respect, & make us the Idols of an unthinking Croud; but Knowledge and Learning alone recommend us to the Love of those in a superior Class, who admire more the Merits of our Understanding, than the Advantages of our Birth & Fortune.

Samuel Vaux scrip.

HANDWRITTEN LETTERING DEFINES THE **LUSH BRAND,** ENDOWING IT WITH AN **ENERGETIC & DISTINCT** PERSONALITY.

Above: Lush Handwritten Custom Font, Dalton Maag, 2015.

Opposite: Published as Issue 27 of *The Universal Penman* by George Bickham the Elder, 1743. An example of the kind of 18th-century 'hands' revived for 20th-century formal scripts.

A third category is 'calligraphic scripts', which fit roughly between 'formal' and 'casual' and are inspired by calligraphy styles, often with letters that do not connect, and sometimes featuring stroke styles that approximate the irregularities and imperfections of handwriting in ink or paint.

The energy and human feel of script fonts have made them a popular choice for a variety of areas of graphic design, although they are often misused, and once popular choices like Mistral or Brush Script have become widely disliked. In the digital age new features available to type designers, such as 'contextual alternates', variable widths and alternate glyphs, have helped improve the realism of fonts that imitate handwriting, reducing the repetition of identical letters that are such a giveaway that you are looking at a font, not real handwriting.

Non-Latin Fonts

Typography as a discipline has historically been Latin-centric; dominated by the creation and discussion of typefaces designed for Latin-alphabet-based languages, to the detriment of the alternative scripts used throughout the world and read by billions.

The historical categorizations that dominate typography are often predicated on Latin alphabet typefaces and involve distinctions that are not always applicable beyond this narrow confine – for instance, serif and sans-serif, or roman and script. The conventions of Western, Latin typography are by no means universal. Every alphabet and writing system has a rich history and legacy, but many have been ignored by type foundries, whose focus on Latin causes typographic inequality.

Efforts are now being made to tackle this issue, as part of a wider drive towards cultural decolonization, with designers pushing to create fonts for under-served scripts, or multilingual typefaces that can be used by a wider audience, thanks to greater language support and larger glyph sets. It is increasingly common for foundries to release non-Latin versions of their key fonts. Often, these are created in collaboration with a typeface designer for whom the non-Latin script is a first language or special area of expertise. However, this often comes long after the release of the original Latin face, often due to the increased number of glyphs found in many of the most widely used scripts, which makes the process more time-consuming. Socio-political reasons aside, this is a key factor in the lower number of typefaces being created for many languages and scripts; the number of glyphs required can be exponentially higher. Take Ming Romantic as an example. This is a typeface being created by design studio Synoptic Office for the Chinese script, based on a 'modern interpretation of a style of printed type originating from the Song and Ming dynasties'. In a 2018 interview with AIGA, its designers, Caspar Lam and YuJune Park, point out that 'a minimum Western typeface uses the Adobe Latin 2 set of 250 glyphs. For a Chinese typeface, we will assume a minimum set of 2–3,000 glyphs for a display face, or 7–8,000 glyphs for a text face. For completeness, a number ten times the number of glyphs in a text face would be required for a font encompassing the entire Chinese character set.'[5] Economics are also a factor: scripts used by small populations are usually more poorly served, as foundries cannot bank on finding enough customers.

Like many creative industries, typeface design is an area with diversity problems. Typeface designers whose backgrounds are in 'Latin' languages are often fascinated by the multitude of other scripts found globally. However, designing a typeface in a script that you cannot read, or did not grow up using, must be done with sensitivity, and often requires extended study to get right. Conventions in typesetting, letter construction and usage can vary hugely between scripts and languages, and it is not always the case that the principles that serve a Latin font can be applied to a non-Latin script without errors.

Designers must be careful not to thoughtlessly apply the forms and ideals

一丁七丈三上下不丐丑且世丘丟並中串
丹主乃久之乎乏乘乙九也乾亂企伊伍伏
休伙伯估伴仲似但位低住佔何四回因困
固圈國始姐姑姓委姥姻姿威娃娘娜婆婚
撞撤撥撫播撲擁擇擊擋操擔據擠擦擬擲
請諒論諸諾謀謂講謝謹證識譜警譯議護
譽讀變願顛類顧顫顯風飄飛食飾養餐餓
館饒香馬馮馳駐駕駛騎騙騰驅驗驚驪體

Разнообразный
и богатый опыт
новая модель
организационной
деятельности
обеспечивает
широкому кругу
(специалистов)
участие в
формировании
позиций, занимаемых
участниками
в отношении
поставленных задач.

ลักษณะของตัวพิมพ์
แต่ละตัวสามารถ
แสดงออกได้ถึง
ระดับเสียง

Top: Ming Romantic, Chinese script font, Synoptic Office, 2018.

Above: Thonglor bold, Vietnamese script font, Cadson Demak, 2016.

Left: Steinbeck font shown in Cyrillic, Roman Gornitsky, The Temporary State, 2018.

新しい時
代のここ
ろを映す
タイプフ
エイスデ
ザイン

शब्दों और
वाक्यों की तरह
ही अक्षराकृतियों
के भी स्वर, ध्वनि
और व्यक्तित्व
होते हैं ।

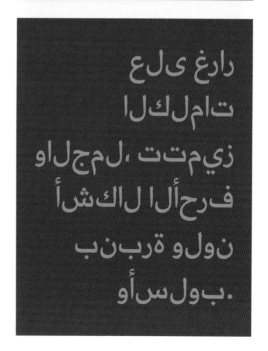

Above Left: WanpakuRuika, Japanese
script font, using both Kana and Kanji
characters, Yutaka Satoh, Type Labo, 2013.

Above Right: ITF Devanagari Marathi,
Satya Rajpurohit, Indian Type Foundry,
2011.

Below: Amariya Bold, Arabic script font,
Nadine Chahine Monotype, 2017.

Further Reading →

Futuress, 'A Resource Hub for Decolonizing
Typography' (Sept, 2022) www.futuress.org/
stories/decolonizing-typography-resources/
Ben Wittner, Sascha Thoma & Timm Hartmann,
*Bi-Scriptual: Typography and Graphic Design
with Multiple Script Systems* (Niggli, 2018)

of Western, Latin-based typography to diverse global scripts. Although aiming to create a multi-scriptural world, and fonts with diverse language support, is an important endeavour, it should not be done by simply imposing dominant Latin ideals imperialistically. Globalism and technology are increasing the need for scripts with broad language support, but they can also help to spread the idea that Latin should be the default. As pointed out by the authors of the article 'Multi scripts: Blended type family stories', published in *Forum+* magazine in 2022:

> globalization in a post-colonial reality tends to generate uniformity at numerous levels. It standardizes cultures, ways of thinking and ways of seeing. As a central visual interface to culture, scripts – the visual representations of languages – are subject to this process. Latin, a globally successful script, has an outsize influence on the way languages are shaped and used, and its colonial heritage is reflected in its cultural and technological hegemony on a global scale.[6]

Practically speaking, designers who have set multilingual text will know the frustration of discovering a typeface that lacks glyphs used in a required language. This causes the missing character box, sometimes nicknamed 'tofu', to appear □□□□ (some fonts have custom symbols instead of the generic box). The 'tofu' problem would lead Google and Monotype to collaborate on Noto, an open-source typeface family whose goal was support for the 800-plus languages included in the Unicode Consortium standard. Doing this required using over 150 writing systems, including some classified as endangered.

Lettering

Lettering is distinct from (though related to) typography, as it refers to the creation of letters without using the prefabricated characters of existing typefaces. Lettering implies the creation of something bespoke to fit the needs of the piece of text being rendered. Many lettering artists are adept at calligraphy. However, the two are different disciplines: one definition has it that lettering is the art of 'drawing letters' while calligraphy is the art of 'writing letters'. The implication is that in calligraphy consistency is expected – the same 'hand' writing a piece of text in a sustained style with a tool designed for writing. Lettering has no insinuation of uniformity or any limitations on how it is created. The term 'hand-lettering' was used when all lettering was created by hand, but in the computer age lettering is often digital.

Historically, lettering was an area for creative expression, not just the dissemination of textual information. In Islamic art, where representational forms were avoided, lettering of quotations from the Qur'an flourished as an art form, with many different regional styles and varieties – some flowing and organic, others geometric and mathematical. Even during the late 19th century lettering remained important, especially on signs, where printed typography could not compete for permanence and impact. The sign painters who created these works often had manuals featuring instructions on the construction of letters and alphabets to copy.

By the early 20th century the Arts and Crafts movement reinvigorated interest in hand-lettering with typographers like Edward Johnston, Rudolf Koch and Eric Gill valuing the craftsmanship of hand-work, alongside designing typefaces. Different aesthetic trends each influenced designers' approach to lettering: Art Nouveau hand-lettering was organic, ornate and flowing, while Art Deco was more regular and streamlined, often imitating typefaces rather than calligraphic traditions. Although typography was more available than ever, most 'commercial artists' creating the posters and advertising of the twenties and thirties preferred to do their own lettering, unifying text and image.

Modernism would shun the hand of the designer, instead prioritizing the mechanization that came with typefaces, However, in the mid-century modern era (see pages 34–7), hand-lettering was favoured by many designers. It was often more economical and faster than using a typeface, plus many printers, in their struggle to keep up with fashion, carried only a limited range of typefaces. The informality and immediacy of handwriting meant it remained popular, while it allowed mid-century designers to literally put a personal stamp on their work, in contrast to the anonymity of the Swiss Style (see pages 38–41). David Crowley notes that, in the fifties, 'handwriting became a code for modern individualism, allied to jazz and classical music […] and to the modern novel in book covers by Alvin Lustig and Paul Rand.'[7] By the sixties and seventies lettering was even more exuberant and changed rapidly with

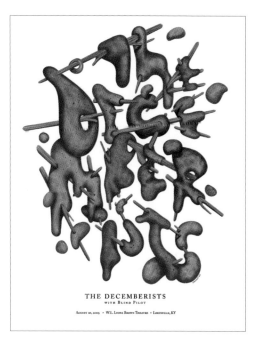

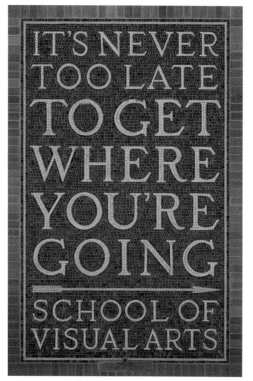

Above Left: 'The Decemberists' gig poster, Alex Trochut, 2009.

Above Right: School of Visual Arts subway poster, Louise Fili Ltd, 2018.

Below Right: EP cover for *Laughing at the System* by Total Control, Wei Huang, 2017.

Below Left: Jordan Metcalf for *Money* magazine, 2018.

THE BEST REASON TO Paint IS THAT THERE IS NO Reason TO PAINT

Above Left: Seb Lester, 2010.

Above Right: Oli Frape, 2021.

Opposite: Keith Haring quotation, Aries Moross for Adobe, 2020.

new fashions and designers often looked backwards for inspiration.

Rather than making lettering obsolete, digital software introduced new techniques, giving lettering a new lease of life away from the reliance on hand-drawing skills. Computer-generated imagery and 3D-modelling software have added dimensionality to lettering that was not easy to achieve by hand, while the motion opened up by the move from paper to screen adds animation possibilities. Traditional lettering is created digitally, too, with designers using Béziers (which, in vector-based graphic software, model smooth lines parametrically) to create perfect curves with the same attention to detail as any historical draughtsperson. There has also been a resurgence of interest in hand-lettering, in part due to saturation of the digital and a desire to go back to

screen-free methods. Lettering artists like Jessica Hische (b. 1984) and Seb Lester (b. 1972) have gained huge online followings, with people keen to watch videos of them working.

Lettering is essentially an illustration of a piece of text, so it should come as no surprise that professional lettering artists are more likely to also work as illustrators than as graphic designers. Another aspect of lettering is in the realm of visual identity, where brands want their logotypes to be bespoke, unique and, most of all, 'ownable', rather than using widely available fonts. Sometimes this just means custom typography, perhaps adapted from existing fonts, rather than something akin to handwriting.

Above Left: Martina Flor, 2014.

Above Right: Shiva Nallaperumal, 2022.

Below: Alison Carmichael, 2020.

Opposite Page: Lebassis, 2021.

Further Reading →

Ken Barber, *House Industries Lettering Manual* (Watson-Guptill, 2020)

Martina Flor, *The Golden Secrets of Lettering* (Thames & Hudson, 2017)

Jessica Hische, *In Progress* (Chronicle Books, 2015)

Postmodern Typography

The ripping up of old rules that came with postmodernism (see pages 56–63) had a huge impact on typeface design, particularly as the emergence of the Apple Macintosh and commercially available typeface design software allowed designers to experiment with creating their own typefaces that could quickly be used in digitally designed work. Many fonts that came out of the postmodern period made use of the possibilities that computers opened up, or embraced the limitations of early digital technology, such as Zuzana Licko's (b. 1961) Lo-Res font family; a collection of bitmap fonts designed on a tiny pixel grid. Licko was one of the founders of the influential *Emigre* magazine. Designed by co-founder Rudy VanderLans (b. 1955) on an Apple Mac, *Emigre* showcased Licko's innovative digital fonts, and the pair soon established Emigre Fonts to make them available. The magazine was at the forefront of postmodern graphic design, and its foundry became a nexus for designers creating new experimental and conceptual typefaces unconcerned with tradition.

Typical of postmodern typography were Dead History, designed by P. Scott Makela (1960–99) in 1990 and a mash-up of a serif (Centennial) and a sans-serif (VAG Rounded), and Keedy Sans, designed by frequent *Emigre* contributor Jeffery Keedy (b. 1957) in 1989. Keedy Sans was intentionally incongruous and inconsistent, giving it a look that was distinctive but also – like most Emigre fonts – divisive. Postmodern typography was wilfully combative in its rejection of both classical tradition and modernist dogma; attractiveness and clarity were not primary concerns, and the ease of producing and distributing fonts digitally meant designers were less concerned by whether typefaces would sell, although many Emigre fonts – the height of countercultural fashion – were successful.

Alongside retro and vernacular influences, many postmodern typefaces fit into the era's trend for 'grunge': they were messy and dirty and deliberately looked unfinished. One example that fits this category, but notable for its mechanics too, is FF Beowolf. Designed by Just van Rossum (b. 1966) and Erik van Blokland (b. 1967) in 1990 and the first release of FontFont (a digital foundry started by Erik Spiekermann [b. 1947] and Neville Brody [b. 1957]), Beowolf at first appears to be a slightly odd serif face with a jagged, curve-less finish. However, due to a tweak made to the PostScript code, when printed the font randomizes to varying degrees so no two instances of a glyph come out the same.

New ways of distributing fonts, such as on disks or online, meant postmodern typefaces spread quickly among tech-savvy designers looking to subvert the rules of good taste imposed on them by earlier generations. Alongside *Emigre*, another influential publication was *FUSE*, founded by Neville Brody and Jon Wozencroft (b. 1958) in 1991. Each quarterly issue had an overarching theme, and featured four invited designers (such as Barry Deck, Peter Seville, David Carson and Malcolm Garrett) who each produced a typeface (included on a floppy disk) and poster. As with many postmodern fonts, those that came

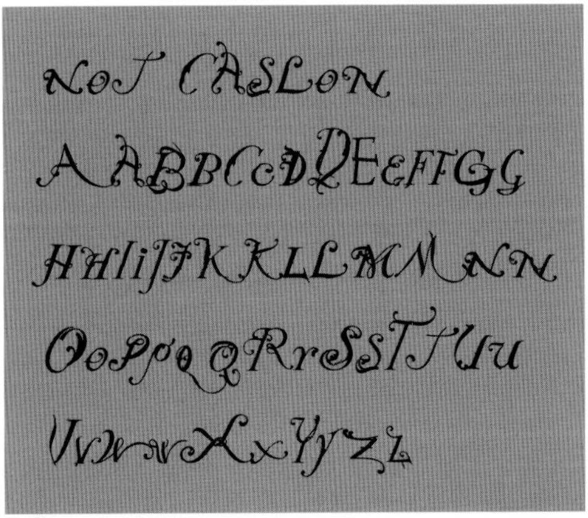

Keedy Sans Bold
AaBbCcDdEeFfGg
HhiiJjKkLlMmNnOo
PpQqRrSsTtUuVv
WwXxYyZz

Dead History
AaBbCcDdEeFfGg
HhIiJjKkLlMmNn
OoPpQqRrSsTtUu
VvWwXxYyZz

NoT CASLoN
A ABBCcDEeFFGG
HHliJK KLLMN Nn
OopºQ RrSSTUu
VvWwXxYyZz

Above Left: Keedy Sans, Jeffery Keedy, Emigre, 1989.

Above Right: Dead History, P. Scott Makela, Emigre, 1990.

Below Right: Dogma Outline, Zuzana Licko, Emigre, 1994.

Below Left: Elliotts OT JigsawDropshadow, Elliott Peter Earls, Emigre, 1998.

Centre: NotCaslon, Mark Andresen, Emigre, 1991.

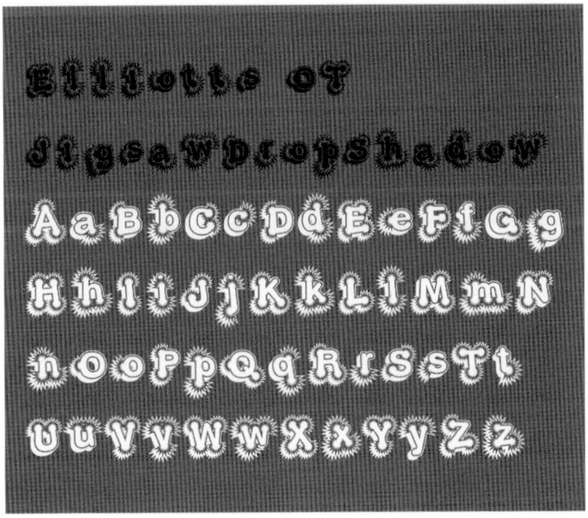

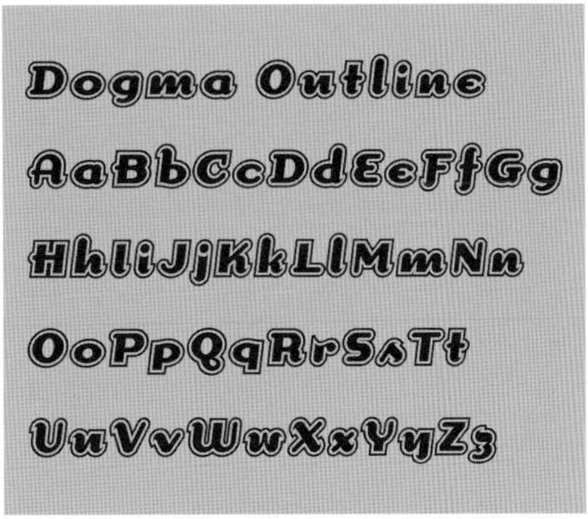

Elliotts OT
JigsawDropshadow
AaBbCcDdEeFfGg
HhIiJjKkLlMmN
nOoPpQqRrSsTt
UuVvWwXxYyZz

Dogma Outline
AaBbCcDdEeFfGg
HhIiJjKkLlMmNn
OoPpQqRrSsTt
UuVvWwXxYyZz

THE
QUICK
BROWN
FOX
JUMPS
OVER
THE
LAZY
DOG

with *FUSE* were usually explorations of ideas – experiments meant to challenge the boundaries of the discipline, rather than designed for practical use.

Postmodern fonts – taken out of context or viewed from a conservative standpoint – infuriated many designers who saw them as abominations or self-indulgent. However, most were not designed to fit typography's previous role of functionality. Postmodernism had shaken up binary notions – such as 'right' and 'wrong' or 'high' and 'low' culture – and language (which typography expresses) itself was no longer considered objective: it became a carrier of meaning to be deconstructed and decoded. It was no surprise, then, that typography became more subjective, too, as designers sought to better understand their role.

Typography was no longer simply a vehicle for improving communication or attracting customers but became an area to express oneself, or to reflexively interrogate and challenge. Of course, not everyone approved. Famously, Steven Heller (b. 1950) and Massimo Vignelli (1931–2014) were prominent critics of postmodern typography, and such debates sparked the so-called 'Legibility Wars' – fierce arguments around legibility and typography's purpose. Opinions still vary widely, but postmodernism's influence on typography has resulted in a richer field in the long term and its anything-goes attitude has become normal, to the point of no longer being subversive. Many designers who began in the postmodern era have gone on to have long careers producing a variety of type styles, including more traditional typefaces such as Licko's Mrs Eaves

Template Gothic
AaBbCcDd
EeFfGgHhIi
JjKkLlMmNn
OoPpQqRr
SsTtUuVvWw
XxYyZz1234
56789!?

Above: Template Gothic, Barry Deck, Emigre, 1991.

Opposite: Exocet, Jonathan Barnbrook, Emigre, 1991.

(1996), proving that they had the skills to produce conventional and functional typefaces all along, despite what their critics thought.

Digital Typography

From the invention of the printing press to the 'cold' process of phototypesetting – typography has evolved with technology, becoming ever faster and less labour-intensive. The shift from print to digital has had a radical impact, turning an entire industry upside-down in a matter of decades. The early limitations of basic screens and the requirements that came from digital processes gave typeface designers new constraints to work within, leading to a technological aesthetic that was new and exciting.

An early designer to experiment in this area was Wim Crouwel (1928–2019; see page 130). The Dutch grid devotee drew his New Alphabet typeface in 1967, in response to the large pixel size of cathode-ray-tube (CRT) monitors, whose dot-matrix grid made curves and fine details impossible. Crouwel's still-futuristic font is hard to read, due to its many unconventional letters, and uses exclusively horizontals, verticals and 45-degree angles and a consistent line width. It was meant as a theoretical exercise exploring new technology, rather than for actual use, although Peter Saville used it for Joy Division's *Substance* album cover in 1988, and a digital revival was produced by The Foundry in 1997.

One technology that led to new typographic forms in the sixties was the need for optical character recognition (OCR) – a typeface readable by a machine, turning printed text into digital data. One of the first was ATF's OCR-A, a monospaced, monoline sans-serif released in 1968. Like Crouwel's experiment, it features minimal curves, giving it a distinctive look, while the rudimentary abilities of OCR technology meant that certain characters have unconventional constructions to differentiate them. Although text-recognition technology has advanced to the level where most fonts can be read, OCR-A is still used often. The weirdness of OCR-A's forms led to the development of OCR-B (1968), designed by Adrian Frutiger for Monotype. This is much more conventional looking, yet could still be read by sixties technology.

OCR-A's forms were less exaggerated than the slightly earlier typefaces designed for magnetic ink character recognition (MICR), which featured idiosyncratic thick strokes in places to aid recognition and avoid confusion between glyphs. This quickly became synonymous, along with the lack of curves, with the public image of computers, leading to the design of many fonts that, though not OCR-compliant, imitated the construction and style of those fonts. These included Gemini (1964) by Franco Grignani, Westminster (1965) by Leo Maggs (b. 1939) and Data 70 (1970) by Bob Newman. Although not actually digital typefaces (most were produced for phototypesetting and dry-transfer lettering), they quickly epitomized a technological look for typography by the seventies.

The first truly digital typefaces were designed for the Digiset typesetter, a 1965 invention of Rudolf Hell (1901–2002), who also invented the first fax machine and colour scanner. In the Digiset process, typography was beamed as light through a cathode-ray tube, and while the end result still involved photographic exposure, the typefaces themselves were stored as digital

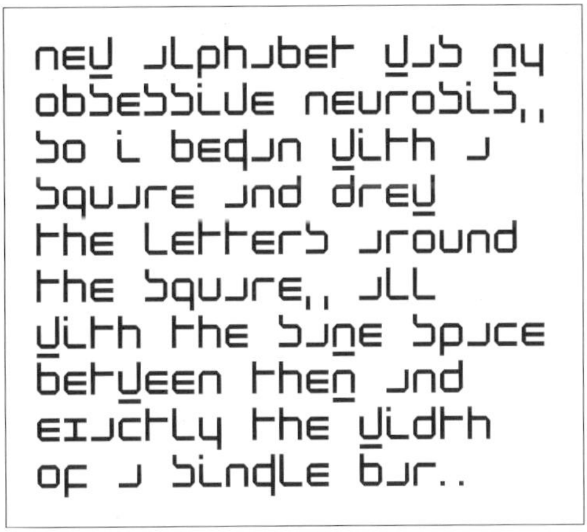

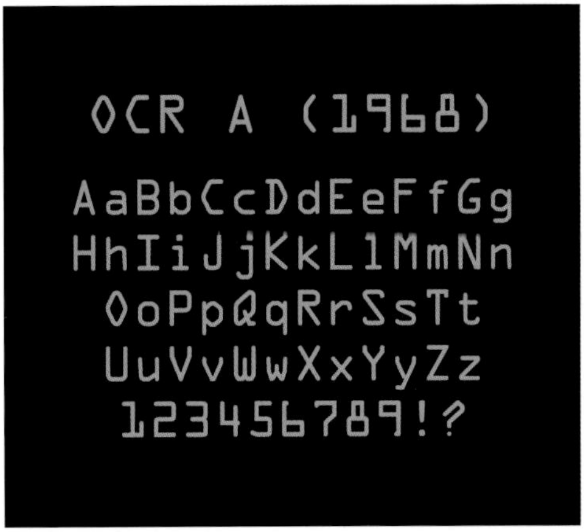

neu ⊔lphⱼbet ⊔ⱼⴝ nᵧ
obⴝeⴝⴝⱼⱱe neuroⴝⱼⴝ,,
ⴝo ⱼ bed⊔n ⊔ⱼth ⱼ
ⴝqu⊔re ⊔nd dreᵧ
the Letterⴝ ⱼround
the ⴝqu⊔re,, ⱼLL
⊔ⱼth the ⴝⱼne ⴝp⊔ce
betᵤeen then ⊔nd
eⱼⱼⱼtLy the ⊔ⱼdth
of ⱼ ⴝⱼnqLe b⊔r..

OCR A (1968)

AaBbCcDdEeFfGg
HhIiJjKkL1MmNn
OoPpQqRrSsTt
UuVvWwXxYyZz
123456789!?

Data 70 [1970]

AaBbCcDdEeFfGg
HhIiJjKkLlMmNn
OoPpQqRrSsTt
UuVvWwXxYyZz
123456789!?

Above Left: New Alphabet, Freda Sack and David Quay for The Foundry, 1997, designed by Wim Crouwel in 1967.

Above Right: OCR-A typeface, ATF, 1968.

Below Right: Amelia, Stan Davis for Visual Graphics Corporation, 1966.

Below Left: OCR-B, Adrian Frutiger for Monotype, 1968.

Centre: Data 70, Bob Newman for Letraset, 1970.

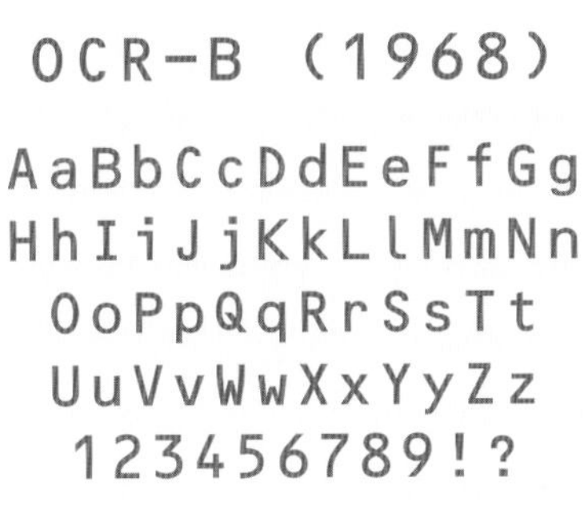

OCR-B (1968)

AaBbCcDdEeFfGg
HhIiJjKkLLMmNn
OoPpQqRrSsTt
UuVvWwXxYyZz
123456789!?

Amelia 1966

AaBbCcDdEeFfGg
HhIiJjKkLlMmNn
OoPpQqRrSsTt
UuVvWwXxYyZz
123456789!?

AaBbCcDdEeFfGg
HhIiJjKkLlMmNn
OoPpQqRrSsTtUu
VvWwXxYyZz12345
6789!? AaBbCcDdEeFfGgHh
IiJjKkLlMmNnOoPpQqRrSsTtUu
VvWwXxYyZz123456789!?

Above: LoRes typeface family: LoRes 21 Serif Regular (in black) and LoRes 22 Narrow Regular (in red), Zuzana Licko for Emigre, 1985/2001.

data - a first. Fonts had to be created especially for the machine, with each glyph constructed using a 100 × 200 square grid. The first was Digi-Grotesk, based on Neuzeit-Grotesk. As the technology took off, Holl Digiset had digital typefaces designed by Gerard Unger (1942-2018) and Hermann Zapf.

These original digital typefaces could be called 'bitmap', 'raster' or 'pixel' fonts as they were constructed in a grid matrix of square units, rather than having clean curves. When the Macintosh debuted in the early eighties, it came with some excellent bitmap fonts designed by Apple's Susan Kare (b. 1954). Technological advancements involving complex mathematics and automation, such as hinting (the distortion of letter shapes to better fit on a pixel grid), subpixel rendering, anti-aliasing (where gradations of grey pixels are used to mitigate jagged lines) and interpolation, have improved the smooth appearance and legibility of typefaces at lower resolutions and smaller sizes in the last few decades. However, the best results are still achieved through painstaking manual attention by typeface designers and engineers.

Smooth digital curves would come with the invention of vector graphics and Bézier curves (see page 229). Adobe's 1984 release of the PostScript programming language ushered in the 'desktop publishing' revolution but also had a huge impact on digital font design, allowing fonts to be designed as vectors and then outputted to a device with different resolutions. This, in turn, led to new font creation program available on personal computers that democratized type design. The first on the Apple Mac

- Fontastic - could create only bitmap fonts. By 1986 came Fontographer, the first Bézier curve editing software for a personal computer - hugely influential on a new generation of font designers. For many designers, the bitmap aesthetic was visually exciting and remained of interest even once vector graphics were technologically feasible. Over the years many more font design programs would be developed - such as FontLab, FontForge, RoboFont and Glyphs - which, combined with the internet, have been responsible for the proliferation of free typefaces, of all imaginable varieties, available to designers today.

Digital typefaces have historically come in multiple file formats (e.g. TrueType and OpenType), with the differences between them rooted in competition between companies. A font format development of practical importance to designers was the emergence of web fonts, which allowed websites to use remotely loaded typefaces rather than relying on fonts that would already be installed on the user's device. Prior to this, 'web-safe' fonts were the defaults that came with most computers, such as Arial, Verdana, Times New Roman, Georgia, Courier New, Comic Sans and Impact, making it difficult for web designers to achieve anything unique.

Technology has advanced to the point where there are few limitations on digital typography and its possibilities have long surpassed print. Developments in programming scripts have introduced elements of automation into the type design process, although it remains a time-consuming and labour-intensive task to do well. A recent innovation is the 'variable font' format, which allows

AAAAAAAAAAAAAA
AAAAAAAAAAAAA
AAAAAAAAAAAAA
AAAAAAAAAAAAA

'Gilbert is sans-serif typeface, a tribute font to honor the memory of Gilbert Baker, the creator of the LGBT Rainbow Flag.
This colorful typeface was supposedly designed to "express diversity and inclusion", specially made for striking headlines and statements that could live on banners for rallies and protests. It is part of the TypeWithPride initiative, a collaboration between NewFest, NYC Pride, Ogilvy and Fontself'

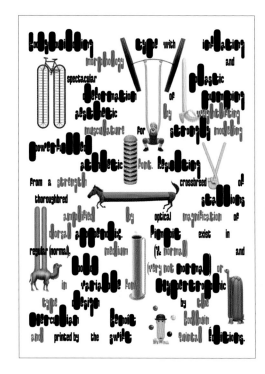

Top: Acumin variable font, Robert Slimbach, Adobe, 2018.

Above Right: Pimpit variable font poster, Benoît Bodhuin / BB-Bureau, 2021.

Above Left: Gilbert colour font, Robyn Makinson Kazunori Shiina & Hayato Yamasaki, 2017.

a single font file to contain a range
of variations, controlled by a slider
axis that controls characteristics like
weight, width and slant. The benefits
of variable fonts include lower file
sizes, which means that websites can have
more variations of a typeface without
slower loading times; more variations
than a traditional multi-style typeface
mean that designers have greater control
over what they want. Another area of
innovation is 'colour fonts', which
are stored in the SVG (scalable vector
graphics) format and 'embed additional
data to display more graphic properties
than the contour shapes of a character',[8]
which usually means pre-set colours,
tones or gradients. The development
of colour fonts came from companies
searching for a way to display emojis on
their operating systems.

Typeface Psychology

In his 1986 identity presentation booklet for Steve Jobs's NeXT computer company, Paul Rand wrote that 'attributing certain magical qualities to particular typefaces is largely a subjective matter'.[9] Subjective it may be, but typefaces undoubtedly have their own personalities, evoking varied psychological feelings and emotions, whether we perceive them or not. Multiple factors influence the subliminal meanings and associations that we receive when presented with a typeface. The most obvious is the forms themselves; this is where subjectivity is less pronounced, as qualities are linked to universal characteristics. A font with rounded forms is considered softer, friendlier and more approachable, while a spiky font is perceived as more aggressive or challenging. Weight, too, has a large impact: thinner forms are more delicate and subtle, while boldness implies confidence, strength and volume. Forms that lean forwards imply speed, movement and dynamism, especially if they seem aerodynamic. The solid construction of a slab serif is sturdy and makes us think of reliability. A casual script font evokes our understanding of handwriting and its personal nature.

Although forms play their part, most associations that are provoked by typefaces come from cultural conditioning and learned associations gained through experience, and as such they are subjective, even if often widely shared. Our understanding of a typeface is more likely to be communal, coming from common contextual use, but it can still also be highly personal. Understanding how we read and understand visual signs is a complex process shaped by many different factors, but repetition over time is one way in which we make sense of non-verbal meaning.

One way to think of fonts is as different voices: we may hear the same message said in different ways but the subtle differences in accent, pronunciation, tone and delivery will impact how we interpret what is being said. This was pointed out by Beatrice Warde (1900–69) in her famous 1930 essay 'The Crystal Goblet', where she writes: 'Type well used is invisible as type, just as the perfect talking voice is the unnoticed vehicle for the transmission of words.'[10] Warde was thinking of book typography here, where legibility is key, but her point holds: on a subconscious level, we understand if a typeface is appropriate for the given context and thus often pay it little attention; when it is used inappropriately, we notice and it disrupts.

Serious

Sophisticated

STRONG

Casual

Childish

𝕲𝖔𝖙𝖍𝖎𝖈

Soft

DYNAMIC

Friendly

Traditional

Elegant

Confident

high-tech

CLASSICAL

Personal

Fun

Further Reading →

Sarah Hyndman, *Why Fonts Matter* (Virgin Books, 2016)
Ellen Lupton, *Thinking with Type* (Princeton Architectural Press, 2010)

Chapter 5:
Mediums

Posters

'The function of the poster is, of course, to speak its message with the greatest possible impact in the least possible time. It must arrest, hold, persuade, implant an idea and give specific information. Pictorial elements may achieve the first ends, but text is almost always a necessity for the latter. Thus, in judging a poster there are three considerations: how eloquently do the pictorial elements make their point; how effectively does the text deliver the specific information; how well are these integrated to create a successful design entity.' Aline B. Louchheim, 'Posters: Challenge to the Artist', *New York Times* (9 March 1952)

The poster is arguably the medium in which graphic design, as we now know it, first emerged, and remains one of the most archetypal, and purest, examples of what constitutes the discipline. In seeking to define the poster, American critic Susan Sontag (1933–2004) contrasted it with a related form, the 'public notice', writing:

> the poster, as distinct from the public notice, presupposes the modern concept of the public – in which the members of a society are defined primarily as spectators and consumers. A public notice aims to inform or command. A poster aims to seduce, to exhort, to sell, to educate, to convince, to appeal. Whereas a public notice distributes information to interested or alert citizens, a poster reaches out to grab those who might otherwise pass it by. A public notice posted on a wall is passive, requiring that the spectator present himself before it to read what is written. A poster claims attention – at a distance. It is visually aggressive.[1]

The poster was born in the age of mechanical reproduction, particularly with the advent of colour lithography.

However, the innovations of its early pioneers (e.g. Jules Cheret, Henri de Toulouse-Lautrec, Eugene Grasset, Alphonse Mucha and The Beggarstaffs) were not particularly stylistic ones – they used approaches found elsewhere in painting – but lay, rather, in applying fine art approaches in a commercial context and marrying their images with text. Most of the significant early posters of the 19th and early 20th century were intended to be seductive pieces of advertising, for everyday products or exciting events (such as theatre performances or cabaret nights), although in the United States many of the best were produced to advertise magazines.

Posters, then as now, were not seen in isolation, but were in prominent public spaces competing with other posters for the attention of passers-by. Posters reflected the commerce and culture of their time, as well as general aesthetic trends. For instance, the earliest posters were in an Art Nouveau style, but soon designers such as Cassandre (1901–68), Edward McKnight Kauffer (1890–1954) and Vera Willoughby (1870–1939), would be working in an Art Deco style, which proved ideal for a new area – the travel poster. The sleek forms of new technological innovations like giant cruise ships and

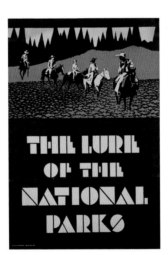

Above (L→R): 'Chat Noir', Théophile Alexandre Steinlen, 1896; 'Austria', Atelier Binder, c.1935; 'Light', Lester Beall, c.1930.

Below (L→R): 'Exactitude', Pierre Fix-Masseau, 1932) 'The Lure of the National Parks' Dorothy Waugh, c.1935, 'San Francisco' for TWA, David Klein, 1957.

Previous Spread: Posters for adidas Football, Yarza Twins, 2018.

fast cross-continent trains proved well suited to the angular stylings of Art Deco. Travel posters would remain an important area of poster design for much of the 20th century, particularly as air travel expanded. The interwar avant-gardes each had their own approach to poster design, while the two world wars gave designers a new type of poster, one outside the usual confines of commerce – propaganda. Another new industry that would generate some of the most iconic posters was cinema, with Hollywood blockbusters and European arthouse films often having distinctive print marketing. The best-known exponent of the movie poster was American designer Saul Bass (1920-96), but many countries had their own take on the form. For instance, the Polish School of Posters, from the fifties through the eighties, gave designers freedom to take a conceptual approach or put their personalities into their work, though in the context of communism rather than capitalism.

Poster design would be one of the main formats in which the modernist Swiss Style (see pages 38-41) emerged in the post-World War II era, and would also be, by the sixties, an area for countercultural expression and at the forefront of pop culture. As posters became more political, commercial designers also reflected on the responsibility of producing such public work and the role of the poster in increasingly visually overwhelming urban spaces. Writing in 1952, Walter Allner (1909-2006) – a Bauhaus graduate who moved to America in 1949 – declared: 'Those who use outdoor posters should recognize their aesthetic obligation toward the public: they are to a large degree

responsible for forming the public's taste, even to the point of involving its intelligence and morality; it is in their power to educate or to defile, to exalt or to debase.'[2] New forms of media, like radio, television and glossy full-colour magazines, made the poster no longer the main focus of the advertising industry, but their public prominence remained unrivalled, and the ease with which they could be produced in large volumes meant they continued to be important in areas outside the mainstream for the rest of the 20th century.

In our digital age a poster no longer has to be printed; the language of physicality is still applied in the virtual world – you 'post' an image to Instagram or onto a Facebook 'wall'. Whether a digital jpeg is technically a 'poster' may be up for debate, but a poster that will only be seen on screen has more possibilities: it does not have to be static. Despite the new possibilities enabled by the internet, the printed poster remains a form in which a great many graphic designers want to produce work. Innovations in printing, such as the rise of digital printing, mean that designers can produce more variations of posters, rather than relying on a large print run for one final design. Although many of the most famous posters in history have been singular, the design of a series of posters can often provide the designer with more chances for creativity, alongside the challenges that come with producing in multiples.

Styles, contexts and subject matter have all evolved constantly since the first posters were printed from lithographic stones in the 19th century, but the challenges facing a poster

Above Left: *Vertigo film* poster, Saul Bass, 1961.

Above Right: *Circus Igor Kio* poster, c.1960-1969.

Below: Poster for The Architectural League of New York's Beaux Arts Ball, Michael Bierut and Nicole Trice / Pentagram, 1999.

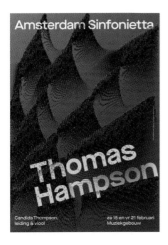

Above: Posters for the Amsterdam Sinfonietta, Studio Dumbar, 2020.

Below: 2-colour Risograph poster for Black Cinema House, designed by James Goggin / Practise, printed by Christopher Roeleveld, 2012.

Opposite: Poster for *Anna Karenina* at Sheffield Theatres, Emilie Chen, 2022.

Further Reading →
Scott Laserow & Natalia Delgado, *Making Posters: From Concept to Design* (Bloomsbury, 2020)
Ellen Lupton, *How Posters Work* (Cooper-Hewitt Museum, 2015)
Gill Saunders & Margaret Timmers, *The Poster: A Visual History* (Thames & Hudson / V&A, 2020)

designer remain much the same: to create something eye-catching, easily digestible, memorable, immediate and economical. The audience for posters, although they have become collector's items or objects of home decoration, is not a captive one: the luxury of attention cannot be taken for granted, whether working with print or for screens. In the words of John Garrigan, design curator at New York's Museum of Modern Art in the 1970s:

A highly developed mass-communication system would seemingly render the poster obsolete. It became however, the group or individual statement in a time of mass electronic messages and proved all the more arresting for that direct one-to-one communication [...] a great poster often becomes the very symbol of a product, cause or event. A synthesis of message and method, the poster can shock or entertain, stir the emotions, and linger in the memory. In this respect, the poster as a means of communication is still unsurpassed.[3]

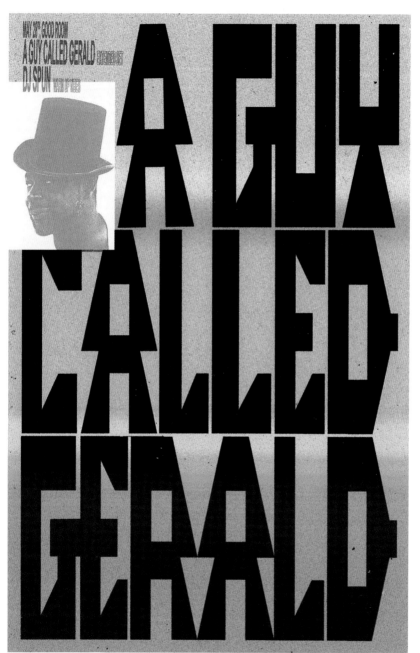

Left and Opposite, Top: Posters for Good Room, Bráulio Amado, 2019, 2022 and 2016.

Opposite Below: Posters for Südpol, Studio Feixen, 2014, 2013 and 2012.

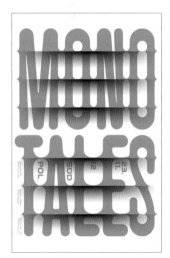

Advertising

'The theory is — and it works — that if an ad hasn't got enough stopping power without all the little words, no amount of talk is going to make any large number of people read it.'

Bill Bernbach, quoted in *Marketing/Communications*, Issue 297 (1969)

Top: Stiller advertisement, Lucian Bernhard, 1908.

Above Right: *Daily Herald* advertisement, Edward McKnight Kauffer, 1918.

Below Left: *Life* advertisement, Walter Allner, c.1952.

Centre: Chrysler advertisment, Ashley Havinden, W.S. Crawford Ltd, 1928.

Not all graphic design is advertising, and not all advertising is graphic design, but the two fields are inherently linked, particularly historically. American art director and writer Steven Heller (b. 1950), in a 1995 *Eye* magazine article titled 'Advertising: mother of graphic design', notes: 'Though graphic design as we know it originated in the late nineteenth century as a tool of advertising, an association today with marketing, advertising or capitalism deeply undermines the graphic designer's self-image.'[4] Not all graphic designers are comfortable with how enmeshed the field is with advertising. This might be for social reasons, such as suspicion of rampant consumerism, or simply because the advertising industry, which is huge and commands large fees, tends to see itself as separate from the graphic design world, despite employing a great number of graphic designers.

The poster (see pages 246–253) was the primary form of advertising for much of the 19th and early 20th centuries, spawning approaches that were ideally suited to the viewer's limited attention span (many posters would have been seen on the move), notably the *Sachplakat*, or object poster, mastered by European designers such as Lucian Bernhard (1883–1972), Otto Baumberger (1889–1961) and Niklaus Stoecklin (1896–1982). A reaction to the maximalism of Art Nouveau, object posters kept it simple by reducing content to the bare minimum, usually just the brand name and its product, which was often rendered monumentally in a hyper-realistic style, or, in the case of Bernhard, its pioneer, a slightly flatter, more graphical approach. The *Sachplakat* was one aspect of what became known as the *Plakatstil*

(German for 'poster style'), developed as designers sought a style appropriate for modern, 20th-century advertising, rather than relying on techniques cribbed from fine art. Over time object posters took inspiration from Surrealism to create more intriguing compositions or, in work epitomized by Swiss designer Herbert Leupin (1916–99), became more light-hearted and playful. Particularly in the wake of the horrors of World War II, humour became vital in advertising design, with anthropomorphized products, fun mascots and smiley illustrated faces commonplace.

Beyond posters, advertising design was mostly found in printed contexts like magazines or newspapers, where the constraints and approaches were much the same, but the more captive audience led to advertisers including more text – what was known as a 'long copy' or 'hard sell' approach. Often, such advertisements were formulaic, with a headline at the top, an illustration or photograph in the middle, and a dense block of text at the bottom, and did little to make consumers want to pay more attention. This would all change by the late fifties and sixties, with what became known as the 'New Advertising'. This was pioneered in New York City and emphasized the importance of a concept, or 'big idea', which tied together text and image into a complete whole, and used intelligence to attract interest, turning viewers into active participants, not passive spectators. Print advertising was working harder to be clever, and in part this was a response to new areas of advertising, like television and radio, that did not involve graphic design.

Advertising came to dominate more and more areas of modern life during the

Above: Marmite Chilli billboard advertisement, Adam&Eve DDB, 2021.

Below: Billboard advertisement for *The Economist*, creative direction by Paul Belford for AMV.BBDO, 2004.

Further Reading →

Pete Barry, *The Advertising Concept Book* (Thames & Hudson, 2016)

D&AD, *The Copy Book* (Taschen, 2022)

Winston Fletcher, *Advertising: A Very Short Introduction* (Oxford University Press, 2010)

sixties and was part of the justification for some of the countercultural, anti-consumerism of the hippie generation. Designers, too, as seen in the 'First Things First' manifesto (1964), were not necessarily happy to be contributing to the 'high pitched scream of consumer selling' - a trend that grew in the following decades, particularly after the founding in 1989 of the Canadian magazine *Adbusters*.

Despite its growing dominance, advertising in the last few decades has tended to appropriate techniques, ideas and aesthetics from elsewhere, rather than innovating itself. Partly this is because graphic design has often been seen in the industry as simply execution or 'styling' for ideas generated elsewhere, rather than as a place for the integration of form and message. That is not to say that good graphic design does not happen in the advertising industry, but it does not always appear to be a primary concern. Television advertisements are given higher prestige, have the most visibility and command larger budgets, so traditional print advertisements often just approximate the same ideas in a watered-down form, serving to remind people of a wider campaign rather than being impactful in their own regard. But with the wide variety of digital and social media platforms that dominate today, the need for campaigns that work broadly is to be expected.

In our social media age of 'viral' content, there is even more rationale for advertising to be designed in a witty way, as a successful campaign will be actively shared and celebrated by people who appreciate its cleverness, thereby reversing advertising's typical role

of the uninvited interruption. To this end, print campaigns may often focus on the design of one particularly creative billboard, rather than a campaign plastered across a nation - safe in the knowledge that this could potentially garner millions of views online with a fraction of the media spend.

Book Covers

While books have existed for centuries, the idea that their covers should be visually appealing is a fairly modern invention. Early books were hardbound, but paper sleeves, known as dust jackets, arrived in the mid-19th century and acted as protection, to be discarded once the book was home. As books got cheaper and more popular, their jackets became a marketing opportunity that artists and designers were hired to produce in a manner that both expressed the book's contents and attracted potential readers.

Book covers have long reflected the aesthetic tendencies of their age. The distinction between books and journals or magazines was blurred in the late 19th century, and it was these serials where covers were more eye-catching, such as *The Yellow Book* with its risqué Art Nouveau covers by Aubrey Beardsley (1872–98), and the so-called 'penny dreadfuls' – cheap sensationalist periodicals featuring lurid artwork. The 'pulp' paperbacks of the 20th century would resume this tradition. The use of artists to create cover images continued into the early 20th century, with a prominent case being Vanessa Bell (1879–1961), a painter who created graphically striking covers for the works of her sister, Virginia Woolf. American covers in the twenties still tended to be painterly rather than graphical, with the most iconic example being Francis Cugat's (1893–1981) 1925 cover for F. Scott Fitzgerald's novel *The Great Gatsby*.

Pictorial covers had become common, even for books of literary merit by the late thirties, but not everyone was quite so enamoured with this development. In some European countries, unadorned functional covers were considered the norm, and many British publishers still preferred a text-only approach. Among these was Penguin, whose Gill Sans type and orange-and-white 'tri-band' (refined by Jan Tschichold [1902–72] in 1947) became iconic.

In the mid-century United States publishers were ahead of the curve commercially, and many put out paperbacks with well-designed, modernist-inspired covers by designers such as Alvin Lustig (1915–55), Leo Lionni (1910–99) and Paul Rand (1914–96). Lustig, working primarily for literary publisher New Directions, was particularly influential for applying European avant-garde principles to covers in a way that was intelligent and sensitive. Across the Atlantic at Penguin, Britain's biggest publisher, visually appealing covers finally began to be embraced in the early sixties, thanks to art director Germano Facetti (1926–2006), but there tended to be a marked separation between type and image, rather than integration into one complete design; the use of templates continued. Facetti hired exciting young designers such as Alan Fletcher (1931–2006), Romek Marber (1925–2020) and Derek Birdsall (b. 1934), and his pairing of novels with contemporaneous, existing (rather than commissioned) works of art for the Penguin Classics series created an evergreen approach.

The late sixties saw the influence of psychedelia coming to book covers through the work of designers such as Milton Glaser (b. 1929), Seymour Chwast (b. 1931), Alan Aldridge (1938–2017) and John Alcorn (1935–92), with eye-catching bright colours the order of the day.

Above (L→R): *The Language of Flowers*, designer unknown, 1896; *Amerika*, Alvin Lustig, 1946.

Below (L→R): *Invisible Man*, Edward McKnight Kauffer, 1952; *The Great American Novel*, Paul Bacon, 1973.

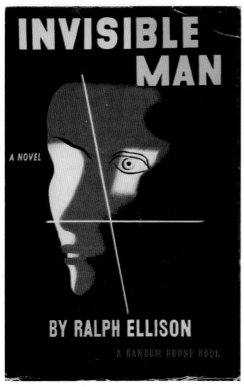

One of the most iconic covers of this era was David Pelham's 1972 cover for *A Clockwork Orange*, which used a striking, flat-colour graphic approach. Airbrushed illustrations also became popular in the seventies and into the eighties, but illustration and 'pure' graphic design would soon lose favour, with photography becoming dominant by the mid-seventies. Often, this came at the expense of type and image working in harmony: text was often put on top of a photograph and felt like something of an afterthought, rather than integral to the design. Some designers, however, managed to use photography in creative ways, and art directors were occasionally able to commission talented photographers to create something bespoke to the book in question. Most publishers were now using an eclectic approach to covers, particularly at the more commercial end of the market. Gone were the days when designers could design hundreds of covers in a consistent 'house style'.

One enduring approach that did not rely on photography was the so-called Big Book Look pioneered by American designer Paul Bacon (1927–95). This was characterized by large eye-catching type, sometimes paired with a small illustrated motif. Two of the best examples of this approach, Tony Palladino's (1930–2014) cover for Robert Bloch's novel *Psycho* (1959) and S. Neil-Fujita's (1921–2010) cover for Mario Puzo's *The Godfather* (1969), have the distinction that their typography was used in the films made of the books (Chip Kidd's [b. 1964] 1993 cover for *Jurassic Park* has a similar distinction). This was in stark contrast to the usual relationship between films and books, where much-derided film-tie-in covers retrofit film posters or use a photographic still to piggyback off the publicity of big-screen adaptation.

Digital design technology would revitalize book cover design. However, it was traditional techniques that became influential around the new millennium, with covers such as Jon Gray's cover for *Everything Is Illuminated* (2003) and Jeff Fisher's for *Captain Corelli's Mandolin* (1998) significant in bringing hand-lettering and naive illustration styles back into vogue among fiction publishers. While digital technology would herald a long-term decline in book sales, it meant that many publishers were keen to embrace the physicality of books, celebrating the medium through the use of special print effects and beautifully designed clothbound editions. The rise of eBooks and online bookshops, particularly Amazon, has meant that covers are often judged as small thumbnails rather than their real size, which has led to designers increasingly using larger typography and often simpler graphics, too. Designers sometimes have to contend with a large amount of extra marketing copy on their covers, such as quotations from other authors or reviewers. These are added in the hope of convincing potential buyers that a book is worth reading, but often dilute the design.

Further Reading →

David J. Alworth & Peter Mendelsund, *The Look of the Book* (Ten Speed Press, 2020)
Alan Powers, *Front Cover* (Mitchell Beazley, 2006)
Ned Drew & Paul Sternberger, *By Its Cover* (Princeton Architectural Press, 2005)

Despite such pressures in the digital age, book covers remain an area that many graphic designers dream of working in, and somewhere where you can find eye-catching typography, clever conceptual ideas, striking illustration and innovative use of photographic imagery. The American designer Ivan Chermayeff (1932–2017) described the cover design process in 1964 as 'the essence of graphic design problems: the challenge and the solution in a simple format' one with 'the luxury of minimum copy'.[5] This is what still draws designers to book covers, alongside the very direct relationship between design and commercial success – a cover can make or break a book, and social media has only made this more obvious.

Above: *Jacob's Room*, Vanessa Bell, 1922.

Above (L→R):
What White People Can Do Next, Jahnavi Inniss, 2021; *Fight Night*, Anna Morrison, 2022.

Below (L→R):
Everything Is Illuminated, Gray318, 2002; *Riot Days*, Tom Etherington, 2017.

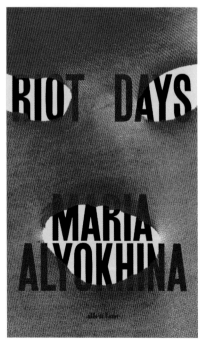

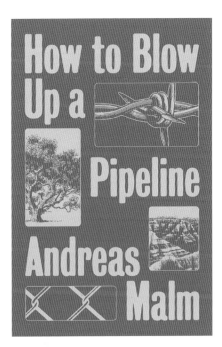

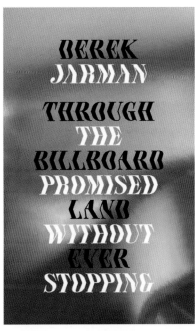

Above (L→R):
How to Blow Up a Pipeline, Chantal Jahchan, 2021; *Through the Billboard Promised Land Without Ever Stopping*, Theo Inglis, 2022.

Below (L→R):
The Age of Skin, Jack Smyth, 2021; *The Waste Land*, Jamie Keenan, 2013.

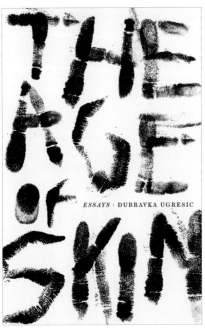

Books

'Creativity in book design is best applied to problems so as to make them appear never to have existed – no signs of a messy manuscript or a haphazard supply of copy and pictures.' Derek Birdsall, *Notes on Book Design* (2004)

In a speech given to the London Bibliographical Society in 1893, artist, writer and designer William Morris (1834-1896) declared that 'a book quite un-ornamented can look actually and positively beautiful, and not merely un-ugly, if it be, so to say, architecturally good', later going on to define what this meant:

> First, the pages must be clear and easy to read; which they can hardly be unless.
> Secondly, the type is well designed; and
> Thirdly, whether the margins be small or big, they must be in due proportion to the page of letter.'[6]

The standard book – by which I mean the small, handheld paperbacks or hardbacks that contain mostly text – has evolved over hundreds of years into a format that is ideal for reading: the two pages and central spine mirror the symmetrical human form. For designers, laying out the interiors of these text-based books can be more about following conventions and achieving clarity, rather than creativity or personality. Perhaps the most apt scenario for the central dictum of Beatrice Warde's (1900-69) manifesto 'The Crystal Goblet' (1930), is that the design of a book should be almost invisible, feeling inevitable rather than distracting the reader from the content.

Deciding an appropriate format, picking the paper stock, choosing the ideal typeface and corresponding size, spacing and justification, opting on the style for page furniture (e.g. page numbers and running heads), and creating a pleasing text block and grid are the upfront jobs for a book designer. Once the architecture of the book has been decided, the main job of the designer is to ensure that the typesetting is correct, avoiding problems like widows, orphans and rivers. If text is fully justified, the designer also has to make sure that tracking and hyphenation are used to avoid lines that are either too compacted or loose, while text that is left justified (centred setting is rarely appropriate for extended texts, while right justification is used only for languages that write right to left) raises the issue of 'ragging'. The 'rag' of a text is the pattern made by its unjustified ends, which in an ideal world would be as even as possible, rather than having lines that vary widely in length. Often, this can be fixed through letter spacing or the use of hyphenation, but not all publisher's house style guides allow words to be split across different lines (over pages, however, is universally avoided).

It is in designing larger, illustrated books (containing photographs, artworks

Opposite: *FLORIDA!*, design and art direction by Studio Elana Schlenker and Jordi Ng, with illustrations by Gabriel Alcaca, 2022.

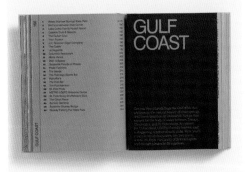

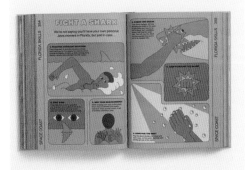

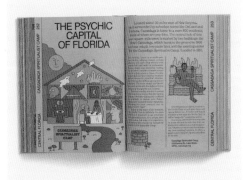

or images of any kind) – often described somewhat disparagingly as coffee-table books – that graphic designers get to be more creative. However, these, too, present challenges in organization; again, the main job for the designer is to develop a system that is flexible enough to present different types of content, at different scales, in a consistent way. Often, this involves having a few different double-page spread (DPS) templates, rather than relying on a one-size-fits-all approach that can quickly become monotonous for the reader. Different kinds of illustrated books present their own challenges. Cookbooks, for instance, combine recipe instructions and ingredient lists, often of widely varying lengths, with large-scale photography; children's books require close integration between text and image, which is usually illustrative; while the designers of art books have been known to go to painstaking lengths to ensure that all the artworks displayed are in correct proportion to one another, rather than risk showing a large painting small and a small painting large.

When done well, the book designer's role should become secondary to the content, while still being visually engaging yet appropriate for the content itself. Illustrated books still present opportunities for creativity, not least in their covers, but also in one-off pages like titles and content lists, as well as in details like endpapers or section dividers. Unlike, say, the average fiction book, an illustrated book is likely to be designed as a complete package, with the same person or studio creating both inside and out. Book design is a highly collaborative endeavour nonetheless, with designers often having to work closely with authors, editors and publishers. Considering the book itself as an object, rather than as just a series of flat pages, is often integral to a successful publishing design project. Elements such as fancy print finishes and luxury materials have helped printed books to continue to compete with their digital rivals.

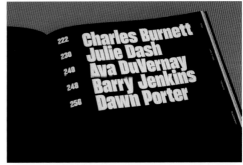

Above: Spreads from *Regeneration: Black Cinema, 1898–1971*, designed by Eddie Opara / Pentagram, 2022.

Further Reading →

A Book on Books: Celebrating the Art of Book Design Today (Victionary, 2020)
Jost Hochuli, *Systematic Book Design?* (Éditions B42, 2020)
Michael Mitchell, *Book Typography: A Designer's Manual* (Libanus Press, 2005)

Editorial

A broad field, of which book design is often considered a part, editorial design refers to the design of publications – for instance newspapers, magazines and journals. Editorial design was once a purely print-based discipline, but as each of these types of media has expanded into the digital world, the design of, say, a magazine's website or newspaper's app can be considered editorial design, as they have the same primary concern: the clear and engaging presentation of text and image, usually in unison.

What differentiates editorial design from book design more generally, at least to my mind, is the different context: editorial brings together a variety of content by different authors, and often of different types, in a format that is serialized (part of a series), rather than a one-off. Although many of the issues faced by a book designer (e.g. balancing text and image, properly setting typography, creating well-designed layouts) are shared by the editorial designer, there are different challenges when content is more varied (for instance, editorial projects will also often include advertisements) and when the systems put in place have to fit this variety, and be effective repeatedly, whether that is every day, week, month or a few times a year.

The system is key for editorial design; it needs to be flexible and adaptable, allowing for individual variations and excitements, yet needs to be coherent overall. An effective editorial design, once established, will, in the words of graphic designer Adrian Shaughnessy (b. 1953), create 'a compelling visual and editorial experience […] an intimate "voice" that, over time, becomes the voice of a well-liked friend.'[7]

Different types of editorial design have their constraints, conventions and additional roles that the designer may be expected to be involved in. Newspapers, for instance, have a long history and as such can be very set in their ways, rarely having much room for radical change on the part of the designer. Newspapers have a lot to cram in, mostly text but often photographs too, as well as the advertisements that help to cover costs, so they often rely on tight columns of text and heavy use of strictly defined grids. Often, it is in back sections of big newspapers, away from the main news (e.g. culture or sport) where designers can be a bit more expressive and get to design more creative covers. The relentless pace, particularly at papers published daily, can put a damper on visual experimentation. Tight deadlines mean instinct is vital, leaving little room for the kind of umming and ahing that is commonplace elsewhere; sometimes this is to the advantage of designers as their ideas are less likely to be diluted. One area of newspaper work handled by designer–art directors, particularly in the United States, is the commissioning of editorial illustrations to accompany the main articles. Sometimes designers will also be involved in directing photoshoots or the design of infographics and diagrams.

Magazines are one of the most archetypal and visible areas of graphic design. They have historically been

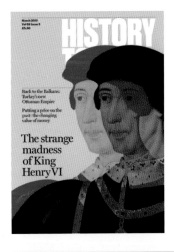

Top: *History Today* redesign, Holly Catford / Esterson Associates, 2018.

Above: *The Masses* magazine cover, February 1916. Illustration by Frank Waltz.

Left: *Bloomberg Businessweek* cover, Richard Turley, 2012.

the site of much visual innovation. From the 19th-century lithographic covers of *Harper's* and *The Chap Book* to the little magazines of the interwar European avant-garde, on to mid-century titles such as *Fortune* and *Esquire* and the underground press of the sixties, punk fanzines of the seventies, and cutting-edge pop culture magazines of the eighties such as *The Face* and Andy Warhol's *Interview* – magazines have often been at the forefront of trends. Through their work, magazine art directors such as Alexey Brodovitch (1898–1971), Cipe Pineles (1908–91), Mehemed Fehmy Agha (1896–78) and George Lois (1931–2022) helped to define the role of the modern graphic designer.

The covers of magazines, as the element most crucial to attracting readers, can be the place where designers get to be creative. Often,

though, they follow a particular template, which at the very least usually means a consistent masthead; the wordmark (see page 88) for the magazine's name is most commonly placed prominently top and centre. Covers for most magazines utilize a combination of typography and image, which can be either photography, illustration or artwork; many magazines will mix it up on this front for their covers, but some areas (e.g. fashion) focus on photographs. The genre of the magazine and its intended audience have a big impact on the design of covers, as noted by writer Ellen McCracken: 'The cover serves to label not only the magazine but the consumer who possesses it.'[8]

Designing the inside of magazines well requires ability in typography, layout and art direction, as well as a good sense of the magazine's

Right: Spread from
The Big Issue,
design by Matt
Willey / Pentagram,
art director Mark
Neil, 2022.

Opposite, Left: The
Guardian Journal
cover, deputy
creative director
Chris Clarke,
executive creative
director Alex
Breuer, 2018.

Opposite, Right: The
Guardian cover,
design by Tomato
Košir and Steven
Gregor, creative
director Chris
Clarke, 2019.

editorial voice and a feel for pacing
and narrative. Layouts need to be
visually related but with enough room
for surprise; Alexey Brodovitch's
catchphrase during his tenure at
Harper's Bazaar (1934–58) was reportedly
'Astonish me'. Alongside all this,
editorial designers also need to have a
good grasp of working with images and
in-depth knowledge of print production
techniques – unless they work in
digital areas of editorial design, that
is, which is a growing area but has
not quite managed to yet bring on the
foretold 'death of print'. Although
sales of magazines and newspapers have
been steadily dropping, niche and indie
publications have blossomed in recent
decades and are where some of the most
interesting design work is being done.

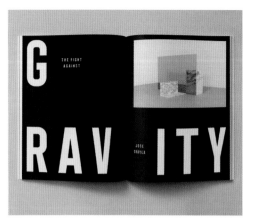

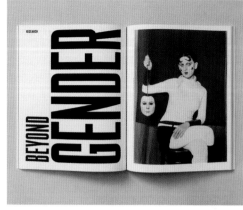

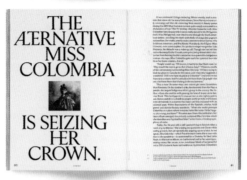

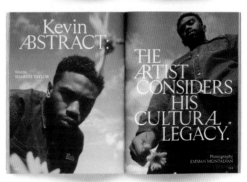

Above: Spreads from *Kinfolk* magazine, Issue 40, designed by Alex Hunting Studio, 2022.

Opposite: Spreads from *Elephant* magazine, designed by Astrid Stavro / Atlas, 2014–17.

Further Reading →

Cath Caldwell & Yolanda Zappaterra, *Editorial Design* (Laurence King, 2016)

Robert Klanten & Sven Ehmann, *Turning Pages: Editorial Design for Print Media* (Gestalten, 2010)

Angharad Lewis, *So You Want to Publish a Magazine?* (Laurence King, 2014)

Album Covers

Like the book jacket, the earliest packaging for vinyl discs was primarily protective: slips of paper holding the easily damaged record were placed in cardboard sleeves, onto which only basic information was printed. The American designer Alex Steinweiss (1917-2011) – who joined Columbia Records as an art director in 1939 – is credited with designing the first pictorial record sleeve (for *Smash Song Hits by Rodgers and Hart*). Other record companies soon followed Columbia's lead. The invention of the long-playing record (LP) in the late forties, combined with increasing levels of home stereo ownership, led to a booming music market in the mid-century United States, with competition between labels giving ample work to graphic designers. Steinweiss, the original innovator, was prolific during the fifties, developing a distinctive style combining illustration, abstract graphics and hand-lettering. Fellow designer Will Burtin (1908-72) said of Steinweiss in 1947: 'He always seems to direct his efforts at the right people's eyes and at the right time, with the correct means in colors, shapes and type.'[9] Most graphic designers working in the United States during the mid-century turned their hands to album covers at various times, with some of the most prolific being those who, like Steinweiss, designed many covers for a particular label, such as Jim Flora (1914-88), S. Neil Fujita, Erik Nitsche (1908-98) and Rudolph de Harak (1924-2002).

Most mid-century album covers, designed for genres like classical and easy listening, were illustrative or graphical rather than photographic, and the large 12-inch sleeve gave plenty of space for impact. Musical tastes would change rapidly in the second half of the 20th century, and the new emphasis on performers rather than composers or band leaders would result in photography soon becoming dominant over illustration or abstraction. Jazz was one genre where this new approach gained early prominence, with Reid Miles's (1927-93) covers for the Blue Note label being particularly iconic. Miles used vibrant modern typography and worked with excellent photographs of jazz stars, often taken during recording sessions by Francis Wolff (1907-71) or Miles himself.

The explosion of rock 'n' roll and pop, and youth culture more generally, in the early sixties would revolutionize approaches to the design of album covers, with styles becoming more connected to the type of music and associated fashions. A good example was the rise of psychedelic rock, which had an accompanying exotic, hallucinogenic aesthetic inspired by Art Nouveau. Writing in 1974, Bob Cato (1923-99) – who created covers for the likes of Barbra Streisand, Bob Dylan, Miles Davis and Janis Joplin – noted that 'the designer of the record cover had to deal with a "real and human" product that was just as concerned, if not more so, about its own image, its own message on its own package!', adding: 'Designing for the pop/rock album is the one area of design that undoubtedly demands the most commitment and involvement on the part of the design/photographer artist.'[10] During the sixties and seventies it was often photographs of the stars that were the key selling points for music, and thus dominated covers, but there was also a great deal of more conceptual,

  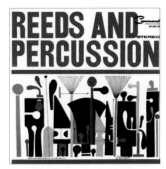

Top (L→R): Alex Steinweiss, 1957; Paul Bacon, 1961; S. Neil Fujita, 1961.

Centre (L→R): Reid Miles, 1966; Reid Miles, 1964; Sylvia Abernathy, 1967.

Below (L→R): Milton Glaser, 1969; Barney Bubbles, 1979; Azar Kazimir, 2018.

Further Reading →
John Foster, *Album Art: New Music Graphics* (Thames & Hudson, 2018)
Michael Ochs, *1000 Record Covers* (Taschen, 2022)
Aubrey Powell, *Vinyl . Album . Cover . Art: The Complete Hipgnosis Catalogue* (Thames & Hudson, 2017)

high-minded approaches that used photography or illustration in creative ways, often relegating band names or titles to small text, or removing them entirely. Notable for a diverse and distinctive take on album cover design was the London-based group Hipgnosis, which created iconic and often surreal covers for artists like Pink Floyd, Peter Gabriel and Led Zeppelin. At times album design was about more than just a cover, with packaging involving wrap-around designs, long 'gatefolds' or additional printed material alongside the disc. This was particularly true of the 'concept albums' associated with prog rock.

At the other end of the scale, many bands and musicians would bring a branded method to their designs, using consistent approaches to album covers or even developing a logo. Notable examples of band logos include the Rolling Stones' lips and tongue symbol (John Pasche [b. 1945], 1970) and Chicago's cursive wordmark (John Berg [1932–2015], 1970), which appeared prominently on their albums. Rejecting slick approaches and high-minded concepts, punk would rip up the rulebook. This laid the groundwork for many alternative and underground genres and labels in the last few decades of the 20th century, which would use music packaging as a chance to develop a distinct aesthetic radically different from that used by the corporate world. In the wake of punk, many prominent designers, such as Peter Saville (b. 1955), Barney Bubbles (1942–83) and Vaughan Oliver (1957–2019), took approaches that were typical of wider postmodernism (see pages 56–63).

Technological changes have had a huge impact on design for music. The 12-inch LP sleeve became the much smaller tape cassette and compact disc (CD), and later the digital thumbnail, which may only be seen at the size of a postage stamp. With the internet, and streaming services particularly, music sales have declined hugely, making the album cover less significant than it once was (in tandem with music videos becoming of greater importance). Nonetheless, covers are still important for setting the tone of an artist's music and often provide a foundation for wider cross-media campaigns. Often, it is the smaller indie labels where design for music is at its most interesting or innovative, while designers remain keen to create images for music: its non-visual nature provides both an interesting challenge and an opportunity to be at the cutting edge of fashion.

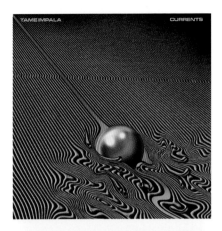

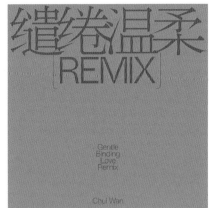

Top (L→R): Robert Beatty, 2015; Qingyu Wu, 2020.

Centre (L→R): Alex McCullough and Jacob Wise, 2018; Hassan Rahim / 12:01AM, 2016.

Below: Wei Huang, 2019.

Brand Identity

A brand identity – also known as visual identity, corporate identity, corporate image, house style or branding – is how a business, company or organization identifies itself visually to distinguish itself from its rivals. Brand identity is the image the organization presents to the world, and should reflect what it does, what it is, its corporate 'personality', its 'values', and the products or services it offers. While the logo is the most prominent aspect of a company's design, the full extent of a brand identity encompasses so much more than a single mark (e.g. colour schemes, typefaces, image styles like illustration or photography, layout approaches, copywriting tone of voice and even the brand name itself) and should be consistently applied across every form of communication – be it in physical space, through print, on screen or via direct interaction with a product. Paul Rand, widely considered one of the most influential designers of brand identities, writing in 1968, declared: 'Unless it consistently represents the aims and beliefs as well as the total activity and production of a company, a corporate image is at best mere window dressing, and at worst deception.'[11]

Marks of ownership and identification have existed for thousands of years, and some businesses have been going for hundreds of years, but the concept of 'corporate identity' was only really popularized in the mid-20th century. One of the most important pioneers in the field was German architect Peter Behrens (1868–1940), employed as a consultant by Berlin-based electrical manufacturer AEG in 1907. Behrens designed buildings and products for the company as well as a corporate identity that was consistently applied to print publicity, packaging and building signage. Another early example of a strong corporate identity was that of the London Underground under the direction of Frank Pick (1878–1941). Behrens's office staff during the AEG years included future giants of modern architecture – Le Corbusier, Ludwig Mies van der Rohe and Walter Gropius – and it was under the broader influence of modernism that corporate identity systems became widespread. Modernist tenets and imperatives – such as consistency, efficiency and the use of systems – were well suited to the design of identities for companies that were becoming bigger and more multinational by the fifties. Leading agencies and individual designers, such as Saul Bass, Paul Rand, Otl Aicher (1922–91), the Design Research Unit and Unimark International, designed identities and provided extensive 'brand guidelines' and 'corporate identity manuals' that laid down the law to other designers or printers on how to correctly apply branding. These manuals thus maintained a consistent approach to visual communication across projects, formats, mediums and territories. Steven Heller describes these manuals as 'sacred texts, revered for how they help shift graphic design from simply an intuitive practice to a rigorously strategic one'.[12]

Modernism's formalist influence on identity design remains strong, and brand guidelines are still a large part of the design of a new corporate identity or rebrand. But as consumerism expanded in the sixties and seventies the field of corporate identity design became more

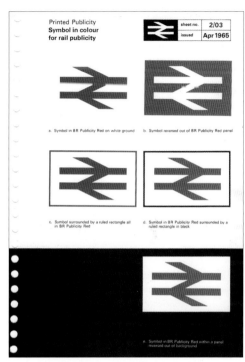

This Page: Pages from British Rail's Corporate Identity Manual. Designed by Design Research Unit (DRU), 1965. The 'Double Arrow' logo was designed by DRU staff member Gerry Barney. British Rail's typeface 'Rail Alphabet' was designed by Jock Kinnear and Margaret Calvert.

emotive and responded to market research and studies of consumer behaviour. Designers, increasingly acting like consultants and managers in the rapidly expanding business world of corporate design, wanted to dig deep into the companies they were working for to truly comprehend what they represented, as well as understand how they were perceived by the public, in the hopes of making the two match up. The stated goal was to create an identity that accurately reflected the company, rather than just 'dressing it up', although, ultimately, increasing profits was what mattered to most businesses. Many of the leading agencies creating corporate branding were British, but became global, such as Michael Peters and Partners, Pentagram, Conran Design Group and Wolff Olins, whose co-founder Wally Olins (1930–2014), although not a graphic designer, was one of the most vocal advocates for the evolving role of corporate identity, particularly through his book *The Corporate Personality* (1978). Olins's writing encapsulates why branding was becoming such a lucrative and expensive business, one in which graphic designers were not necessarily top of the heap. 'It is manifestly impossible', he wrote, 'for a graphic designer by himself to comprehend clearly the nature of an organisation's identity. Too many cultural, organisational, political and psychological factors are involved for which the designer has no training.'[13]

Postmodernism provided another context for the explosion of branding; individualism was more important than ever, and consumerism presented a way for people to define themselves as traditional social identities declined in importance. Stuart Hall (1932–2014), the pioneering cultural theorist, writing in 1988, observed that the post-industrial, postmodern 'new times' were marked by 'a greater emphasis on choice and product differentiation, on marketing, packaging and design, on the "targeting" of consumers by lifestyle, taste and culture rather than by categories of social class.'[14] While the march of seductively branded consumerism had its detractors, notably Naomi Klein's polemic *No Logo* (1999), branding became an inescapable idea. Cultural organizations, cities, countries and even people increasingly saw themselves as 'brands' that required well-designed visual identities to help them stand out and define themselves. Writing in a 2004 article titled 'The Steamroller of Branding' for *Eye* magazine, designer Nick Bell (b. 1965) notes: 'Corporate identity and branding, conceived and reared in the corporate sector, is now being welcomed into the cultural field by arts institutions that now share similar commercial ambitions to their corporate sponsors.'[15]

Bell goes on to say: 'Graphic designers practise corporate identity. It is a kind of science, a method, a theory, a particular kind of way in which a group (a company, an organisation) is given the appearance, character and behaviour of an individual. Branding is where the same thing happens to products. It works very well in the corporate sector. Why don't graphic designers, as part of their armoury of approaches, have something called "cultural identity"?' The question of whether consistency and a fixed identity work so well outside the most obviously commercial areas, into wider society and culture, remains pertinent today. Many critics over the last few

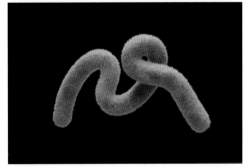

This Page: Flexible brand identity for the Mellon Foundation, Eddie Opara/ Pentagram, 2022.

Overleaf: Rebrand of the Roundhouse, a live performance space in London, Studio Moross, 2022.

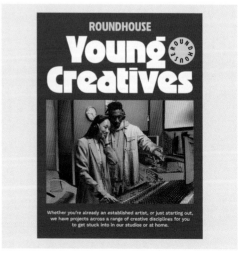

decades have been keen to point out
that 'identity' itself is a complex idea,
difficult to pin down, let alone express
visually in a way that is not shallow
or superficial. In a 2008 interview with
Adrian Shaughnessy, Brian Boylan (b. 1945)
of Wolff Olins explained that, for the
agency, 'the brand is the platform, the
brand is flexible, the brand is a place
of exchange, and it is not fixed, so there
is not one logo. There is recognisable
form and recognisable communication
and behaviour, but it's not one type
of constrained and fixed thing.'[16] This
statement was prescient of the direction
branding was moving in, and predicted
trends in the last decade for identities
that are flexible and responsive and
create entire 'worlds', rather than
relying on the traditional emphasis on
a single logo. That said, the interview
with Shaughnessy was in the context of
Wolff Olins' London 2012 Olympics branding,
which was harshly judged in 2008 on logo
alone and remained unpopular once the
full identity was in use by 2012 - many
could not see past their initial dislike
of the main symbol. The logo remains
the most publicly judged aspect of any
new brand or rebrand, a trend that has
only been accelerated by social media.
For all the complex justifications and
questionable post-rationalizations that
are commonplace in branding case studies,
people often still judge primarily on
first impressions.

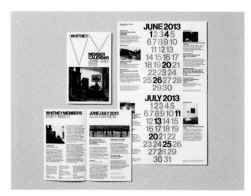

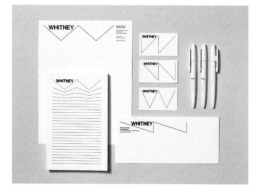

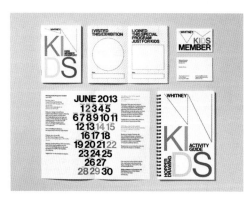

Above: Whitney Museum of American Art rebrand, initial design concept developed by Experimental Jetset, implemented by the Whitney's Design Department, 2015.

Opposite: London Centre for Book Arts visual identity, Studio Bergini, 2021.

Further Reading →

David Airey, *Identity Designed: The Definitive Guide to Visual Branding* (Rockport, 2019)

Catharine Slade-Brooking, *Creating a Brand Identity: A Guide for Designers* (Laurence King, 2016)

Michael Johnson, *Branding In Five and a Half Steps* (Thames & Hudson, 2016)

Packaging

The graphic design of packaging – materials for enclosing or protecting products for distribution, storage, sale and consumer use – is one of the most competitive areas of marketing. Companies usually compete with near-identical products in environments, such as the supermarket, where they must sit alongside their rivals, and where design is often a key factor in guiding buyer decisions. To this end, many different approaches have been taken, including: distinctive three-dimensional forms; eye-catching materials; clever designs that require a second look for the viewer to 'get' them; bright colours and consistent ranges which create a 'blocking' effect when on a shelf together; and large graphics that are clearer from farther away (something that has also proved helpful with the shift to online shopping). The addition of extra point of sale (POS) elements that attract consumers are also common, such as shelf ready packaging (SRP) boxes that contain individual units on the shelf and provide additional space for printed branding and marketing.

Packaging was once utilitarian, but became gradually more sophisticated in tandem with the rise of brand identities and the general growth of consumer culture. Where once a consumer would ask a shopkeeper behind a counter for a product, the development of self-service shelves and aisles gave consumers more choice and meant packaging design became more important. 'Stand out' is now a key consideration for packaging design, but a whole shelf of products standing out in the same way can be overwhelming for consumers, or lead to nothing being unique. Packaging design, particularly in products where there is much direct competition (such as in what is known as FMCG – fast-moving consumer goods), can feel like an arms race, with brands both copying and constantly striving to outdo each other. For designers working for big brands, the challenge can be not just finding something that is eye-catching yet clear and evocative of the product, but also working out a design that can be applied across a vast range of products and variants and for different global territories. The scope of work needed by huge global corporations means that packaging design is dominated by big agencies, often with offices in multiple countries. The stakes are incredibly high for big brands, and consequently they can be risk-averse and quick to change something that isn't performing well in the shops.

Most areas of packaging design – such as food and drink, household goods, toiletries or cosmetics – have developed codes and conventions, cues that help consumers to buy the right thing, or feel confident in the effectiveness or quality of what they are getting. Yet some of the best examples of packaging have been 'disruptive', often for what is called 'challenger brands' that can take more risks and be more distinctive in their efforts to shake up an established area dominated by more conservative rivals. Luxury is another area, across different products, that has its own particular signposts for consumers; often, a costlier product can be more minimal and elegant in its packaging design, alongside the use of better-quality materials. At the other end of the spectrum, budget brands tend

Top: Mast Night chocolate packaging, Astrid Stavro / Atlas, 2016.

Above Right: L'Atypique Cidre packaging, Counter Studio, 2010.

Above Left: Fountain of Youth coconut water packaging for Michelberger, Azar Kazimir, 2019.

Top: MIOK milk beer packaging, IBEA Design, 2022.

Right: Kadoya Kankitsu Juice packaging, Maru inc., 2022.

Above: Piccolo seed packaging, Here Design, 2018.

Opposite: Fountain CBD-infused sparkling water packaging, Pentagram, 2020.

Further Reading →
Gavin Ambrose & Paul
Harris, *Packaging the
Brand* (AVA, 2011)
www.thedieline.com
Julius Wiedemann,
*The Package Design
Book* (Taschen, 2021)

to keep design to the bare minimum, while
many shops will sell 'own-brand' products
designed to look similar to more expensive
branded goods.

Packaging, being one of the most
consumeristic areas of design, has
always had its detractors who see it
as selling out or generally low-brow
– relying on cheap tricks and lowest-
common-denominator approaches. Although
there are, of course, areas where the
pace of change or variety of packaging
is excessive, packaging can still be a
discipline where you find innovative,
sophisticated approaches to graphic
design, sometimes paired well with
corresponding three-dimensional forms.
There are, moreover, areas of packaging
design that are more about clarity
of information than seduction – for
instance 'over-the-counter' medicines.

Environmental issues are having a
large impact on contemporary packaging
design, with most companies looking to
reduce their amount of waste packaging
(particularly plastic), use more recycled
and recyclable material, and introduce
reusable and refillable packaging.

Wayfinding & Signage

An element of the wider field of environmental design – designs which exist in the physical space of the built environment – signage refers to designed items found in the world around us that give information. Although advertising can technically involve signs (e.g. billboards), as an area of graphic design, signage usually refers to contexts that are about information rather than persuasion. Signage usually provides instruction, direction, identification or warnings. There are widespread conventions, particularly in governmentally provided signage in contexts like roads. These might include specific colours and shapes (e.g. triangular for warnings and danger, circles for instructions, and rectangles for general information), or the use of pictograms (see page 146), which is encouraged in contexts where the audience is multilingual.

Wayfinding – a term popularized by American urban planner Kevin A. Lynch (1918–84) in his 1960 book *The Image of the City* – is defined by the Society for Experiential Graphic Design as 'information systems that guide people through a physical environment and enhance their understanding and experience of the space'.[17] Signage is a key part of the wayfinding process and, when used successfully, can help people to orient themselves and go in their desired direction. Signage, because of its primarily informational purpose, is an area of graphic design where functionality often trumps aesthetics. Usually, there are regulations about safety and accessibility that need to be followed, and extensive user testing to make sure that information reaches all potential users.

However, there are examples of signage that is more visually appealing or intriguing, for instance 'supergraphics' – large-scale pieces of graphic design that cover entire walls, buildings or floors. Some of the best examples of this field have been created by individuals such as Barbara Stauffacher Solomon (b. 1928), Morag Myerscough (b. 1963) and Lance Wyman (b. 1937), or have formed an element of an identity system applied in three-dimensional space. Signage is often a part of branding projects, particularly for clients who operate buildings, such as art centres or museums, or have extensive outdoor spaces. Exhibitions are another area where signage can be more creative, with a well-designed exhibition delivering a combination of text and objects, giving designers the chance to create a unique experience and a distinctive identity.

Above: Wayfinding and signage for The Barbican, London, designed by Cartlidge Levene and Studio Myerscough, 2007.

Infographics

Infographics, short for 'information graphics', is an umbrella term that covers many types of graphics produced to aid the visual display of information, such as data visualizations, graphs, charts, maps and diagrams. The goal of infographics is to make complex information (statistics, facts, figures) more accessible, understandable and visually engaging. Developed over centuries, the field of infographics had many unexpected pioneers, such as Scottish Enlightenment figure William Playfair (1759-1853), social reformer Florence Nightingale (1820-1910), famed for her work as a nurse in the Crimean War, American sociologist W.E.B. Du Bois (1868-1963) and Austrian philosopher Otto Neurath (1882-1945).

American professor Edward Tufte (b. 1942) has been a key figure in formalizing ideas around infographics, particularly in his 1983 book *The Visual Display of Quantitative Information*. Tufte, early in his influential book, wrote that 'excellence in statistical graphics consists of complex ideas, communicated with clarity, precision, and efficiency', adding that 'graphics *reveal* data. Indeed, graphics can be more precise and revealing than conventional statistical computations.'[18] When working with data, the infographic designer has a responsibility to be accurate: careless design (or malign intent) can result in visuals that confuse, manipulate or mislead. Politics is one area where infographics can be questionable, with parties, for example, using bar charts that make it seem like past elections were closer than the data shows. Most infographics rely on accurate representations of data to be effective, but there are cases where exactness is not the clearest method. Maps are one example: some of the most famous – such as Harry Beck's (1902-74) London Underground tube map (1931-3) – are topological, meaning they are simplified and not geographically accurate. Beck's approach, inspired by electrical circuits, was revolutionary and would soon be mimicked by almost all city transit diagrams, for instance Massimo Vignelli's (1931-2014) 1972 New York City Subway map.

In our social media age, where information is taken in more quickly and at smaller sizes than in the print-dominated past, infographics are vitally important. Though easily made on software like Excel and PowerPoint, infographics are hard to do well, especially in a visually pleasing way, so professionals are still needed. However, there is an argument that, if they become too aesthetically attractive, the information itself can become secondary or risks oversimplifying complex situations.

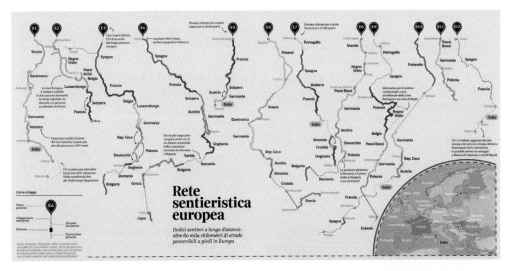

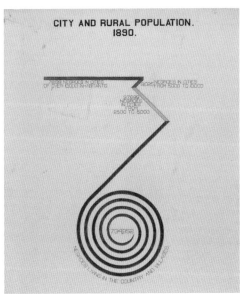

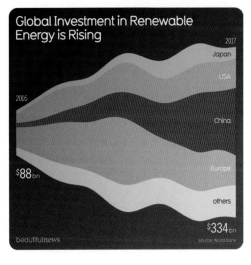

Top: Infographic for *La Lettura, Corriere della Sera*, Tiziana Alocci, 2020.

Above Right: Infographic for *beautifulnews*, Information is Beautiful, 2020.

Above Left: Infographic 'prepared by Du Bois for the Negro Exhibit of the American Section at the Paris Exposition Universelle in 1900', W.E.B. Du Bois.

Further Reading →

Sandra Rendgen & Julius Wiedemann, *History of Information Graphics* (Taschen, 2021)

Edward R. Tufte, *The Visual Display of Quantitative Information* (Graphics Press, 2001)

Motion Graphics

The vast majority of graphic design has historically been static – unchanging due to the finality of print. However, motion graphics, which are durational and incorporate movement, are rapidly expanding, with agencies keen to hire designers fluent in animation. Digital technology has been a major factor in the growth of kinetic design, with screens increasingly replacing print in the public sphere. What distinguishes motion graphics as an area of design from traditional moving-image disciplines like film-making and animation is usually a question of intent, context and the components used (e.g. typography), but the boundaries are blurrier than ever.

Many early experimental animation techniques – pioneered by Oskar Fischinger (1900-67), Norman McLaren (1914-87) and Len Lye (1901-80) – used abstraction in a graphical way. Simple shapes were easier to capture in movement but their films were akin to works of art, not design. It was in film where the first truly moving pieces of graphic design emerged, especially in opening titles and credits. Figures like Saul Bass, Pablo Ferro (1935-2018) and Maurice Binder (1918-91) designed innovative sequences in the fifties and sixties that combined typography with moving images and animation. Film titles, and their small-screen television cousins, remain some of the most prominent examples of motion graphics. In early motion graphics, it was difficult to animate the actual graphic elements; the BBC's first ident (a short film identifying the channel between programmes), created by Abram Games (1914-96) and debuted in 1953, was a kinetic 3D model captured on film, making it more of a sculpture than a traditional piece of graphic design. Digital software like Macromedia Flash (1996), Adobe After Effects and Cinema 4D would finally give designers the power to animate their work without the need for a film camera.

Attempting to create dynamism was often a primary concern for designers of static graphics, but with motion graphics this became a reality, unlocking new considerations such as rhythm, pacing, transitions, duration, looping, and – perhaps most importantly – interaction with sound and music. Considering how a logo or identity elements will work in motion is often now a key motivation in branding projects. Web design and digital spaces where interaction is possible are particularly dominated by motion graphics (often these can be subtle), while augmented reality (AR) is providing a new frontier in which kinetic design will play a major part, something the likes of New York City-based studio DIA are exploring.

Above: Posters from a series of analogue typographic films promoting the release of Klim Type Foundry's Söhne typeface family, DIA Studio, 2019.

Below: 'Cities in Motion' electronic billboards for Exterion Media, Studio Dumbar / DEPT, 2019.

Further Reading →

Wang Shaoqiang, *Motion Graphics - 100 Design Projects You Can't Miss* (Promopress, 2017)

Wang Shaoqiang, *Typography for Screen: Type in Motion* (Hoaki, 2021)

Austin Shaw, *Design for Motion: Fundamentals and Techniques of Motion Design* (Routledge, 2019)

Websites

The World Wide Web, released in 1990 following Tim Berners-Lee's invention of the Hypertext Transfer Protocol (HTTP), was the first browser capable of opening web pages written in Hypertext Markup Language (HTML; an early, simple type of coding) and ushered in the website as a new medium for the transfer of information – changing the world forever.

Early websites – limited to basic code, default typefaces and the capabilities of low-resolution CRT monitors – were a utilitarian affair, with design options severely limited. Images, once they were supported, were very slow to load over dial-up systems that ran through telephone lines, and their positions within text could barely be altered. For the nascent field of web design, the mid-nineties development of new programming languages such as JavaScript and Cascading Style Sheets (CSS) gave designers a little more freedom over stylistic choices. But web pages remained relatively unsophisticated, often just plain text and images over a wallpaper-like background. Macromedia's Flash software, although it required website users to install a plugin, would dominate web design around the turn of the millennium. The software allowed designers to create webpages that they had much more control over and which could incorporate animations and music. Flash sites were usually slow to load, and their unique designs often made them hard for unfamiliar users to navigate.

Flash, as well as sites such as GeoCities that allowed average users to create their own webpages, encouraged experimentation, and site designs were often more about what was possible, rather than what looked good. The aesthetic of the early internet was somewhat unrestrained and chaotic, often involving clashing patterns and looping animated GIFs. Some of the earliest HTML site-building software can be described as WYSIWYG (what you see is what you get), whereby the design interface accurately reflects the appearance of the finished site, rather than relying on users to code manually to see how something will look when live. Software would eventually evolve into the even more user-friendly 'drag and drop' site-builders.

As technology improved and the number of internet users grew, what became known as Web 2.0 was developed. This was faster, more dynamic and more interactive, with greater emphasis on user-generated content, social networks and commerce. The internet during the 2000s became much more integrated into people's lives, rather than something to be looked at occasionally. Subsequently, web design became less about gimmicks and experiments and began to focus more on usability, information architecture and slicker techniques. This trend was accelerated by the rapid expansion of mobile browsing. On these smaller screens, websites had to be lightweight and simpler, leading to a more minimalist aesthetic. Websites were increasingly responsive; they responded to the user's environment, be it screen size, window size, screen orientation or platform.

By the early 2010s web fonts were giving designers more choice over typography on the web, rather than being

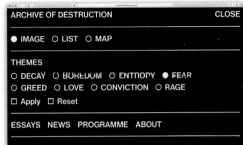

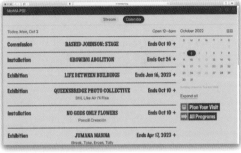

Above: Archive of Destruction website (www.archiveofdestruction.com) for Jes Fernie, design by Daly & Lyon, built by Matthew Luke, 2021.

Centre: MoMA PS1 website (www.momaps1.org), 2022. Website designed and developed by Linked by Air; visual identity developed by a Design Working Group, including Vance Wellenstein, Dante Carlos, Anna Kulachek, Other Means and Julia Schäfer, with advisors Nontsikelelo Mutiti and John Lee; type design by Berton Hasebe.

Below: Identity and website design for Metamorphoses (www.metamorphosesobjects.com), design by A Practice for Everyday Life, website development by Kieran Startup, 2022.

limited to what the user had installed on their device. One trend found around the same time in web design, and digital products more generally, was a backlash against skeuomorphism (digital design features that imitate their real-world counterparts - e.g. highlights and shadows to make buttons look three-dimensional) towards 'flat design' that was more minimalistic, using flat colours rather than textures and eschewing unnecessary ornament.

Emphasis on usability and speed has continued to grow in contemporary web design, particularly as mobile devices have become the dominant source of traffic to sites. Often, designers will take a mobile-first approach, ensuring that sites look best on smaller, portrait-orientated screens. As speeds on smartphones have improved thanks to 4G/5G networks, images have become more important again, with new file formats also resulting in faster loading times without loss of quality. Web design, perhaps more than any other area of graphic design, has been hamstrung by technical limitations, but nowadays almost anything is possible. Today, many graphic designers working across various disciplines have a working knowledge of coding, but bringing a bespoke (rather than a templated) website design to fruition, particularly a complex one with many pages, often requires the expertise of a professional programmer or backend developer, particularly as the technologies and programming languages are constantly evolving.

Above: Website for Trevor Jackson (www.trevor-jackson.com), design and development by All Purpose Studio, 2018.

Opposite Top + Centre: Website design for Sternberg Press (www.sternberg-press.com), design by Wkshps and Knoth & Renner, 2020.

Opposite Below: *Power: Infrastructure in America* project website for Columbia University's Temple Hoyne Buell Center for the Study of American Architecture (power.buellcenter.columbia.edu), design and development by Partner & Partners, 2019.

UI / UX Design

'Let me argue that the actual dawn of user interface design first happened when computer designers finally noticed, not just that end users had functioning minds, but that a better understanding of how those minds worked would completely shift the paradigm of interaction.'
Alan Kay, 'User Interface: A Personal View' (1989) [19]

User experience (UX) and user interface (UI) are two of the newest and fastest-growing areas of contemporary graphics (many new designers will likely never work in print media); they are also some of the most concerned with prototyping, iterative developments, user-testing, interactivity, research and psychology. UX and UI are an element of the trend towards what has been called 'user-centred design'. This is a key aspect of the broader (though somewhat vague) area of 'design thinking', which is defined by Tim Brown (b. 1962) – CEO of IDEO, one of its leading proponents – as 'a human-centred approach to innovation that draws from the designer's toolkit to integrate the needs of people, the possibilities of technology, and the requirements for business success'.[20]

While some graphic design can be said to be oriented towards a viewer or audience, rather than a 'user' per se, there are plenty of pre-digital examples of graphic design creating a user interface – the book, for instance, has evolved over centuries to become the ideal way of delivering printed text to readers. UI as a field, however, is concerned with the creation of the interfaces of digital products or services for end users and consumers to interact with. Although there are now cases where such interfaces are non-visual (e.g. ones controlled by voice or gesture), the majority of a UI designer's work will be on graphical user interfaces (GUIs), a term coined in the early 1980s that first gained prominence after the release in 1984 of the Apple Macintosh, with its iconic blocky, greyscale GUI designed by Susan Kare (b. 1954). GUI design involves static elements, such as text and images, and active elements – the interactive parts such as buttons, sidebars, forms, drop-down menus, checkboxes and controls. According to Adobe, the essential properties of a well-designed UI are: 'Clarity, Familiarity, Consistency, Forgivingness and Efficiency'.[21] The mainstays of UI design have been

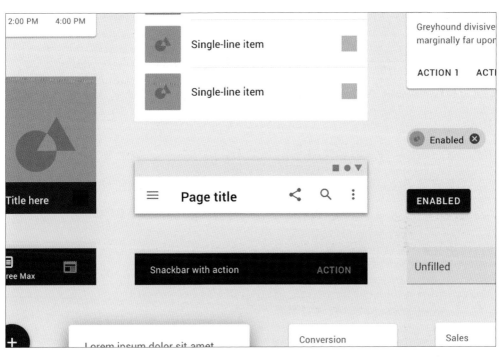

2:00 PM   4:00 PM

Single-line item

Single-line item

Greyhound divisive
marginally far upor

ACTION 1   ACTI

Enabled ✕

Title here

☰   **Page title**   <   🔍   ⋮

ENABLED

ree Max

Snackbar with action   ACTION

Unfilled

＋

Lorem ipsum dolor sit amet

Conversion

Sales

900 800 700 600 500 400 300 200 100 50

Primary
Purple

500   #6200EE

700   #3700B3

Secondary
Teal

200   #03DAC5

≡ Analytics   🔍 ⋮

Marketing
123.4 M

Conversion
537
+22% of target

Conversion
432.1M
+12.3% of target

Sales
345.8 M
+11% of target

Users
45.5 M

Avg. session
4:53 H
+56.6% of target

Sessions
23,242

Bounce rate
12%   ＋

Pageviews

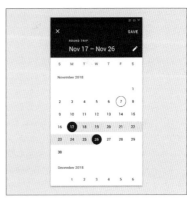

✕   SAVE

ROUND TRIP:
Nov 17 – Nov 26   ✎

S   M   T   W   T   F   S

November 2018

1

2   3   4   5   6   7   8

9   10   11   12   13   14   15

16   17   18   19   20   21   22

23   24   25   26   27   28   29

30

December 2018

1   2   3   4   5   6

This Page: Google's Material
Design 2 system, 2018

websites, apps and software, but with screens becoming increasingly more common everywhere – for instance, in cars, on watches or 'smart' home appliances – the need for UI designers, and for the clear, usable GUIs they can create, has grown exponentially.

Although often conflated, or combined into the dual role of the UI/UX designer, UI is only one aspect of user experience design. First coined by Don Norman (b. 1935) – author of the influential book *The Design of Everyday Things* (1988; revised 2013) – user experience refers to a broader field that considers all stages of the user journey, not just their final interactions with interfaces. Norman defined UX as encompassing 'all aspects of the end-user's interaction with the company, its services, and its products', adding that, 'It's important to distinguish the total user experience from the user interface (UI), even though the UI is obviously an extremely important part of the design. As an example, consider a website with movie reviews. Even if the UI for finding a film is perfect, the UX will be poor for a user who wants information about a small independent release if the underlying database only contains movies from the major studios.'[22]

Generally speaking, UI design is more detail-oriented and concerned with nitty-gritty decisions about individual features and functions, while UX design is more strategically minded, thinking about the bigger picture and requiring wider skills in strategy, research and information architecture. Scott Jenson (b. 1954), a former product strategist at Google, sees UI as 'focusing on the product, a series of snapshots in time' but UX as focused on 'the user and their journey through the product'. He adds: 'The UX is the path through a product, escaping the screen and articulating the user's journey and motivations, justifying why things are in the UI and even more importantly, why things are left out. The UI copes with constraints; the UX challenges them.'[23] Although it is important to understand the difference between UX and UI, the two are inseparable.

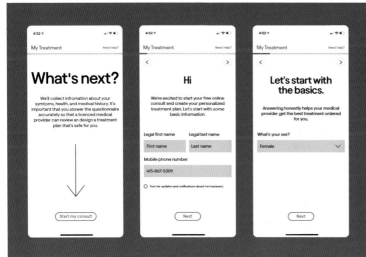

Above: iO Academy coding school identity, Fiasco Design, 2020.

Below: Evernow identity design, Natasha Jen / Pentagram, 2022.

Further Reading →

Bill Moggridge, *Designing Interactions* (MIT Press, 2006)

Don Norman, *The Design of Everyday Things* (MIT Press, 2013)

Social Media

Social media has had an enormous impact on graphic design, particularly as visually dominated platforms such as Instagram and TikTok have begun to dominate, especially among younger users. Research has consistently shown that engagement rates are higher for posts that include images rather than just text, although on social networks a quality design is no guarantee of success. Algorithms often decide what gets seen, and many platforms have begun to prioritize videos over static imagery.

Primarily viewed on small screens amid an endless scroll of competing material, graphic design for social media usually has to strive to be eye-catching through the use of bright colours, simple illustrations (e.g. emojis), saturated photography and fast-moving elements. Copy is usually made as snappy as possible, with large typography often the most effective way to get a message across. The challenge of creating designs that work across the various platforms and their different size requirements can be time-consuming for designers, whose work in this field is becoming increasingly obsolete thanks to free software and websites like Canva which provide templates that anyone can use for professional-looking designs. Yet such tools often lead to uniformity, and something bespoke stands out more. Whether they realize it or not, many users sharing content on social media platforms will be creating graphic design, through their combination of text and image.

Most social media networks are designed to encourage short attention spans, and graphic design is just another part of the creation of 'content' that is quickly consumed by users, and often barely registered. This is particularly true for the invasive advertisements that punctuate the posts that people have actively subscribed to see.

Graphic design itself, as an area of creativity and practice, has become widely popular on social media, introducing a new generation to the field, while also making trend cycles faster and hugely driving up the volume and variety of work that designers are exposed to. One negative of this has been the conflation of popularity, quantified through 'likes' or reshares, with quality and effectiveness.

Above: Branding for Stompy wine subscription service, & Walsh, 2022.

Opposite Above: Branding for Manuvo, Marina Willer / Pentagram, 2021.

Opposite Below: Twitch rebrand, Collins, 2019.

Further Reading →
INSTA-PERFECT: Creative Photography For Social Media Today (Victionary, 2018)

Sources

Introduction

1 https://designobserver.com/feature/thoughts-on-paul-rand/39426
2 Tibor Kalman, J. Abbott Miller and Karrie Jacobs, 'Good History/Bad History', *Print*, Vol. 47, No. 2 (March/April 1991).
3 Steven Heller (ed.), *The Education of a Graphic Designer* (Allworth Press, 2015), 375.
4 David Reinfurt, *A *New* Program for Graphic Design* (Inventory Press, 2019), 16.
5 Sigfried Giedion, *Space, Time and Architecture: The Growth of a New Tradition* (Harvard University Press, 1959), 5.
6 Paul Rand, 'Confusion and Chaos: The Seduction of Contemporary Graphic Design', *AIGA Journal*, Vol. 10, No. 1 (1992).

Chapter One: History

1 William Addison Dwiggins, 'New Kind of Printing Calls for New Design', *Boston Evening Transcript*, 29 August 1922.
2 www.etymonline.com/word/design#etymonline_v_46757
3 Rob Roy Kelly, 'The Early Years of Graphic Design at Yale University', *Design Issues*, Vol. 17, No. 3 (Summer 2001), 7.
4 Sara De Bondt and Catherine de Smet (eds), *Graphic Design: History in the Writing, 1983–2011* (Occasional Papers, 2012), 7.
5 Ulrich Conrads (ed.), *Programs and Manifestoes on 20th-Century Architecture* (MIT Press, 1971), 66.
6 Caitlin Condell and Emily Orr, *McKnight Kauffer: The Artist in Advertising* (Rizzoli Electa, 2020)
7 Filippo Tommaso Marinetti, *Manifesto of Futurism*, 1909.
8 Ezra Pound, 'Vortex', *BLAST*, June 1914.
9 Marinetti 1909.
10 https://designmanifestos.org/kazimir-malevich-the-manifesto-of-suprematism/
11 *LEF*, Issue 1 (1923).
12 https://bauhausmanifesto.com/
13 www.moma.org/documents/moma_catalogue_2735_300190238.pdf
14 *bauhaus journal*, 1 (1926).
15 Helen Armstrong (ed.), *Graphic Design Theory* (Princeton Architectural Press, 2009), 35.
16 Ibid.
17 *House Beautiful*, Vol. 97 (1955), 37.
18 Steven Heller, *The Graphic Design Reader* (Allworth Press, 2002), 172.
19 Holland R. Melson Jr. (ed.), *The Collected Writings of Alvin Lustig* (1958), 43–4.
20 Bob Levenson, *Bill Bernbach's Book* (Villard, 1987).
21 Theodore Roszak, *The Making of a Counter Culture* (Doubleday, 1969).
22 *Texts and Posters by Atelier Populaire* (Bombs-Merrill, 1969).
23 www.tate.org.uk/art/art-terms/p/postmodernism
24 Robert Venturi and Martino Stierli, *Complexity and Contradiction in Architecture* (MoMA, 1977).
25 Rick Poynor, *No More Rules: Graphic Design and Postmodernism* (Laurence King, 2003), 12.
26 https://walkerart.org/magazine/clearing-the-haze-prologue-to-postmodern-graphic-design-education-through-sheila-de-bretteville-2
27 Rand 1992.
28 www.emigre.com/Essays/Magazine/GraphicDesigninthePostmodernEra
29 www.eyemagazine.com/feature/article/katherine-mccoy
30 www.eyemagazine.com/feature/article/cult-of-the-ugly
31 www.emigre.com/Essays/Magazine/GraphicDesigninthePostmodernEra
32 Helen Armstrong (ed.), *Digital Design Theory* (Princeton Architectural Press, 2016), 61.
33 Rand 1992.
34 Armstrong 2016, 64.
35 https://historyofinformation.com/detail.php?entryid=3721
36 https://walkerart.org/magazine/muriel-cooper-turning-time-into-space
37 De Bondt and de Smet 2012, 37–44.
38 Ibid.

Chapter Two: Theory

1 Roland Barthes, *Mythologies* (Hill & Wang, 1972), 10–11.
2 www.vam.ac.uk/articles/an-introduction-to-the-aesthetic-movement
3 https://psychclassics.yorku.ca/Wertheimer/Forms/forms.htm
4 Johannes Itten, *The Elements of Colour* (John Wiley & Sons, 1970).
5 Johannes Itten, *The Art of Colour* (Van Nostrand Reinhold Inc, 1961).
6 Josef Albers, *Interaction of Color* (Yale Universty Press, 1963).
7 Conrads 1971, 20.
8 Denise Gonzales Crisp, 'Toward a Definition of the DecoRational', in Brenda Laurel (ed.), *Design Research: Methods and Perspectives* (MIT Press, 2003), 99.
9 https://linedandunlined.com/archive/default-systems-in-graphic-design/
10 www.merriam-webster.com/dictionary/vernacular
11 *Print* (Jan/Feb 1990).
12 Edward Bernays, *Propaganda* (Horace Liveright, 1928), 9–10.
13 Norman Potter, *What is a Designer?*, 4th edn (Hyphen Press, 2002).
14 Victor Papanek, *Design for the Real World* (Bantam Books, 1973), 14.
15 Susan Sontag, 'Posters, Advertisement, Art, Artefact, Commodity', *The Art of Revolution: 96 Posters From Cuba* (McGraw Hill, 1970).
16 Jean-François Lyotard, *Postmodern Fables* (UM Press, 1999), 40.
17 Armstrong 2009, 102.
18 Lucienne Roberts, *Good: An Introduction to Ethics in Graphic Design* (AVA, 2006), 28.
19 www.eyemagazine.com/feature/article/first-things-first-manifesto-2000
20 Elizabeth Resnick, *Developing Citizen Designers* (Bloomsbury, 2021), 12.
21 De Bondt and de Smet 2012, 139.
22 http://letterformarchive.org/news/view/the-black-experience-in-graphic-design-1968-and-2020
23 Ibid.
24 Ellen Lupton et al., *Extra Bold: A Feminist, Inclusive, Anti-racist, Nonbinary Field Guide for Graphic Designers* (Princeton Architectural Press, 2021), 109.
25 www.nypl.org/blog/2013/11/22/silence-equals-death-poster
26 www.britannica.com/story/what-is-cultural-appropriation
27 www.designweek.co.uk/issues/9-15-march-2020/cultural-appropriation-in-design/
28 Lupton et al. 2021, 197.
29 https://linedandunlined.com/archive/new-black-face/
30 Bruno Munari, *Design as Art* (Penguin, 1971), 12–13.
31 Roland Barthes, *Image, Music, Text* (Fontana, 1977), 146.
32 Beatrice Warde, *The Crystal Goblet: Sixteen Essays on Typography* (Sylvan Press, 1955), 13.

[33] Marshall McLuhan and Quentin Fiore, *The Medium is the Massage* (Penguin, 1967), 26.
[34] www.eyemagazine.com/feature/article/the-designer-as-author
[35] https://2x4.org/ideas/2009/fuck-content/

Chapter Three: Practice
[1] Josef Müller-Brockmann, *Grid Systems in Graphic Design* (Niggli, 1981), 10.
[2] Armstrong 2009, 87.
[3] *Looking Closer 5: Critical Writings on Graphic Design* (Allworth Press, 2006), 115
[4] Mark Foster Gage (ed.), *Aesthetic Theory: Essential Texts for Architecture and Design* (W. W. Norton, 2011), 229.
[5] *Graphis* 276 (November/December, 1991) p.99
[6] www.designboom.com/interviews/designboom-interview-stefan-sagmeister-2/
[7] https://theaoi.com/2016/09/22/the-varoom-report-style-v26/
[8] www.creativereview.co.uk/bob-gill-design-illustration/
[9] Josef Müller-Brockmann, *The Graphic Artist and His Design Problems* (Niggli, 1968), 7.
[10] Papanek 1973, 68.
[11] *Communication Arts*, 6 (1964), 55.
[12] Paul Rand, *A Designer's Art* (Yale University Press, 1968).
[13] Rudolf Arnheim, *Visual Thinking* (University of California Press, 1969), 64.
[14] Rand 1968, 79.
[15] Susan Doyle, Jaleen Grove and Whitney Sherman (eds), *History of Illustration* (Fairchild Books, 2018), 40.
[16] Lucienne Roberts, *Drip-dry Shirts: The Evolution of the Graphic Designer* (AVA, 2005), 42.
[17] Bob Gill and John Lewis, *Illustration: Aspects and directions* (Studio Vista, 1964), 95.
[18] https://t-y-p-o-g-r-a-p-h-y.org/media/pdf/The-New-Typography.pdf
[19] Ken Garland, *Graphics Handbook* (Studio Vista, 1966), 25.
[20] https://www.dandad.org/en/d-ad-become-art-director-new-blood-advice/
[21] Steven Heller and Veronique Vienne (eds), *The Education of an Art Director* (Allworth Press, 2006), ix.

[22] www.oed.com
[23] Wassily Kandinsky, *Concerning the Spiritual in Art* (1910).
[24] *The Universal Design File* (NC State University, The Center for Universal Design, 1998), 4.
[25] Ibid.
[26] Adrian Shaughnessy, *Ken Garland: Structure and Substance* (Unit Editions, 2012), 39.
[27] Papanek 1973, 241.
[28] Philip Thompson and Peter Davenport, *The Dictionary of Graphic Images* (St. Martin's Press, 1980), v.
[29] Ibid., vii.
[30] *A Dictionary of Modern and Contemporary Art* (Oxford University Press, 2009)
[31] Fredric Jameson, *The Cultural Turn: 1983-1998* (Verso, 1998), 7.
[32] www.moma.org/documents/moma_catalogue_2914_300190234.pdf
[33] Armstrong 2009, 33.

Chapter Four: Typography
[1] Emil Ruder, *Typography: A Manual of Design* (Verlag Niggli, 1967), 10
[2] Jan Tschichold, *The New Typography: A Handbook for Modern Designers* (University of California Press, 1998), 73-4.
[3] Walter Tracy, *Letters of Credit: A View of Type Design* (David R. Godine, 2003), 14.
[4] Ibid.
[5] https://eyeondesign.aiga.org/ming-romantic-a-complete-reimagining-of-chinese-type/
[6] www.forum-online.be/en/issues/winter-2022/multi-scripts-blended-type-family-stories
[7] David Crowley 'Out of Hand', *Eye*, 80 (Summer 2011), 65.
[8] www.colorfonts.wtf/
[9] www.paulrand.design/work/NeXT-Computers.html
[10] Armstrong 2009, 41.

Chapter Five: Mediums
[1] Sontag 1970.
[2] W. H. Allner (ed.), *Posters* (Reinhold, 1952), 5.
[3] *Images of an Era: The American Poster 1945-75* (Smithsonian, 1975), 10.
[4] www.eyemagazine.com/feature/article/advertising-mother-of-graphic-design-extract
[5] Richard Hollis, *Writings about Graphic Design* (Occasional Papers, 2017), 29.

[6] Edward M Gottschall (ed.), *Typographic Directions* (Art Directions Books Co., 1964), 199.
[7] Adrian Shaughnessy, *Graphic Design: A User's Manual* (Laurence King, 2009) 186.
[8] Ellen McCracken, *Decoding Women's Magazines* (Macmillan, 1993), 10.
[9] Jennifer McKnight-Trontz and Alex Steinweiss, *For the Record: The Life and Work of Alex Steinweiss* (Princeton Architectural Press, 2000), 139.
[10] Walter Herdeg (ed.), *Graphis Record Covers* (The Graphis Press, 1974), 8-9.
[11] Rand 1968, 238.
[12] https://qz.com/200959/the-sacred-texts-of-corporate-graphic-design
[13] Wally Olins, *The Corporate Personality: An Inquiry Into the Nature of Corporate Identity* (Design Council, 1978), 157.
[14] Stuart Hall 'Brave New World', *Marxism Today*, October 1988.
[15] www.eyemagazine.com/feature/article/the-steamroller-of-branding-text-in-full
[16] Shaughnessy 2009, 44.
[17] https://segd.org/what-wayfinding
[18] Edward Tufte, *The Visual Display of Quantitative Information* (Graphics Press, 2001), 13.
[19] Randall Packer and Ken Jordan (eds), *Multimedia* (W. W. Norton & Co., 2002), 121.
[20] https://designthinking.ideo.com/
[21] https://xd.adobe.com/ideas/process/u
[22] www.nngroup.com/articles/definition-user-experience/
[23] www.usertesting.com/resources/topics/ui-vs-ux

Bibliography

Many books are mentioned in the sections they relate to, or are quoted from and listed on the previous pages. What follows are some further suggestions of useful books on graphic design and typography:

Sean Adams, *The Designer's Dictionary of Type* (Abrams, 2019)

Gavin Ambrose and Paul Harris, *Typography: Basics Design* (Bloomsbury, 2016)

Gavin Ambrose, Paul Harris and Nigel Ball, *The Fundamentals of Graphic Design* (Bloomsbury, 2019)

Helen Armstrong (ed.) *Graphic Design Theory: Readings from the Field* (Princeton Architectural Press, 2009)

Russell Bestley and Ian Noble, *Visual Research* (Bloomsbury, 2018)

Michael Bierut, *79 Short Essays on Design* (Princeton Architectural Press, 2012)

Michael Bierut and Jessica Helfand (eds), *Culture is Not Always Popular: Fifteen Years of Design Observer* (MIT Press 2019)

John R. Biggs, *An Approach to Type* (Blandford, 1961)

Robert Bringhurst, *The Elements of Typographic Style* (Hartley & Marks, 2004)

Hazel Conway (ed.), *Design History: A Students' Handbook* (Routledge, 1987)

David Crowley and Paul Jobling, *Graphic Design: A Critical Introduction: Reproduction and Representation since 1800* (Manchester University Press, 1996)

David Dabner, Sandra Stewart and Abbie Vickress, *Graphic Design School: The Principles and Practice of Graphic Design* (Wiley, 2020)

Meredith Davis, *Graphic Design Theory* (Thames & Hudson, 2012)

Peter Dawson, *Type Directory* (Thames & Hudson, 2019)

Sara De Bondt and Catherine de Smet (eds), *Graphic Design: History in the Writing 1983-2011* (Occasional Papers, 2012)

Johanna Drucker and Emily McVarish, *Graphic Design History: A Critical Guide* (Pearson, 2012)

Stephen J. Eskilson, *Graphic Design: A History* (Laurence King, 2019)

Ken Garland, *Graphics Handbook* (Studio Vista, 1966)

Steven Heller, *Design Literacy: Understanding Graphic Design* (Allworth Press, 2014)

Steven Heller (ed.), *The Education of a Graphic Designer* (Allworth Press, 2015)

Steven Heller and Gail Anderson, *The Typography Idea Book* (Laurence King, 2016)

Steven Heller and Veronique Vienne, *100 Ideas That Changed Graphic Design* (Laurence King, 2019)

Richard Hollis, *Graphic Design: A Concise History* (Thames & Hudson, 2001)

Michael Horsham, *Hello Human: A History of Visual Communication* (Thames & Hudson, 2022)

David Jury, *What is Typography?* (Rotovision, 2006)

Robin Kinross, *Modern Typography* (B42, 2019)

Robin Kinross, *Unjustified Texts* (B42, 2019)

Paul Luna, *Typography: A Very Short Introduction* (Oxford, 2018)

Ellen Lupton, *Design is Storytelling* (Cooper Hewitt, 2017)

Ellen Lupton and J. Abbott Miller, *Design Writing Research* (Princeton Architectural Press, 1996)

Ellen Lupton and Jennifer Cole Phillips, *Graphic Design: The New Basics* (Princeton Architectural Press, 2015)

Jens Müller and Julius Wiedemann, *The History of Graphic Design Vol. 1. 1890-1959* (Taschen, 2016)

Jens Müller and Julius Wiedemann, *The History of Graphic Design Vol. 2. 1960–Today* (Taschen, 2022)

Josef Müller-Brockmann, *A History of Visual Communication* (Niggli Verlag, 1999)

Titus Nemeth (ed.), *Arabic Typography* (Verlag Niggli, 2022)

Quentin Newark, *What is Graphic Design?* (Rotovision, 2007)

Oscar Ogg, *The Twenty-six Letters* (Crowell, 1971)

Craig Oldham, *Oh Sh*t What Now?: Honest Advice for New Graphic Designers* (Laurence King, 2018)

Richard Poulin, *The Language of Graphic Design* (Rockport, 2018)

David Reinfurt, *A *New* Program for Graphic Design* (Inventory Press, 2019)

Caroline Roberts, *Graphic Design Visionaries* (Laurence King, 2015)

Adrian Shaughnessy, *Graphic Design: A User's Manual* (Laurence King, 2009)

Adrian Shaughnessy, *How to be a Graphic Designer without Losing Your Soul* (Laurence King, 2010)

Erik Spiekermann and E.M Ginger, *Stop Stealing Sheep & Find Out How Type Works* (Adobe, 2003)

Deyan Sudjic, *B is for Bauhaus* (Penguin, 2015)

Alice Twemlow, *What is Graphic Design For?* (Rotovision, 2007)

Armin Vit and Bryony Gomez Palacio, *Graphic Design, Referenced* (Rockport, 2009)

Alina Wheeler, *Designing Brand Identity* (Wiley, 2017

Judith Williamson, *Decoding Advertisements: Ideology and Meaning in Advertising* (Marion Boyars, 2010)

Index

Picture Credits

Ilex Press would like to thank all the designers, their representatives, and agencies for their help in providing images for publication in this book.

6a Boston Public Library. Digital Commonwealth, Massachusetts Collections; 6b, 9bl & br, 10 Library of Congress, Prints and Photographs Division, Washington; 9al & ar The New York Public Library, Digital Collections; 12 TTWKennington, CC BY-SA 4.0, via Wikimedia; 13 Anja Kaiser; 14 Photo12/Alamy; 17 Matt Lamont, Design Reviewed; 19al The Metropolitan Museum of Art, New York, Harris Brisbane Dick Fund, 1932; 19bl Rijksmuseum, Amsterdam; 19br Smithsonian Institution. Museum purchase through gift of Mrs. Gilbert W. Chapman and Ely Jacques Kahn; 21a, 21br Library of Congress, Prints and Photographs Division; 21bl The New York Public Library, Digital Collections. © & TM. MOURON - AM.CASSANDRE. Lic 2023-02-15-02 www.cassandre.fr; 22l The Picture Art Collection/Alamy Stock Photo; 22r, 24r The New York Public Library, Digital Collections, 23l © ADAGP, Paris and DACS, London 2023; 24l Everett Collection/Alamy Stock Photo; 27, 28al & br Letterform Archive © DACS 2023; 28ar Universal Art Archive/Alamy Stock Photo; 31al & ar Letterform Archive; 31bl Swim Ink 2, LLC/Corbis via Getty Images © DACS 2023; 32 Museum für Gestaltung Zürich, Graphics Collection, ZHdK; 35b Courtesy Kenji Fujita © Columbia Records, 1959; 37al & ar Design © Estate of Elaine Lustig Cohen; 39, 41b Museum für Gestaltung Zürich, Poster Collection, ZHdK, 40 © DACS 2023, 41a © Estate Karl Gerstner, courtesy Galerie Knoell; 43al Bart Solenthaler/Flickr; 43ar, 47al, 51br, 54ar & br, 57r Library of Congress, Prints and Photographs Division; 45 Courtesy of the family of Alan Fletcher and permission of Pirelli & C. SpA; 47ar permission of Pirelli & C. SpA; 47bl Standards Manual; 49al Courtesy of the RIT Cary Graphic Arts Collection; 49ar Matt Lamont, Design Reviewed; 49bl © Westminster Recording Corporation, 1960; 51al Courtesy Geoff & Olwen Stocker; 51ar The New York Public Library, Digital Collections; 51bl Collection of the Smithsonian National Museum of African American History and Culture; 52r McMaster University Libraries, Digital Collections; 54al Courtesy of Milton Glaser Inc. © Milton Glaser. All Rights Reserved; 54bl © Seymour Chwast; 57l, 65 Courtesy April Greiman; 58l © Barney Bubbles Estate; 58r Courtesy Brody Associates; Matt Lamont, Design Reviewed; 59r, 61, 59l permission courtesy Pentagram, 60 used with permission; 62l, 66l Courtesy Émigré; 62r © Barnbrook; 69a Letterform Archive; 69b Courtesy Occasional Papers; 70 Courtesy of California Institute of the Arts Institute Archives; 75al © Paladin, 1973; 75ar Courtesy of Milton Glaser Inc. © Milton Glaser. All Rights Reserved; 77a © Camille Walala for The LEGO Group. Photo: Tekla Evelina Severin; 77b Courtesy Wade & Leta; 80 © The Josef and Anni Albers Foundation/DACS 2023; 81l © Malika Favre; 81r Courtesy A Practice for Everyday Life; 83 Courtesy James Goggin, Practise; 87b Dan-yell (CC by-SA 3.0)/Wikipedia; 89al © United Airlines; 89bl © Deutsche Bank; 89br © SBB CFF FFS; 91al Courtesy Marian Bantjes; 91ar Courtesy COLLINS; 91bl Courtesy Studio Feixen; 91br Courtesy &Walsh; 93al Courtesy Mevis & Van Deursen; 93ar & b Courtesy Gretel; 94b Art Direction: Yani Arabena, Guille Vizzari (YaniGuille&Co.). Design: Yani Arabena, Guille Vizzari, Agustín Pizarro Maire. Illustration: Guille Vizzari, Agustín Pizarro Maire. Production: Planner Group. Photo: YaniGuille&Co.; 96 Courtesy Noah Baker Studio; 97 Courtesy Shiva Nallaperumal; 95 Made at FISK; 99, 100, 101al & br Library of Congress, Prints and Photographs Division; 101ar U.S. National Archives; 103al Courtesy Michael Oswell; 103ar The Museum of Modern Art, New York/Scala, Florence; 103bl Courtesy Other Forms; 104 © Barnbrook; 105 Courtesy Dionne Pajarillaga; 107a Unit Editions. Courtesy the Estate of Ken Garland; 107b Anthony Burrill; 109al The State and Sexist Advertising Cause Illness - Don't Let These Men Invade Your Homes (1974) © See Red Women's Workshop; 109bl Library of Congress, Prints and Photographs Division, 109ar © Faith Ringgold/ARS, NY and DACS, London, Courtesy ACA Galleries, New York 2023, 113bl © Emory Douglas/DACS 2023; 110a & b © Guerrilla Girls, courtesy guerrillagirls.com; 111a Shaz Madani Studio; 111bl Courtesy Chloe Scheffe © Verso, 2018; 111br Courtesy Deva Pardue; 113al The New York Public Library, Digital Collections © Heirs of Aaron Douglas/VAGA at ARS, NY and DACS, London 2023; 113ar Collection of the Smithsonian National Museum of African American History and Culture, Gift of Arthur J. "Bud" Schmidt; 114al Collection of the Smithsonian National Museum of African American History and Culture; 114ar The Metropolitan Musem of Art, New York. Gift of Nappy-negroes in art, 2020; 114br Collection of the Smithsonian National Museum of African American History and Culture, Gift of Samuel Y. Edgerton; 115a Courtesy Jahnavi Inniss; 115bl © Sadie Red Wing; 115br Isometric Studio; 117al Wellcome Collection; 117ar The New York Public Library, Digital Collections; 117bl Grey London/Chaz Mather and Lucy Jones; 119b All-Pro Reels (CC by-SA 2.0)/Wikipedia; 121a & br Courtesy Fraser Muggeridge Studio. Photos by Patrick Jameson; 121bl Courtesy the artist, Sprüth Magers, and Museum of Modern Art, New York; 123 Courtesy the family of Alan Fletcher and Phaidon Press. The Art of Looking Sideways © Phaidon Press, 2001; 124 Courtesy Peter Biľak, Typotheque; 126 Courtesy Tom Etherington; 129l Courtesy Studio Ghazaal Vojdani; 129r © ADAGP, Paris and DACS, London 2023. Photo ADAGP Images; 131a Courtesy Obys; 131b Courtesy Jeremy Jansen; 133al James Goggin, Practise; 133ar Courtesy Yotam Hadar; 133b Courtesy David Pearson © Penguin Books, 2020; 135b Courtesy Order; 137ar Boston Public Library, Digital Commonwealth, Massachusetts Online, CC BY-NC-ND; 137al, 141ar, 144al, 149ar & b Library of Congress, Prints and Photographs Division; 137b Courtesy of Milton Glaser Inc. © Milton Glaser. All Rights Reserved; 139al Courtesy David Rudnick; 139ar 12:01AM. © LuckyMe, 2017; 139bl Courtesy Studio Moross. BFI Flare: London LGBTQIA+ Film Festival, 2020. Courtesy of the BFI; 139br Courtesy of Bráulio Amadio © The Vinyl Factory, 2018; 141bl The Partners; 141br Mucho; 143a The Click; 143b Unit Editions. Courtesy the Estate of Ken Garland; 144ar Courtesy Ben Denzer © Verso, 2021; 144b Courtesy Counter Studio; 145 Courtesy Paul Belford Ltd. © The TNT Book Company, 2017; 147al Courtesy Francesco Muzzi; 147ar © Gerd Arntz Estate, DACS/Pictoright 2023; 147b Courtesy Lance Wyman; 149al Reprint Courtesy of IBM Corporation; 151a Courtesy Bráulio Amado; 151b Courtesy Mark El-khatib; 154a Courtesy Studio South. Illustration by Jean Jullien; 154bl Courtesy Lebassis; 154br Courtesy Javier Jaén; 157al Courtesy Estate of Hans Hillmann; 157ac, 157br, 163a Library of Congress, Prints and Photographs Division; 157ar Design Reviewed © Design Council Archive, University of Brighton/Estate of Keith Cunningham; 157bl © Columbia Records, 1940; 159a Courtesy Pit magazine; 159b Courtesy Hingston Studio, Photography Julia Noni © Ninja Tune, 2018;

Bibliography

My utmost thanks go to all the designers who shared their work for inclusion in this book, the designers' estates and relatives who gave permission for reproducing pieces and all the collectors who kindly shared material, particularly Matt Lamont of the fantastic resource Design Reviewed. Thank you to Ben, Ellie, Giulia, Jen, Sybella and Pete at Ilex Press for all your hard work and patience. Thank you to my friends Apsi and Livio for German translation advice, second opinions and moral support. Finally, thank you to Kirstie and Eliza for always being there.

MIX
Paper | Supporting responsible forestry
FSC® C016973
www.fsc.org